BUSINESS SKILLS
for the 21ST CENTURY

Marc G. Baaij

BUSINESS SKILLS
for the 21ST CENTURY

Sage

1 Oliver's Yard
55 City Road
London EC1Y 1SP

2455 Teller Road
Thousand Oaks
California 91320

Unit No 323-333, Third Floor, F-Block
International Trade Tower
Nehru Place, New Delhi – 110 019

8 Marina View Suite 43-053
Asia Square Tower 1
Singapore 018960

Editor: Matthew Waters
Editorial assistant: Charlotte Hanson
Production editor: Imogen Roome
Copyeditor: Sarah Bury
Proofreader: Leigh Smithson
Marketing manager: Lucia Sweet
Cover design: Francis Kenney
Typeset by: C&M Digitals (P) Ltd, Chennai, India
Printed in the UK

Library of Congress Control Number: 2023938277

British Library Cataloguing in Publication data

A catalogue record for this book is available from the British Library

ISBN 978-1-5296-0001-8
ISBN 978-1-5296-0000-1 (pbk)

At Sage we take sustainability seriously. Most of our products are printed in the UK using responsibly sourced papers and boards. When we print overseas we ensure sustainable papers are used as measured by the Paper Chain Project grading system. We undertake an annual audit to monitor our sustainability.

DEDICATION

For Ellen and Sophie

ENDORSEMENTS

'This is a superb practical skills text employing a central area of Problem Solving to provide an extremely focused and rounded way of delivering this subject. The text delivers its key concepts and academic knowledge in a highly structured and engaging manner and there is an exceptionally good balance between knowledge, higher learning, and opportunities for reflection. This text provides students at any level of higher education to meet the challenges ahead.'

Joel Arnott, Senior Lecturer in Management, Marketing and Strategy at The University of Sunderland

'This book is THE book for anyone who wants to solve problems in a structured manner. The method presented in this book is practical, valuable, and proven. Even for those who are not inclined to approach problem-solving in a structured manner, I highly recommend reading this book as a first step. Marc Baaij brilliantly demonstrates his exceptional writing skills in this book.'

Muel Kaptein, partner at KPMG and professor at Erasmus University Rotterdam

CONTENTS

ABOUT THE AUTHOR

Marc Baaij is an associate professor of strategic management at the Rotterdam School of Management (RSM) at the Erasmus University Rotterdam in the Netherlands. Previously he worked for Boston Consulting Group (BCG) as a manager of research and as a strategy consultant. Marc specializes in methods and techniques for strategy development and implementation, with a focus on stakeholder management and strategic foresight development. He has written professional books and scientific articles on strategic management, management consultancy, and structured problem-solving. Besides teaching bachelor, master, and MBA students, Marc also provides open and in-company training in structured problem-solving and communication for managers, consultants, and other business professionals. Moreover, he serves as a soundboard for managers in cases of strategy development and implementation. Marc holds a master's degree in economics and is a PhD in strategic management.

PREFACE

This book is a practical guide to solving business problems and seizing opportunities in a structured way. Structured problem-solving is the hallmark of the world's leading management consultants, such as McKinsey & Company, Boston Consulting Group (BCG), and Bain & Company. This book is an interpretation of public sources of this problem-solving method (such as Chevallier, 2016; Conn & McLean, 2018; Garrette, Phelps, & Sibony, 2018; Minto, 2003; Rasiel, 1999; Rasiel, Friga, & Enriquez, 2001). This method is suitable for both companies and not-for-profit organizations. Moreover, this method also suits issues in private life. This setup makes the book very suitable for action learning and project-based learning. Figure 0.1 provides an overview of the structured problem-solving process and the supporting twenty-first-century business skills.

Moreover, structured problem-solving follows the scientific method of hypothesis development and testing. By choosing problem-solving as a focus, we place the skills for the twenty-first century in a business context and show how to use these skills in an integrated way. Management consultants are professional problem-solvers, but

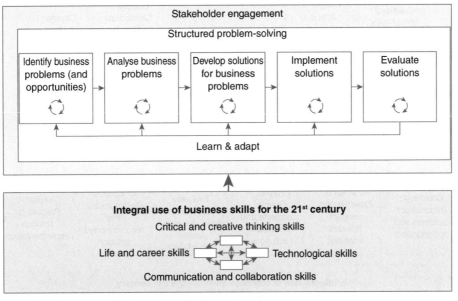

Figure 0.1 **Overview of the structured problem-solving process and the business skills for the twenty-first century**

problem-solving is relevant for all people in business. We emphasize that the target audience of this book is *all* business students instead of only those who want to become consultants. All students who will need to solve problems in their future careers will benefit from this book's method. The acquired skills will provide many benefits to graduates: employment, income, career, job satisfaction, and the potential to have a positive societal impact.

Problem identification, problem analysis, solution development, and implementation are iterative processes of hypothesis development and testing – the arrows and cycles in Figure 0.1 point to these iterations.

We acknowledge the importance of information, media, and technology skills, as well as life and career skills. However, they are out of this book's scope. This book is about structured problem-solving and focuses on the integrated use of skills for critical thinking, creative thinking, communicating, and collaborating. Complex problem-solving, critical thinking, and creative thinking top the list of skills that employers believe will grow in prominence (World Economic Forum, 2020).

MAP OF THE CHAPTERS

The book is structured in 11 chapters. Figure 0.2 plots the chapters on the problem-solving process.

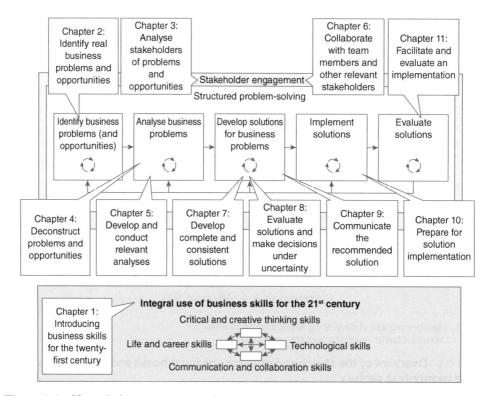

Figure 0.2   Map of chapters on overview of the structured problem-solving process

REFERENCES

Chevallier, A. (2016). *Strategic Thinking in Complex Problem Solving*. Oxford: Oxford University Press.

Conn, C., & McLean, R. (2018). *Bulletproof Problem Solving: The One Skill that Changes Everything*. Hoboken, NJ: John Wiley & Sons.

Garrette, B., Phelps, C., & Sibony, O. (2018). *Cracked It! How to Solve Big Problems and Sell Solutions Like Top Strategy Consultants*. London: Palgrave Macmillan.

Minto, B. (2003). *The Minto Pyramid Principle: Logic in Writing, Thinking and Problem Solving*. London: Minto International.

Rasiel, E. M. (1999). *The McKinsey Way: Using the Techniques of the World's Top Strategic Consultants to Help You and Your Business*. New York: McGraw-Hill.

Rasiel, E. M., Friga, P. N., & Enriquez, J. (2001). *The McKinsey Mind: Understanding and Implementing the Problem-Solving Tools and Management Techniques of the World's Top Strategic Consulting Firm*. New York: McGraw-Hill.

ACKNOWLEDGEMENTS

I would like to thank the many people without whom it would not have been possible to write this book. Teaching the methods and techniques helped me sharpen the book's content. That is why I am grateful to my students for their questions and feedback. The manuscript benefited from the thoughtful feedback from Senior Lecturer Joel Arnott. Without the invitation of publisher Matthew Waters, this book would not have happened. I am thankful to him and the team from Sage for their professional support of the process. I would also like to thank my daughter Sophie for her helpful feedback on both the content and the visualization. Finally, I am very thankful for the support of my wife Ellen and for her patience with a husband who keeps coming up with new book ideas.

ONLINE RESOURCES

This textbook is accompanied by online resources to aid teaching and support learning. To access these resources, visit: https://study.sagepub.com/baaij. Please note that lecturers will require a Sage account in order to access the lecturer resources. An account can be created via the above link.

FOR LECTURERS

- **PowerPoints** that can be downloaded and adapted to suit individual teaching needs
- A **Teaching Guide** providing practical guidance and support and additional materials for lecturers using this textbook in their teaching

FOR STUDENTS

- **Author Videos** that introduce the key concepts for each chapter

Introducing Business Skills for the Twenty-First Century

INTRODUCTION

How to prepare for a successful career?

You study business because you are interested in a business career. You may have family or friends in the business world who have motivated you, or you have seen inspiring stories in the media about successful businesspeople. You do not know what your business career will look like, but you know that you will be active in the business world for about the next forty years.

Pause and Reflect

What will it take to have a successful career in the next twenty years?

What may happen?

Let us do a thought experiment about a fictitious character named Tara. Assume that she was born in 2000 and studied at a business school. After graduating in 2022, Tara got her first job as a Human Resource (HR) professional in a medium-sized company. She will work about forty years, which means that Tara will retire around 2062. What may happen during these years? Figure 1.1 presents the time line of Tara's career with some examples of plausible technological developments during that period.

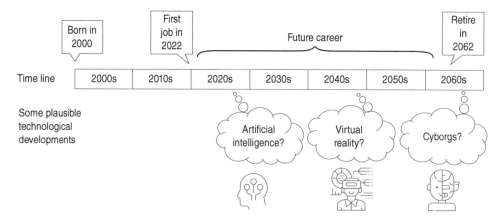

Figure 1.1   The time line of Tara's career in business

MAIN LEARNING OBJECTIVES

After studying this chapter, you should be able to:

- understand:
  - how the workplace is changing
  - what the future of work may look like
  - what the structured problem-solving method is about and why it is so important for your future career
  - what business skills you require for your future career
- know how to:
  - assess your present business skills
  - identify any skill gaps for your future career

In this chapter, we will discuss the importance of business skills to becoming successful in the coming decades of the twenty-first century. The chapter is structured as follows (see Figure 1.2).

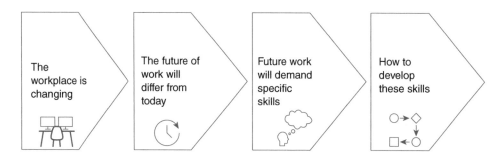

Figure 1.2   Chapter structure

THE WORKPLACE IS CHANGING

Two critical drivers of change

You may ask yourself: *What may happen to work in the business world during the coming forty years?* We cannot predict the future of work, but to get a bit of an idea of how much change may occur in such a period, we may look at the recent past.

Let us look back at what happened to the workplace during the 1980–2020 period. It is just to give you an idea of the amount of change that can occur to the workplace in forty years. Our focus is on the impact of the most critical technological, political, and economic developments on the workplace, without claiming to be exhaustive. We acknowledge that other factors, such as climate change, have an enormous impact on society. Still, we concentrate on the factors that we perceive to be most important to the workplace. Figure 1.3 provides an overview of two critical drivers that changed the workplace during the 1980–2020 period: technological developments and the spread of neo-liberalism.

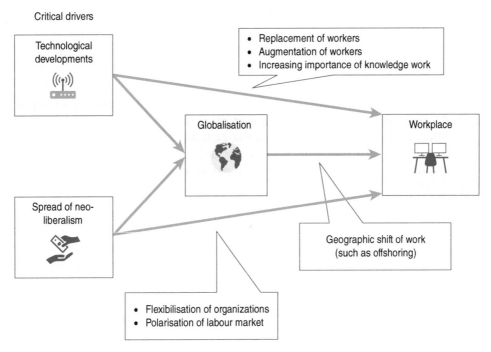

Figure 1.3 **Two critical drivers that changed the workplace during the 1980–2020 period**

Driver 1: Technological developments change the workplace

Technology, defined as the practical application of knowledge to fields, such as communication, construction, and manufacturing, plays such an essential role in the development of the business world. Think of the role of technology in the Industrial

Revolutions. The invention of the steam engine led to the First Industrial Revolution (1760–1840). The discovery of electricity and the invention of the automobile, airplane, and telephone contributed to the Second Industrial Revolution (1870–1940). We are currently still in the Third Industrial Revolution, which began in the 1950s, with the invention of the integrated circuit or 'chip'. This revolution spurred the development of increasingly powerful computers and the expanding connectivity of computers in the form of the Internet. This chapter focuses on the impact of information and communication technologies (hereafter ICT) on jobs and employment. But we also recognize the importance of other technologies, such as biotechnology, for society.

Technology creates new jobs

The development of ICT led to innovative products and new types of jobs, such as app developers, drone operators, and digital marketers. Furthermore, ICT led to 'big data', creating new jobs, such as data analysts. Cloud services specialists, social media specialists, and influencers are other examples of jobs that arrived with the Internet. Moreover, apps and digital platforms led to 'gig jobs', such as Uber-drivers and Airbnb-hosts.

Technology replaces workers

ICT also destroyed jobs as computers and robots took over jobs. Take the example of the bank teller. Until the 1990s, banking customers would go to a local bank branch. At the office, a bank teller handed them the cash money. Later, the automatic teller machine (ATM), or cash machine, became an attractive substitute. Nowadays, computers and the Internet allow for electronic payment. ATMs will be redundant in a cashless society.

Technology augments workers

The replacement of people by machines suggests a choice between *either* people *or* machines. But there are also situations where the solution is *both* people *and* technology. Technology can also *support* people in fulfilling a job. Individuals are not replaced by technology but work *with* technology. Before the invention of the personal computer and the spreadsheet software in the 1980s, office workers made calculations using pocket calculators. Spreadsheet software augmented the calculation capabilities of these workers. More recently, we see the advance of data analytics software that enables office employees to analyse 'big data' or data sets that are too large for a spreadsheet.

Technology impacts industries

ICT impacted whole industries. Technology-enabled automation reduced employment in sectors like agriculture. Technology increased employment in other industries, such as the ICT industries. In some other sectors, technology caused employment to shift from one type of company to another. For example, the Internet introduced web shops and parcel deliverers in the retail industry. Web shops and parcel delivery companies benefited from e-commerce, but 'brick-and-mortar' stores suffered.

Technology transforms society

In the 1960s, developed countries started to transform from an industrial society to a post-industrial or knowledge-based society. This transformation implied the increasing importance of knowledge work at the expense of manual labour. Knowledge workers (a term coined by management guru Peter Drucker in 1959!) are persons whose jobs are about developing and using knowledge rather than producing products and services. Examples of knowledge workers in the business world are accountants, management consultants, and managers.

Driver 2: Neo-liberal politics change the workplace

In the 1980s, the United States and the United Kingdom embraced 'free market' thinking or 'neoliberalism'. Later, this ideology spread to other countries across the globe. Towards the end of the 1980s, the then state socialist countries (such as China, India, the Soviet Union, and Eastern Europe) began to open to the capitalist world and restructure their economy towards a market system. We discuss the two main consequences of neo-liberalism for organizations and labour markets: the flexibilisation of organizations and the polarisation of labour markets.

Neo-liberal politics contribute to the flexibilisation of organizations

Neo-liberalism came with an increasing focus on shareholder value. Creating value for shareholders became the main driver for companies in the 1980s. Focus on the 'core business' and outsourcing the other activities became the mantra for shareholder value creation. The 'non-core' activities and employees had to be organized flexibly and efficiently to enable quick responses to any market changes. For these 'non-core' people, temporary and part-time contracts, or contracts on an on-call basis, replaced permanent and full-time jobs.

Neo-liberal politics contribute to the polarisation of labour markets

The division of a company into a core business and a flexible shell was accompanied by a division of the labour market. The labour market position of the people at the core business improved considerably. The pay of these employees rose, but the remuneration of the top managers took off thanks to earnings and bonuses linked to the stock price: shareholder value creation. The improvement in pay for the core people contrasted sharply with the deteriorating income for the unfortunate who fell outside the core. This income decline resulted from the deterioration of labour's bargaining position due to automation and the offshoring of work to low-wage countries. A class of vulnerable workers emerged. These so-called 'precarious' workers had insecure jobs with poor pay.

Technological developments and spread of neo-liberalism contribute to globalisation

Technological developments contribute to globalisation

ICT and transportation technologies allow people to exchange knowledge and goods over (large) geographic distances. During the twentieth century the invention of (jet) airplanes allowed fast cross-continental travel for people. The invention of the container revolutionized the transportation of goods around the world. Due to these technologies, geographic distance no longer seemed to matter.

Spread of neo-liberalism contributes to globalisation

The spread of neo-liberalism across the globe in the 1980s and the opening-up of state socialist countries led to large-scale international trade and foreign investment liberalisation. The resulting international trade and investment streams contributed to globalisation, or the interaction, and integration among people, businesses, and governments worldwide. For example, in 2001, China opened its borders to foreign investment and Western companies massively invested in this country.

Globalisation changes value chains

Globalisation of the markets caused work shifts across national borders as multinational enterprises transferred capital investments and employment from the West to the East. Many companies created global value chains, which is when a company's value chain is broken down into activities that are carried out in different countries. ICT facilitated the globalisation of work by allowing globally distributed workers to operate as a virtual team. But the COVID-19 pandemic exposed the fragility of global value chains.

 Pause and Reflect

What may the business world be like twenty years from now? Imagine what may happen in the next twenty years.

THE FUTURE OF WORK WILL DIFFER FROM TODAY

How far may automation of work go?

What will the future of work look like? How will the workplace change in the coming decades? We do not have a crystal ball to predict the future. But we can imagine *plausible* futures or scenarios. A critical scenario driver is technology. We briefly touch upon two scenarios.

- An *optimistic* scenario is that technological developments positively impact work. In this scenario, advanced robots and computers take over the dull, dirty, dangerous, and hard work. At the same time, technology creates new, engaging, and rewarding jobs for people.
- A *pessimistic* scenario is a future where robots and computers rule the workplace. They replace many, if not most, workers. In this gloomy future, technological development does not lead to new jobs. On a large scale, people lose their job and cannot find new work. The fear of replacement of labour by capital is not new. In the early nineteenth century, English textile workers, known as the Luddites, destroyed textile machines to protest the First Industrial Revolution.

What factors limit work automation?

The growth of artificial intelligence (AI), such as ChatGPT, may make you wonder: Is there no limit to the automation of knowledge work? Will the technological developments still leave work for me? The fear of automation of *all* knowledge work is unfounded. We discuss several limits to work automation.

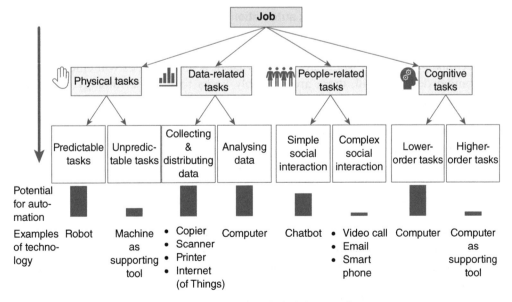

Figure 1.4   An example of a deconstruction of a job into tasks

Tasks not jobs

We should not look at *whole* jobs if we want to understand the real influence of technology. Technology does not intervene at the job level, but at the lower level of the *tasks* that together form the job. A job consists of tasks, and technology may affect one or more of the activities that comprise these tasks. We can deconstruct a job into its component tasks. The automation potential varies by task (see Figure 1.4).

Six critical limits to automation

You may ask why some tasks seem less susceptible or even immune to automation. We will discuss six critical limits of automation (see Figure 1.5).

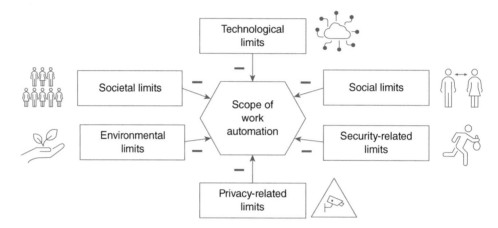

Figure 1.5   Six critical limits to work automation

- *Technological limits*: We do not know what new technologies will emerge in the coming decades. Still, there are probably limits to what technology can do. It seems highly unlikely that intelligent robots will make *all* human workers *completely* redundant. There will remain tasks that require skills that cannot be automated. We will discuss these skills in the next section.
- *Social limits*: In various situations where a pleasant demeanour is essential, people prefer face-to-face interaction with another person over digital interaction or interaction with smart (AI) machines. For example, think of in-person service workers such as nursing staff, hospitality workers, hairdressers, beauticians, daycare workers, and live entertainers.
- *Security-related limits*: Work automation can mean the exchange of sensitive and secret data over telecommunication networks and storage in computers. A task's dependency on automation may cause exposure to hacking and other attacks on networks and computers.
- *Privacy-related limits*: Work automation can also mean that data of customers, employees, and other stakeholders is stored on computer systems and shared

across various parties. There are already many examples of errors where sensitive data about people became public. There are also examples where organizations, like 'big brothers', use digital technology to track and watch people. The fear of privacy breaches and mass surveillance by 'big brothers' may limit automation.

- *Environmental limits*: Global warming and natural resource constraints may put limits on the use of computers. For example, computers require rare metals, consume electricity, and require cooling. Recycling computer parts, such as batteries, is a challenge.
- *Societal limits*: Suppose the automation of work is not (entirely) compensated by the creation of new jobs. In that case, unemployment in society will rise. History teaches us that rising unemployment may contribute to economic inequality and social tensions. Governments can provide people a basic income, but jobs are more than making a living. To prevent a large part of the working population from being out of work, governments can set limits on work automation. Then, people will have jobs that can be automated well. But governments subsidize these jobs to incentivize employers.

 Pause and Reflect

What tasks for business professionals will likely be 'future-proof' in the coming twenty years?

What is future-proof work?

Here we limit ourselves to the *technological* limits to automation. We look for tasks where workers can add value beyond what smart (AI) systems can do. Our focus is on tasks characterized by:

- higher-order cognitive activities
- complex social interaction
- unpredictability

High-order cognitive activities

Figure 1.6 shows two scenarios about the influence of technology on the future of cognitive work. The literature distinguishes between higher-order and lower-order cognitive skills (Bloom, 1956). In the scenario "Humans for higher-order work", the scope of work automation is limited to lower-order cognitive skills. But according to the scenario "Technology takes over" the scope of work automation encompasses *both* lower-order and higher-order cognitive skills. We note that the latter scenario is less likely because of technological limits to the automation of higher-order cognitive work.

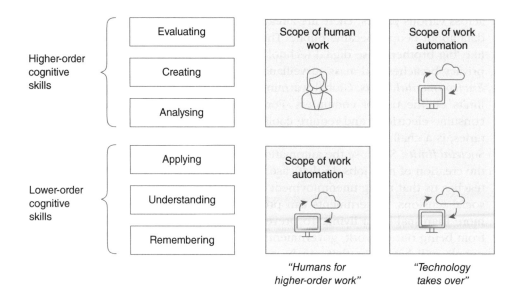

Two scenarios about the influence of
technology on cognitive work in 2040

Figure 1.6   Two scenarios about the influence of technology on cognitive work in 2040

Complex social interaction

Figure 1.4 distinguishes between simple and complex social interaction, which refers to communication and collaboration. This chapter focuses on tasks that require complex social interaction, such as people management, teamwork, and deal-making. Interacting with people with diverging interests, values, and views can provide important benefits but it can also make social interaction more complex and put higher demands on communication and collaboration skills.

Unpredictability

In the twenty-first century the business world will likely remain volatile, uncertain, complex, and ambiguous (abbreviated as VUCA). In the 1980s the US Army War College coined the term 'VUCA' to describe the world after the Cold War. Later the concept spread to business and other fields. We would like to briefly explain these four characteristics (see Figure 1.7).

- *Volatility*: The volatility of the business world refers to changes in various aspects. A few examples are the volatility of stock markets, interest rates, and energy prices. It is about both the speed and the magnitude of changes. Volatility is not only about how fast changes are, but also how significant the changes are.
- *Uncertainty*: The business world's uncertainty refers to the unpredictability of the future.

○ At low levels of uncertainty, we may extrapolate trends from the past.
○ At intermediate levels, we may distinguish between different scenarios.
○ At high levels, we have no idea how the future might look like.

- *Complexity*: The complexity of the business world refers to the number of factors that play a role (such as political, economic, social, technological, environmental, and legal developments) and the interconnections between these factors. If the number of factors is large and there are many interconnections, then the situation is complex. An example of a complex system is a stock market (many interconnected factors drive stock prices).

- *Ambiguity*: The business world's ambiguity refers to the multiple interpretabilities, or vagueness, of a specific situation. Ambiguity means it is unclear how to interpret that situation because there is no objective, correct interpretation. The ambiguity is based on

  ○ a lack of information about that situation
  ○ the diversity of beliefs and values of individuals who need to observe that situation.

VUCA has implications for business workers. Under these conditions, we cannot make (long-term) plans of action. We do not know upfront whether these actions will be effective in the future. Therefore, we must experiment with activities, learn from our experiences, and adapt our efforts accordingly. VUCA requires a 'trial and error' or agile approach rather than a planning approach.

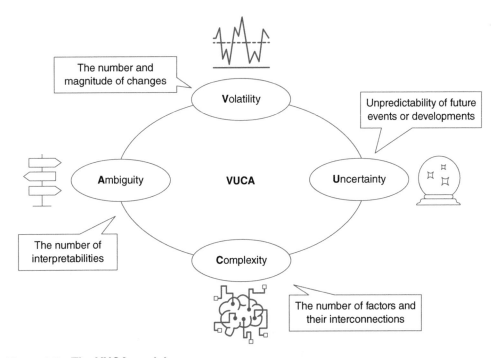

Figure 1.7   The VUCA model

Solving complex problems is an example of future-proof work

Figure 1.8 distinguishes between three dimensions of work and visualizes the scope of work automation as a box. Automation requires low levels of each dimension. The low levels determine the box of automatable work. Outside this box, we find work that is not or less susceptible to automation. We focus on the high levels of each dimension.

An example of a combination of high levels of higher-order cognitive tasks, complex social interaction, and unpredictability is *complex problem-solving*. We may define a problem as a situation that we regard as unwelcome or harmful and needing to be dealt with and overcome. For example, a hotel chain sees the emergence of apartment-sharing platforms like Airbnb as a problem. Complex problems have many interconnected factors. Problem-solving equates to finding a solution to that problem. Complex problem-solving, together with critical and creative thinking, tops the list of skills that employers believe will grow in prominence (World Economic Forum, 2020).

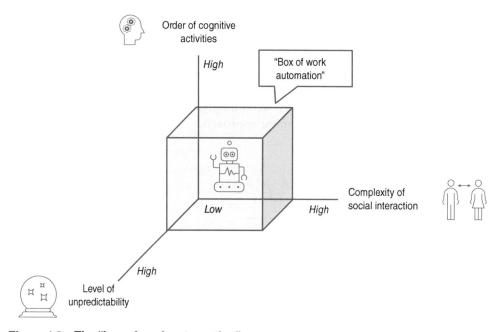

Figure 1.8   The "box of work automation"

How leading management consultancy firms solve complex problems for clients

The literature provides various methods for complex problem-solving. But we want procedures that are field-tested and proven to be effective. Moreover, we prefer practical approaches that are tailored to the business. Managers and many professionals in business must solve problems as part of their job, but problem-solving is the *profession* of management consultants. We focus on the problem-solving methods of the world's leading management consultancy firms, such as McKinsey & Company, Boston Consulting Group (BCG), and Bain & Company. This book is based on the author's interpretation of public sources of these methods (such as Chevallier, 2016; Conn & McLean, 2018; Garrette et al., 2018; Minto, 2003; Rasiel, 1999; Rasiel et al., 2001).

These consultants use a scientific method for successful problem-solving

These consultancies have in common that they solve their clients' complex problems according to a structured method. They use this method for all client problems in all industries and countries. This method, which has become the hallmark of these renowned consultancies, is named '*structured problem-solving*' (see Figure 1.9). This approach is based on the scientific method, which we define as: 'the principles and procedures for the systematic pursuit of knowledge involving the recognition and formulation of a problem, the collection of data through observation and experiment, and the formulation and testing of hypotheses' (Merriam-Webster, 2021). A hypothesis is a testable statement about an explanation or another idea that is based on (limited) known factors but has not yet been proved. A business example of a hypothesis is: Apartment-sharing platforms like Airbnb lowered the revenue of hotel chains.

These consultants engage stakeholders for successful problem-solving

The problem-solving process is embedded in stakeholder engagement. Problem-solving is about stakeholders. There are people inside and outside the focal company who have a stake in that company's problem. To solve this problem, we must engage the relevant stakeholders. We distinguish between:

- internal stakeholders inside the focal company (business owners, managers, and professional employees)
- industry-level stakeholders (such as customers, distributors, suppliers, other business partners, producers of complementary products, producers of substitute products, and competitors)
- stakeholders in society (such as the public, (social) media, regulators, governments, non-governmental organizations, and politicians)

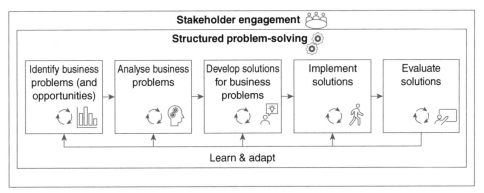

Iterative process of developing and testing hypotheses about problems, solutions, and implementation

Figure 1.9   Structured problem-solving with stakeholder engagement

Follow five steps for successful problem-solving

We briefly outline the steps in identifying and analysing business problems, and subsequently, developing and implementing solutions for these problems. The book is also about seizing *opportunities*. Whereas we define a problem as a situation that we regard as unwelcome or harmful and needing to be dealt with and overcome, we define an opportunity as a favourable situation that makes it possible to do something that we want to do or must do. For example, the Internet provided the founders of Airbnb with a favourable situation to attain their goals. The method's steps are:

1. *Identify business problems and opportunities*: Is there really a problem (or an opportunity)?
2. *Analyse business problems and opportunities*: *Where* is the problem (or opportunity), and *why* does it exist? Developing and testing hypotheses about possible causes make the analysis more efficient.
3. *Develop solutions*: What is the *best* solution to the problem (or the best way to seize the opportunity)? Hypotheses about possible solutions increase the efficiency of the problem-solving process.
4. *Implement solutions: How* to make the solution work?
5. *Evaluate solutions*: Has the problem been solved (or has the opportunity been seized) in an effective and efficient manner?

Successful problem-solving may require repeating steps

Figure 1.9 may give the impression that problem-solving is a *linear* process. But problem analysis, solution development, and solution implementation use hypotheses. Rejection of hypotheses means that we need to develop and test new hypotheses. Therefore, structured problem-solving is an *iterative* process of learning and adaptation of hypotheses.

The problem-solving method also applies to people and planet problems

This book focuses on business with a focus on *profit*-problems and profit-opportunities. But problem-solving is not limited to profit creation. We acknowledge that companies can also have people and planet goals in addition to their profit goals: the 'triple bottom line'. Figure 1.10 distinguishes between the private goals of the company's *share*holders and the public goals of the company's *stake*holders, in the form of the United Nations' Sustainable Development Goals (SDGs). Structured problem-solving also applies to any people-problems and planet-problems (as well as opportunities) of companies.

Figure 1.10   The 'triple bottom line' of profit, people, and the planet

Source of SDGs: United Nations

 **Pause and Reflect**

To what extent can companies pursue private and public goals simultaneously?

FUTURE WORK WILL DEMAND SPECIFIC SKILLS

Solving business problems and seizing opportunities rests on a combination of knowledge, skills, and attitude.

- *Knowledge* refers to business administration concepts, theories, models, and frameworks.
- *Skills* are the ability to apply that knowledge to do something well.
- *Attitude* is the way we think or feel about someone or something. It is about our values and beliefs.

Though we recognize and value knowledge and attitude, this book focuses on skills. But we do pay attention to the relationship between skills, knowledge, and attitude.

  Pause and Reflect

What skills will you need in order to be successful at work in the business world you have imagined twenty years from now?

What skills does future work demand?

We consider the skills required for future-proof tasks. The literature refers to them as '*twenty-first-century skills*'. Interpretations of these skills in the literature vary, but Figure 1.11 provides some commonalities of these definitions. We conclude that *twenty-first-century skills are the foundational, critical, and essential skills for operating in a highly connected and resourced, globally diverse knowledge-based society.* These skills are about the need to learn and adapt and communicate and collaborate with a wide range of stakeholders.

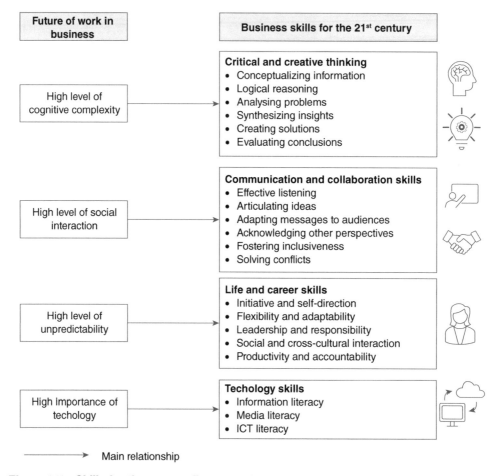

Figure 1.11   Skills for the twenty-first century

How new are these skills?

It is more appropriate to speak of skills *for* the twenty-first century instead of skills *of* the twenty-first century because these skills have always been essential to work. What is new is that in the twenty-first century, success in business more than ever before depends on these skills. Before the twenty-first century, many people in the industry could still be successful without these skills. Then routine manual and lower-order cognitive skills were still in demand as technology had not yet made them obsolete. But technology is pushing up the skills requirements. Technological developments have made the skills for the twenty-first century more important than ever before. Let us briefly review these skills.

Critical and creative thinking skills

Critical thinking

Critical thinking is conceptualizing information, logical reasoning, analysing, synthesizing, and evaluating information to guide a belief and action.

- *Conceptualizing* information refers to 'systems thinking'. We must consider the whole, the big picture, and the connections between the parts. These considerations allow us to define vital problems and raise critical questions.
- We distinguish between various types of *logical reasoning*: induction and deduction.
  - Induction is discovering a general principle from specific examples. It is studying many cases to develop a theory.
  - A deduction is the opposite form of logic as it draws conclusions on instances from a general principle. It is explaining a specific case with the help of a theory.
- *Analysing* means thinking open-mindedly within alternative systems of thought and recognizing and assessing the assumptions and implications of these systems. We must analyse and evaluate stakeholders' assumptions, arguments, beliefs, evidence, and points of view.
- *Synthesizing* is using abstract ideas to interpret information and effectively come to well-argued conclusions and solutions. It combines components, such as ideas and insights, to form a connected and consistent whole that is more valuable than the items considered separately.
- *Evaluating* is testing conclusions and solutions against relevant criteria and standards. The evaluation can also include a judgment of these conclusions and solutions.

Creative thinking

- *Creativity* is the ability to see new opportunities and to create original and valuable ideas. It involves looking at situations from various perspectives, being flexible to adapt to changing conditions, and applying one's imagination to solve complex problems. We distinguish between phases of divergent and convergent thinking.
  - Divergent thinking is creating many ideas, which may benefit from idea-generating techniques, such as brainstorming.

- ○ After divergent thinking we need convergent thinking. Convergent thinking is about evaluating, selecting, and improving ideas.
- *Innovation* transforms a creative idea into new or improved products or value-adding processes to achieve an economic goal. Innovation skills comprise problem-solving, critical thinking, communication, collaboration, and various life and career skills, such as taking the initiative, self-direction, and leadership.

Communication and collaboration skills

Communication

Communication is about effectively listening to others to decipher the meaning of their messages. It is also effectively articulating ideas and other thoughts to inform and persuade others. Effectiveness implies adjusting the message to match the needs of different audiences and environments. Communication can take various forms: oral, written, and nonverbal communication. Moreover, we distinguish between multiple media, such as face-to-face, print, TV, and digital.

Collaboration

Collaboration is working together for a common goal. We may work in a physical place but also in a virtual community. Collaboration has several requirements: willingness to contribute and help, an assumption of shared responsibility, and respect for other team members. Effective collaborators value diversity and appreciate other members' contributions. They are willing to make compromises to accomplish a common goal. Moreover, they know when to speak and when to listen. Finally, they conduct themselves respectably and professionally.

Life and career skills

Initiative and self-direction

We can set goals and tangible and intangible success criteria. To meet these criteria, we can effectively use our time and manage our workload. Moreover, we can define, prioritise, monitor, and complete tasks without direct oversight. To succeed in our careers, we should be self-directed learners with a commitment to lifelong learning. Initiative and self-direction are also about reflecting critically on past experiences to improve. We must go beyond the primary mastery of skills to expand our learning opportunities.

Flexibility and adaptability

To achieve workable solutions, we understand, negotiate, and balance diverse beliefs and perspectives. We can deal positively with criticism and setbacks, and we are also able to effectively incorporate feedback. Moreover, we can effectively adapt to various roles, job responsibilities, time schedules, and environments. Finally, we can also effectively work in a climate that is characterized by ambiguity and fluctuating priorities.

Leadership and responsibility

We can use problem-solving and interpersonal skills to influence and guide others towards a goal. As a leader, we can leverage the strengths of others to accomplish a common purpose. Our role modelling and selflessness inspire others to reach their very best. The use of our power and influence demonstrates integrity and ethical behaviour. Finally, we act responsibly with the interests of the larger community in mind.

Social and cross-cultural interaction

Social and cross-cultural interaction refers to a diverse group with people from various social and cultural backgrounds. We respect social and cultural differences, as well as respond open-mindedly to different ideas and values. Moreover, we can leverage social and cultural differences to create new ideas and increase work quality.

Productivity and accountability

Productivity is the ability to efficiently create a product or service. Accountability is taking a role in creating a product or service and assuming responsibility for that product or service. In doing so we use the following skills: setting objectives, prioritizing tasks, managing our time, working ethically, and, where necessary or desirable, collaborating with others.

Technology skills

Information literacy

Information literacy means that we can efficiently and effectively access information. We can critically and competently evaluate information. It also means that we demonstrate a fundamental understanding of the legal and ethical issues surrounding data access and use. Moreover, we can manage the information flow from a wide range of sources. Finally, we can accurately and creatively use the information for the problem at hand.

Media literacy

Media literacy indicates that we understand how media works and how we can use media. We know how media messages are constructed and how media can influence beliefs and behaviours. It also means that we can examine how individuals interpret messages differently and include or exclude values and points of view. Furthermore, we can effectively utilize the most appropriate media creation tools, conventions, and characteristics for our purpose. Finally, we can effectively use the most appropriate expressions and interpretations in diverse environments.

ICT literacy

ICT literacy implies that we can effectively use digital technology, communications tools, and communications networks to access, create, manage, integrate, and evaluate information. We know how to collect and retrieve data. ICT literacy also entails developing knowledge by inventing, designing, adapting, authoring, or applying information. Our skills for comparing, contrasting, and summarizing information enable us to integrate knowledge. Finally, we can make judgments about the quality, relevance, and usefulness of the data.

Pause and Reflect

How good are your skills for the twenty-first century?

HOW TO DEVELOP THESE SKILLS

What is your skills gap?

You may compare your current level and the required level for each skill. Figure 1.12 uses a scale of 1 to 5, in which 5 is the required level.

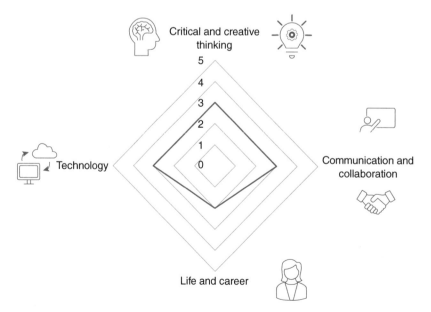

Figure 1.12   Assess your twenty-first century skills

To help you assess your skills, we may benefit from scientific research by Kelley, Knowles, Han, and Sung (2019). We use their validated survey questions as a self-assessment.

Assess your critical thinking skills

I am fully confident in my ability to	Strongly disagree	Disagree	Neither agree nor disagree	Agree	Strongly agree
identify in detail what needs to be known to answer a science inquiry question					
gather relevant and sufficient information from different sources					
develop follow-up questions that focus or broaden inquiry					
develop follow-up questions to gain understanding of the needs and wants of clients or users					
understand questions that lead to critical thinking					
evaluate reasoning and evidence that support an argument					
revise drafts and justify revisions with evidence					
combine different elements into a complete solution					
justify choices of evaluation criteria					

Figure 1.13   Assess your critical thinking skills

Source: Author's interpretation of Kelley, Knowles, Han, & Sung (2019: 589)

Assess your creative thinking skills

I am fully confident in my ability to	Strongly disagree	Disagree	Neither agree nor disagree	Agree	Strongly agree
create ideas geared to intended clients or users					
understand how knowledge or insights might transfer to other situations or contexts					
find sources of information and inspiration when others do not					
elaborate and improve on ideas					

Figure 1.14   Assess your creative thinking skills

Source: Author's interpretation of Kelley, Knowles, Han, & Sung (2019: 589)

Assess your communication skills

I am fully confident in my ability to	Strongly disagree	Disagree	Neither agree nor disagree	Agree	Strongly agree
adapt a communication style appropriate for the purpose, task or audience					
present all information clearly, concisely, and logically					
use appropriate body language when presenting					
organize information well					
use time and run meetings efficiently					
complete tasks without having to be reminded					
track our team's progress towards goals and deadlines					

Figure 1.15   Assess your communication skills

Source: Author's interpretation of Kelley, Knowles, Han, & Sung (2019: 589)

Assess your collaboration skills

I am fully confident in my ability to	Strongly disagree	Disagree	Neither agree nor disagree	Agree	Strongly agree
be polite and kind to teammates					
acknowledge and respect other perspectives					
follow rules for team meetings					
make sure all team members' ideas are equally valued					
offer assistance to others in their work when needed					
improve my own work when given feedback					
help the team solve problems and manage conflicts					
come physically and mentally prepared each day					
follow rules for team decision making					

Figure 1.16   Assess your collaboration skills

Source: Author's interpretation of Kelley, Knowles, Han, & Sung (201: 589)

How this book will help you to increase your skills

Technological developments will push up skills requirements and so cause skill gaps for people without the future-proof skills for the twenty-first century. Business graduates need to develop these skills. Some of those skills can be acquired through experiential learning during business school, while others take more time and practice to develop. This book will focus on a subset of the future-proof skills for the twenty-first century that can be attained while at business school: critical thinking, creative thinking, communication, and collaboration. These skills enable complex, non-routine problem-solving. Communication and collaboration are necessary because problem-solving is more than an intellectual puzzle and implies social interaction with relevant stakeholders.

The method of structured problem-solving has been a success within the world's leading management consultancy firms, such as McKinsey & Company, BCG, and Bain & Company, for many decades. New employees of these consultancies receive extensive training in this method. But business graduates who join other organizations can also benefit from this method. Business students can learn this method while at school. That is why we introduce this method here. Figure 1.17 shows the structured problem-solving process and the underlying skills in a very concise manner. In the coming chapters, we will explain all process steps and introduce the requisite skills.

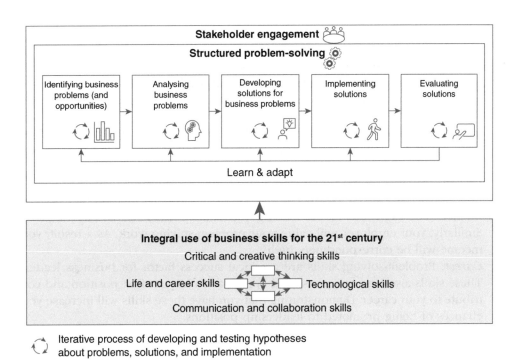

Figure 1.17   Structured problem-solving and skills for the twenty-first century

How you may benefit from your increased skills

This book will help you to understand and use the structured problem-solving method. Learning this method and developing the requisite skills can bring you many benefits. Figure 1.18 presents the main advantages for you. We will go through these benefits in reverse order one by one.

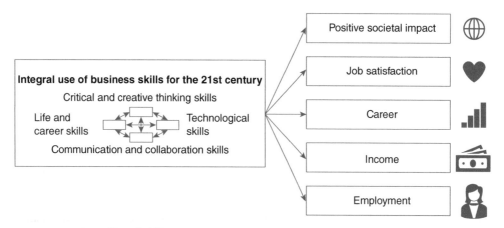

Figure 1.18   Benefits of skills for the twenty-first century

- *Employment*: The structured problem-solving skills are valuable not only in management consultancy but in all sectors of society. Why do you think companies and not-for-profit organizations in all kinds of industries have turned to these consultancies for decades when faced with complex problems? The structured problem-solving skills make you attractive to employers. If you have these skills, you increase your chance of a great job. Moreover, these skills are 'future-proof'. With these skills, you will remain in demand during your working life.
- *Income*: Management consultancy practice shows that (top) managers in companies and not-for-profit organizations greatly appreciate this problem-solving method. The high fees of the leading consultancy firms reflect this valuation. Similarly, your employer will value your problem-solving work. As a result, your income will be correspondingly high.
- *Career*: Problem-solving skills are a critical success factor for business leaders. These skills also lead to success and appreciation in your first position and contribute to your career. Demonstrating that you have these skills will increase your chances of being promoted to leadership positions.
- *Job satisfaction*: If you solve complex issues with stakeholders, you will get the necessary pleasure in your work. The feeling that you have achieved actual results with others is very satisfying. From a certain income level, this sense of achievement becomes even more important than the financial reward.
- *Societal impact*: The feeling of having achieved something societally relevant becomes increasingly important from a certain income level. With problem-solving skills, you can help companies to function better. You can contribute to better products and services, higher efficiency, growing sales, and more employment. Problem-solving cannot only be used for increasing the profitability of companies. The method is not limited to profit goals but can also achieve

other goals, such as social and environmental improvements. The scope of structured problem-solving is not just profit, but also encompasses people and the planet, such as the sustainable development goals (SDG). A growing number of companies is becoming increasingly aware of their corporate social responsibility. With these skills, you can contribute to the societal impact of your company. You can help ensure that your company achieves healthy profit growth and at the same time makes a positive contribution to solving societal and environmental problems.

You will benefit from these skills if you work in business. But if you decide to work in the not-for-profit sector, these skills may also prove valuable. Moreover, you can benefit from these skills in your private life as well.

 Pause and Reflect

Consider how you may use the skills for the twenty-first century in your studies, work, and personal life.

SUMMARY

We briefly outline the main takeaways of this chapter.

- The workplace is changing
  - technological developments lead to both the replacement and augmentation of workers; even knowledge work is subject to automation

- The future of work
  - future-proof work consists of:
    - higher order cognitive activities
    - a high level of complexity of social interaction
    - a high level of unpredictability
    - an example of future-proof work is solving complex business problems

- The structured problem-solving method
  - solving complex business problems is the work of leading management consultancies, which have a method for structured problem-solving. The method has the following steps:
    - identify a business problem
    - analyse a business problem
    - develop a solution

- implement a solution
- evaluate a solution

- Business skills you require for your future career

  ○ for your future career in business, you need the following twenty-first century skills:
    - critical and creative thinking skills
    - communication and collaboration skills
    - life and career skills
    - technology skills

- Assess your present business skills and identify any skill gaps for your future career

  ○ use a survey to assess your present level of these skills and identify any gaps between the present and required levels for your future career

 Mini Exercise

Identify the key concepts and terms in this chapter, define them briefly, and compile your own glossary.

REFERENCES AND FURTHER READING

Acemoglu, D., & Autor, D. (2011). Skills, tasks, and technologies: Implications for employment and earnings. In D. Card, & O. Ashenfelter (Eds.), *Handbook of Labor Economics* (Vol. 4B, pp. 1043–1171). Amsterdam: Elsevier.

Autor, D. H. (2015). Why are there still so many jobs? The history and future of workplace automation. *Journal of Economic Perspectives*, 29(3), 3–30.

Autor, D. H., & Dorn, D. (2013). The growth of low-skill service jobs and the polarization of the US labor market. *American Economic Review*, 103(5), 1553–1597.

Bloom, B. S. (1956). *Taxonomy of Educational Objectives. Vol. 1: Cognitive Domain*. New York: McKay.

Brynjolfsson, E., & McAfee, A. (2014). *The Second Machine Age: Work, Progress, and Prosperity in a Time of Brilliant Technologies*. New York: WW Norton & Company.

Bughin, J., Hazan, E., Lund, S., Dahlström, P., Wiesinger, A., & Subramaniam, A. (2018). *Skill Shift: Automation and the Future of the Workforce*. McKinsey Global Institute, Discussion paper 1, pp. 3–84.

Chevallier, A. (2016). *Strategic Thinking in Complex Problem Solving*. Oxford: Oxford University Press.

Conn, C., & McLean, R. (2018). *Bulletproof Problem Solving: The One Skill that Changes Everything*. Hoboken, NJ: John Wiley & Sons.

Drucker, P. F. (1959). *Landmarks of Tomorrow: A Report on the New*. New York: Harper.

Garrette, B., Phelps, C., & Sibony, O. (2018). *Cracked It! How to Solve Big Problems and Sell Solutions Like Top Strategy Consultants*. London: Palgrave Macmillan.

Goos, M., Manning, A., & Salomons, A. (2014). Explaining job polarization: Routine-biased technological change and offshoring. *American Economic Review*, 104(8), 2509–2526.

Joynes, C., Rossignoli, S., & Amonoo-Kuofi, E. F. (2019). *Twenty-first Century Skills: Evidence of Issues in Definition, Demand and Delivery for Development Contexts*. K4D Emerging Issues Report, August 2019, K4D Knowledge, Evidence and Learning for Development.

Kelley, T. R., Knowles, J. G., Han, J., & Sung, E. (2019). Creating a twenty-first century skills survey instrument for high school students. *American Journal of Educational Research*, 7(8), 583–590.

Kwon, R. (2014). Employment transitions and the cycle of income inequality in post-industrial societies. *International Journal of Comparative Sociology*, 55(5), 404–428.

Lambert, R., & Herod, A. (Eds.). (2016). *Neoliberal Capitalism and Precarious Work: Ethnographies of Accommodation and Resistance*. Cheltenham (UK): Edward Elgar.

Merriam-Webster. *Dictionary*. www.merriam-webster.com Accessed on August 19, 2021.

Minto, B. (2003). *The Minto Pyramid Principle: Logic in Writing, Thinking and Problem Solving*. London: Minto International.

Rasiel, E. M. (1999). *The McKinsey Way: Using the Techniques of the World's Top Strategic Consultants to Help You and Your Business*. New York: McGraw-Hill.

Rasiel, E. M., Friga, P. N., & Enriquez, J. (2001). *The McKinsey Mind: Understanding and Implementing the Problem-solving Tools and Management Techniques of the World's Top Strategic Consulting Firm*. New York: McGraw-Hill.

Reich, R. B. (1992). *The Work of Nations: Preparing Ourselves for Twenty-first Century Capitalism*. New York: Vintage Books.

Santana, M., & Cobo, M. J. (2020). What is the future of work? A science mapping analysis. *European Management Journal*, 38(6), 846–862.

United Nations. *Sustainable Development Goals*. www.un.org. Accessed on October 9, 2021.

Willcocks, L. (2020). Robo-Apocalypse cancelled? Reframing the automation and future of work debate. *Journal of Information Technology*, 35(4), 286–302.

Williams, S., Bradley, H., Devadason, R., & Erickson, M. (2013). *Globalization and Work*. Cambridge (UK): Polity Press.

World Economic Forum (2020). *The Future of Jobs Report 2020*. www.weforum.org/reports/the-future-of-jobs-report-2020. Accessed on October 11, 2021.

Identify Real Business Problems and Opportunities

2

INTRODUCTION

How to do a real-world business problem-solving assignment?

Now, at school or later in your work, you get real-world business problem-solving assignments. There will be principals or problem-owners, such as managers, who assign you to solve their business problems. *What* will you do when you get such an assignment? Most people will simply accept the principal's definition of the problem. But a solution for the principal's problem will not improve the business if the principal's perceived problem is *not* the real problem. For example, a principal of a retail store chain tells us that the store personnel are not customer-centric enough. Our solution is to train and incentivize the personnel to act in a customer-centric way. But after implementation of our solution, store sales remain low. We wonder: Why is that so? The most important problem of this retail business appears to be online competition and not a lack of customer centricity. We have solved the wrong problem. Most people tend to do one of the following on problem-solving assignments:

a. Jump to conclusions: come up with solutions without doing analyses.
b. Dive into the data: endlessly search for more and more data.
c. Do the popular framework analyses, such as the strengths, weaknesses, opportunities, and threats (SWOT) analysis.

What will typically happen in these situations?

a. Recommendations without supporting analyses. Principal asks: "Why would this solution work?"
b. A lot of data but a lack of analysis. Principal: "What are the insights from your data?"
c. Nice analyses but no recommendations. Principal: "What are the implications of your insights?"

MAIN LEARNING OBJECTIVES

In this chapter we show how to avoid such problems with problem-solving. After studying this chapter, you should be able to:

- identify a business problem or opportunity
- verify a business problem or opportunity
- evaluate the suitability of solving a business problem or opportunity
- assess the context of a problem or opportunity
- formulate a key question about a problem or opportunity
- appreciate critical thinking

This chapter is about the first step of structured problem-solving: identify business problems (and opportunities).

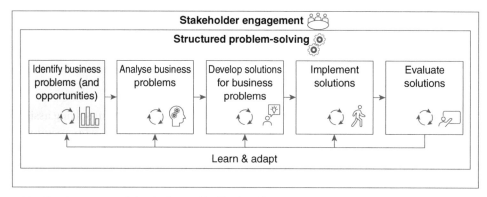

Figure 2.1   Identifying business problems is the first step of structured problem-solving

This chapter will outline how to identify problems (see Figure 2.2). Next, we discuss how to identify an opportunity.

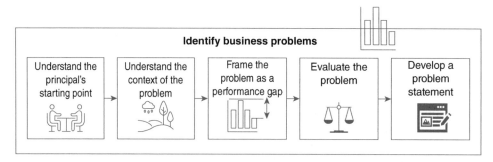

Figure 2.2   Identify business problems in five steps

PART 1: IDENTIFY BUSINESS PROBLEMS

Critical thinking plays a critical role in problem identification. Recall that critical thinking is conceptualizing information, logical reasoning, analysing, synthesizing, and evaluating information to guide a belief and action. To identify real problems, we must:

- conceptualize: use systems thinking to see the 'big picture'
- use logical reasoning: develop arguments why problems exist
- analyse: think open-mindedly about problems, and consider alternative systems of thought
- synthesize: 'connect the dots' to draw conclusions about problems
- evaluate: test assumptions about problems

Understand the principal's starting point

Principals own the problems

Various persons may experience the same problem of a company, but generally, there is one person in the focal company who is responsible for that problem. This person is the so-called 'problem-owner'. The problem-owner *must* solve the problem and *can* do something about the problem. The problem-owner may assign you to solve the problem. If you are an employee of a company, your manager can be your principal. If you are a management consultant, the client is your principal.

 Pause and Reflect

Use your own experience of a recent project from your study or work. During your introductory meeting, did you check whether you were sitting with the principal at the table? Did you ask this person: "If I develop a solution for the problem, can you decide to implement it or do you need the approval of someone else?"

Understanding the principal's starting point is the first step of identifying business problems. We develop such understanding in three steps (see Figure 2.3).

Listen to the principal's question

Principals may respond in various ways to business problems. Their response influences their instructions for you as problem-solver. We distinguish between the following situations.

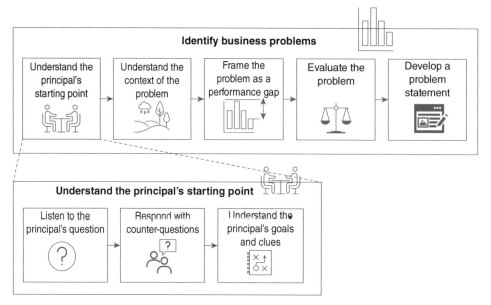

Figure 2.3   Understand the principal's starting point in three steps

- The principal believes she already knows the solution to the business problem
  - Principal's instruction for you: "Implement this solution." For example, implement an agile way of working as a solution for a problem of high costs.
  - Principal's question for you: "How can we best implement this solution?"
- The principal believes she already has alternative solutions
  - Principal's question for you: "What is the best solution?" For example, if the problem is low sales, what is the best solution: discounts, more advertising, or a customer loyalty programme?
- The principal does not yet know the solution, but she believes that she knows the problem
  - Principal's instruction for you: "Develop a solution." For example, the principal perceives that unattractive employment conditions cause too high voluntary employee turnover.
  - Principal's question for you: "How can we best solve this problem?" More specifically: "How should we improve the employment conditions?"
- The principal believes she has a problem, but she is not sure
  - Principal's instruction for you: "Analyse this and analyse that. Collect this data and collect that data." For example, analyse the company's competitors and costs. Collect data about the market and about the customer complaints.
  - Principal's question for you: "Is this a problem?" For example, an increasing number of talented employees resigns. The principal wonders whether the wages are a problem.

- The principal only has feelings and hunches about the problem
  - Principal's question for you: "What is going on? Is there a problem?" For example, absenteeism among production personnel is increasing but the principal has no clue whether the level of absenteeism is problematic or not.

Figure 2.4 shows how a principal's typical response to a problem varies with her *perceived* knowledge about that problem.

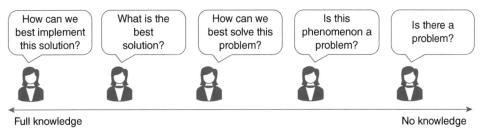

Figure 2.4   **Some examples of how a principal may respond to a problem**

 **Pause and Reflect**

Use your own experience of a recent project from your study or work. Did you ask yourself: Why does the principal ask this question? Is there a question behind the question?

Running Case RobotCo[1]

RobotCo is a medium-sized manufacturer of industrial robots for manufacturing tasks. This company has 75 customers with 1,800 robots installed at customer sites in 20 countries. Its customers are industrial production companies which produce 24 hours a day and 7 days per week. Therefore, robot uptime (time during which a robot can function) is a critical success factor. RobotCo's customer services engineers provide maintenance and repair at customer sites. They replace broken or worn robot parts. RobotCo employs 200 customer services engineers. Monthly, the engineers order 4,500 spare parts for maintenance and repair. The company has several warehouses for spare parts.

(Continued)

---

[1]RobotCo is a fictive company. This case and other cases and examples in this book are inspired by real-world situations but simplified for easy comprehension.

RobotCo faces a problem of late delivery of parts to customers for repair jobs. Late delivery delays repairs, which reduces robot uptime. Customers complain about the delays. The delivery problems arose because the requested parts were not in stock in RobotCo's warehouse. To have the right parts in stock, RobotCo developed software that predicts the demand for parts. Based on the data about the functioning of robots at customer sites during the past years, the software predicts the future demand for parts for the maintenance and repair of robots. Much to the disappointment of RobotCo's management, the software has not solved the problem of the late delivery of parts. Customers continue to complain about delays, and some have switched to one of RobotCo's competitors. The delivery problem is becoming increasingly important and RobotCo's general manager decides that Tara, one of the company's management trainees, should focus on this problem. Tara, who graduated in business administration two years ago, has already solved a few small problems quickly and well. This is an opportunity to show that she can also solve a large problem.

Respond with counter-questions

How to respond to the principal's questions and instructions? Do not take those questions and instructions blindly. The principal might be wrong. We need to find out whether the principal is right by asking critical questions: "*Why* is this perceived problem relevant for the company?" Continue to ask 'Why?' to discover the problem behind the problem.

- The principal believes she already knows the solution
  - For example, the principal asks: "How can we best implement this solution?"
  - Suggested response: Counter the principal's question by asking the principal: "Could you please clarify the problem?" After the principal's clarification of the problem, ask: "*How* will this solution benefit your company?" Subsequently put the following questions to the principal: "*Why* is this the best solution for that problem? Have you considered any alternative solutions? How do you compare these alternative solutions?"
- The principal believes she already has alternative solutions
  - For example, a principal considers two options for solving the problem and she asks you: "*What* is the best solution?"
  - Suggested response: Like the previous situation, counter the question by asking the principal to clarify the problem and the solutions. Continue as outlined in the previous bullet point.
- The principal does not yet know the solution, but she believes that she knows the problem

○ For example, a principal perceives that unattractive employment conditions cause too high voluntary employee turnover. She asks you: "How should we improve the employment conditions?"

○ Suggested response: Counter the question by asking the principal to clarify the problem: "Why is this problem (of high voluntary employee turnover) relevant for your company?"

- The principal believes she has a problem, but she is not sure

○ For example, a principal believes the low wage is a problem. Her question for you: "Is the low wage a problem?"

○ Suggested response: Counter the question by asking the principal to clarify the problem. Question for you to ask: "*Why* would the low wage pose a problem for your company?"

○ A principal gives you instructions: "Analyse this and that. Collect this and that data."

○ Suggested response for the instruction: Ask the principal: "For what analyses do you need these data?" Or ask: "Why do you need these analyses?"

○ If a principal has too many requests, ask that principal to prioritise the analyses. "Which analysis has the highest priority for you?"

- The principal only has feelings and hunches about the problem

○ For example, a principal asks you: "Is the increasing absenteeism a problem?"

○ Suggested response: Ask the principal: "*Why* is increasing absenteeism relevant for your company?"

Understand the principal's performance objectives and problem clues

By asking 'Why?', we find out what performance *objectives* and problem clues the principal may have. For problem-solving, we focus on the company's objectives. We use the term objectives because they are more specific than goals, which we interpret as the broadly defined desired outcomes that indicate the long-term direction of the company. Profit is an objective of all companies. But companies can also have objectives for people and the planet. We distinguish between three types of problem clues or indicators: financial indicators; non-financial, quantitative indicators; and hunches and feelings (see Figure 2.5).

- *Financial indicators*: The principal has financial indicators of a business not running properly. For example, costs are above budget or revenues are below the desired level. The selling price and the sales volume are below the desired levels.

- *Non-financial, quantitative indicators*: The principal has measurable indicators of a business not running properly. For example, the principal receives complaints from customers about a business process outcome, such as the timely delivery of products; or the principal measures a gap between the actual and desired levels of a process indicator. For example, the level of employee absenteeism is too high, or the level of employee satisfaction is too low.

- *Hunches and feelings*: The principal develops hunches and feelings that a business process does not run according to plan. For example, the principal has a hunch that the employees involved in a production process do not collaborate well enough.

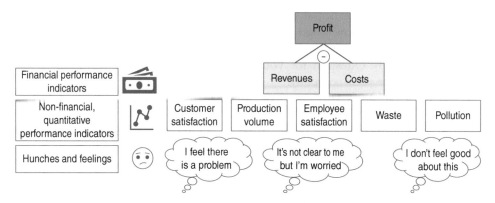

Figure 2.5   Some examples of problem clues that a principal may have

 **How To Do It?**

Not only talk with the principal but also obtain perspectives from other stakeholders inside but also outside the principal's company: speak to other people and collect information from other sources. *Why?* The principal may have cognitive biases that distort his view of the problem. Moreover, the principal may have personal interests that influence his definition of the problem. If you only talk with the principal, you risk a narrow or incorrect definition of a problem. Therefore, look for other knowledgeable people inside and outside the principal's company. Include people who disagree with the principal's problem definition.

Running Case RobotCo

RobotCo's general manager (GM) assigns Tara to solve the delivery problem. During her initial meeting Tara asks the GM: "Can you explain how late deliveries impact your business?" The GM seems surprised: "Is it not quite clear? The late delivery of parts delays the repairs of robots. Repair delays reduce robot uptime. Uptime is an important driver of customer satisfaction. Satisfaction influences customer loyalty. Dissatisfied customers may switch to our competitors. Customer loss means lower revenues. Lower revenues mean lower profit." Tara responds: "Thank you. So, if I understand you correctly, the ultimate impact of the late deliveries is lower profit. Do you have any idea where the late deliveries problem comes from?" The GM replies: "We do not know that yet. That is the reason I assigned you to this problem." Figure 2.6 shows the chain of causality from the waiting time to the company's performance objective.

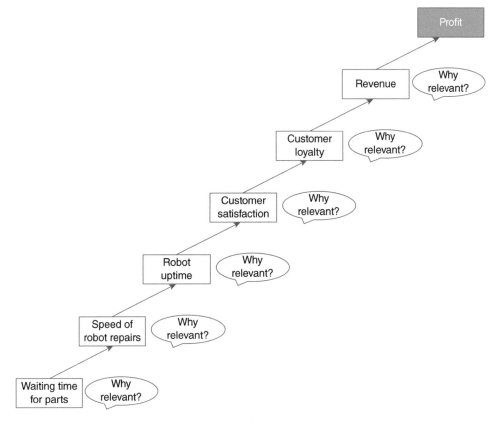

Figure 2.6   An example of a chain of causality from a problem to the company's performance objective

---

 Pause and Reflect

Use your own experience of a recent project from your study or work. Did you ask yourself: Is this problem definition the principal's personal opinion, or is it widely supported in the company?

 **How To Do It?**

Ask: *Why* is this performance gap relevant for the company? Repeat this question until you have reached the level of the company's highest performance objectives: profit, people, and the planet. In practice, a problem does not always have to reach the highest performance level. For example, RobotCo's customers may not care if parts are delivered a little late. Another example is that RobotCo's customers are dissatisfied with a delay of parts but that they continue to buy from the company because there are no (attractive) alternatives. In both examples, the delay does not affect RobotCo's profit. From a *profit* point of view, there is no reason to eliminate the delay.

You identify a problem

We discussed situations where principals identify problems. But *you* may also identify a problem. Then you must convince the principal that she has a problem. You need to explain to the principal why there is a problem. Develop your arguments by asking *yourself* the why-question: Why is this problem relevant for the principal's company? The problem is relevant if it lowers the company performance. The low performance reveals what is at stake for the principal.

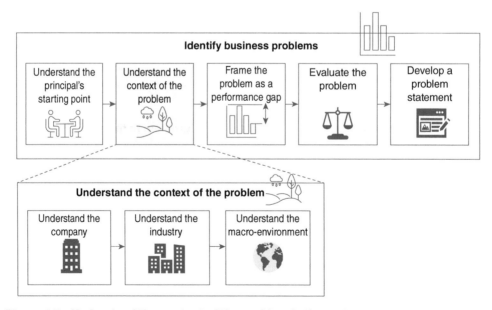

Figure 2.7   Understand the context of the problem in three steps

Understand the context of the problem

Understand who are the stakeholders of the problem

We need to understand the context to solve a problem. The context is the situation or settings in which a problem exists. Most important are the people who have a stake in the problem. We consider the stakeholders as so important that we devote separate chapters to them. Chapter 3 is about identifying stakeholders and Chapter 6 is about collaborating with them.

If the problem is about a business process, then find the persons involved in that process.

- Who are the internal and external providers of the process? Which persons perform the process tasks? Why does the principal use these people?
- Who are the internal and external customers of the process? Why do they use or buy the products, services, or other outputs from this process? What is the added value of the process for the customers?
- Who are the internal and external suppliers of goods and services for the process? Why does the principal use these suppliers?

 How To Do It? ────────────

Combine multiple sources of information:

- Study any documents about the process
- Interview the principal
- Observe the process in action
- Interview involved persons

Understand what the company is about

You may not know the principal's company well because you are a new hire or a management consultant who had not worked for this company before. Then you need to develop a basic understanding of what the company is about. Figure 2.8 shows an approach.

 How To Do It? ────────────

We can use various ways to develop an understanding of the principal's company. Frameworks are a good starting point. Before seizing the valuable time from the

(Continued)

principal and other stakeholders, we do homework in the form of desk research. We start with the principal's company website and company documents, such as annual reports. If answers to our questions are not available via desk research, then we put our questions to stakeholders. We conduct personal interviews or surveys. But people may be unwilling or unable to answer our questions. They may provide politically correct answers. Alternatively, they may not know the answer. For example, they do not have a big picture of a work process. Then we observe people in action at work.

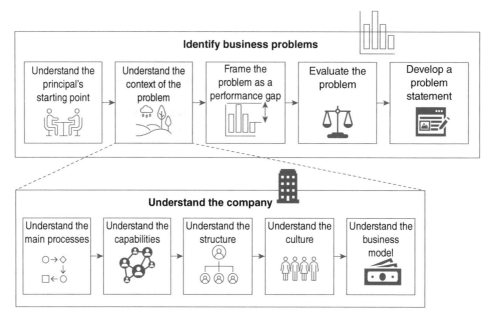

Figure 2.8   Understand the principal's company in five steps

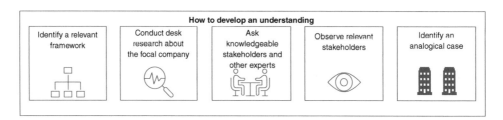

Figure 2.9   Five ways to develop an understanding of the principal's context

Understand what the process is about

What does a business process in the principal's company look like? What are the process steps? We map the process. There are different frameworks we may use.

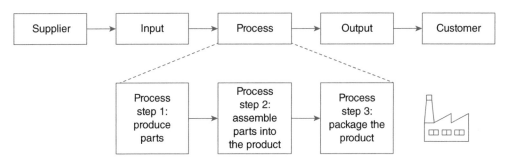

Figure 2.10   An example of a SIPOC framework

Figure 2.10 shows an example of a SIPOC framework. SIPOC is the acronym of Supplier, Input, Process, Output, and Customer.

— **Pause and Reflect** ———————————————————————————

Use your own experience of a recent project from your study or work. Did you ask yourself: Do I understand what the principal's business is about?

————————————————— **Running Case RobotCo** —————————————————

Tara asks the involved managers about the production and delivery of robot parts. Figure 2.11 shows a process flow chart of RobotCo's parts production and delivery process.

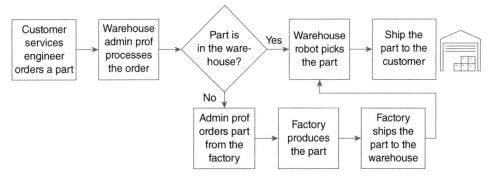

Figure 2.11   An example of a process flow chart of parts production and delivery

Note: 'admin prof' means administrative professional

How To Do It?

1. Ask the principal whether an up-to-date process chart is available. Do not reinvent the wheel.
2. Check whether the official chart matches the reality of practice. People may deviate from the official process.

If there is no up-to-date chart or if practice substantially deviates from the charted process, then create a chart yourself.

1. Interview the principal.
2. Observe the process.
3. Interview persons involved in the process.
4. Make a first attempt. Create a provisional chart. It does not have to be perfect.
5. Share it with the involved persons and ask for feedback. Use the feedback to make improvements.
6. Share the improved chart with the principal and ask for approval or feedback.

 Pause and Reflect

Use your own experience of a recent project from your study or work. Did you ask yourself: Does this process flow chart reflect practice?

Understand the links to other processes

If a problem is about a process, we need to understand the bigger picture as well. How does the process fit in the company's value chain (see Figure 2.12)? For example, we must understand the links between the problematic process and other processes.

In addition, we need to understand any links between the problematic process and any *external* organizations. Therefore, we need to look at the suppliers, complementors (the providers of products and services that are complementary to the principal company's products and services), distributors, and customers. A useful concept is the value system (see Figure 2.13).

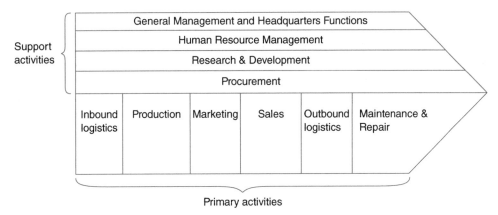

Figure 2.12   An example of a company's value chain (Porter, 1985)

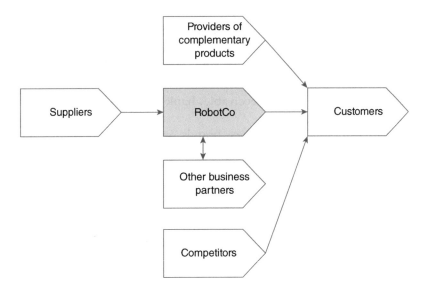

Figure 2.13   RobotCo's value system

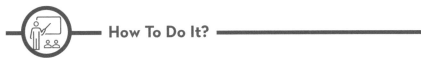

How To Do It?

We ask the principal whether the value chain and value system charts are available. If there are no up-to-date charts, then we create charts ourselves. We interview the principal and other knowledgeable persons. Moreover, we may observe the company's internal processes and relations with external organizations.

Understand the capabilities of the company

A business capability is an ability of an organization (abilities of individuals are skills) for conducting activities or processes. Capabilities define what a company can do. Capabilities are not the same as processes. Therefore, we use nouns for capabilities and verbs for processes. To manufacture robots, RobotCo needs a manufacturing capability. A business capability is based on an organization of people, often in combination with assets, such as machines and equipment.

Understand the resources of the company

Resources are what a company owns or controls. We distinguish between the following categories:

- Human resources: permanent and temporary employees
- Material or physical or tangible resources
    - Fixed or non-current material resources: land, buildings, and equipment
    - Variable or current material resources: inventory of finished goods, work-in-progress, and raw materials and other physical inputs for producing goods
- Financial resources: accounts receivable, bank accounts, cash, as well as bonds and shares of other companies
- Intellectual or intangible resources: brands, copyrights, goodwill, patents, and trademarks

Understand the structure of the company

An organogram or organisational chart shows the reporting structure. Tara discusses the organogram of RobotCo with the GM (see Figure 2.14).

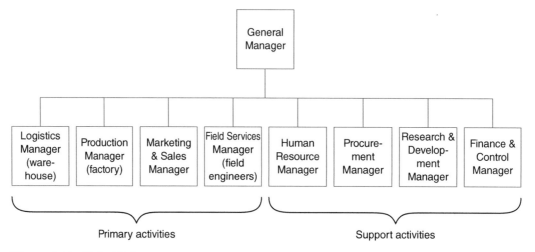

Figure 2.14   RobotCo's organogram

How To Do It?

We ask the principal whether an organizational chart is available. If there is no up-to-date chart, then we create a chart ourselves. We interview the principal and other knowledgeable persons, like the HR manager. In addition, we look at the *informal* organization, which is the network of social and personal relationships between individuals that develops spontaneously when people associate with each other in a work environment.

Understand how a process is organized

We should also understand how a company organizes a business process. Therefore, we look at the division of roles and responsibilities in the process. A RASCI matrix is a tool for mapping the organization of a process (see Figure 2.15).

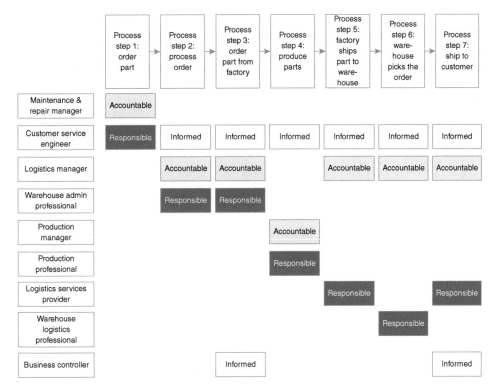

	Process step 1: order part	Process step 2: process order	Process step 3: order part from factory	Process step 4: produce parts	Process step 5: factory ships part to warehouse	Process step 6: warehouse picks the order	Process step 7: ship to customer
Maintenance & repair manager	Accountable						
Customer service engineer	Responsible	Informed	Informed	Informed	Informed	Informed	Informed
Logistics manager		Accountable	Accountable		Accountable	Accountable	Accountable
Warehouse admin professional		Responsible	Responsible				
Production manager				Accountable			
Production professional				Responsible			
Logistics services provider					Responsible		Responsible
Warehouse logistics professional						Responsible	
Business controller			Informed				Informed

Figure 2.15   A RASCI matrix of RobotCo's production process

The acronym refers to the following roles and responsibilities:

- Responsible: a person is responsible for a process step or task
- Accountable: a person has the final responsibility for a step, and has the right of final approval

- Supporting: a person provides support for the completion of a step
- Consulted: a person's expertise is used for a step
- Informed: a person is kept updated on the progress and completion of a step

 How To Do It?

We ask the principal whether a RASCI matrix is available. If there is no up-to-date matrix, then we create such a matrix ourselves. We use job descriptions, and we interview the persons involved in the process. Thereby, we distinguish between formal and informal roles.

Understand the culture of the company

The organizational culture is the set of shared values, beliefs, and behaviours of an organization's people that determines how these persons interact with each other and with external stakeholders. The culture manifests itself in many ways, such as the management style, the communication style, personal relationships, dress style, and the interior design of the office. A company's culture is like an individual's personality.

Understand the business model of the company

A business model is a description of how a company earns money by making and selling a product or service that is of value to customers. The business model canvas is a popular template to map a business model (see Figure 2.16).

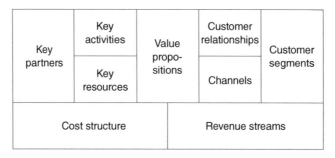

Figure 2.16   A business model canvas (Osterwalder & Pigneur, 2010)

Understand the industry

The Five Forces Framework by Porter (1980) helps us understand the principal's industry. Porter distinguishes between five competitive forces:

- The bargaining power of buyers (for example, the principal's company is a small supplier of commodity parts to very large car manufacturers)
- The bargaining power of suppliers (for example, the principal's company is a computer hardware manufacturer which is highly dependent on the supply of advanced microchips)
- The rivalry among existing competitors (for example, the principal's company is one of many consumer electronics retailers on the web)
- The threat of new entrants (for example, the principal's company is a popular subscription streaming platform but fears that some large entertainment companies will enter the streaming market with rival offerings)
- The threat of substitute products (for example, the principal's company is a car dealer and fears the rise of car sharing)

If applicable, we add the power of complementors and industry regulators as additional forces. To keep Figure 2.17 simple, we group existing competitors, new entrants, and substitutes together under the label 'competitors'.

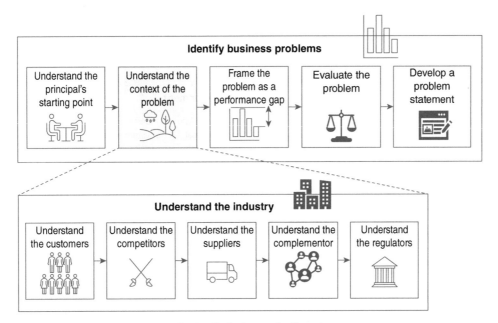

Figure 2.17　Understand the principal's industry in five steps

Understand the macro-environment

The PESTEL Framework can help us understand the principal's macro-environment:

- Political developments (for example, the principal is a fast-food restaurant chain with many employees and a new government raises the minimum wage)
- Economic developments (for example, the principal is a retail bank and a high inflation rate reduces the attractiveness of savings)
- Social developments (for example, the principal is a producer of meat products which faces a trend towards vegetarian food)
- Technological developments (for example, the principal is a producer of wallets that must deal with the digitization of payments)
- Environmental developments (for example, the principal is a coffee producer plagued by crop failures due to long periods of heat and drought)
- Legal developments (for example, the principal is a polluting industrial company that is subject to legal restrictions on greenhouse gas emissions)

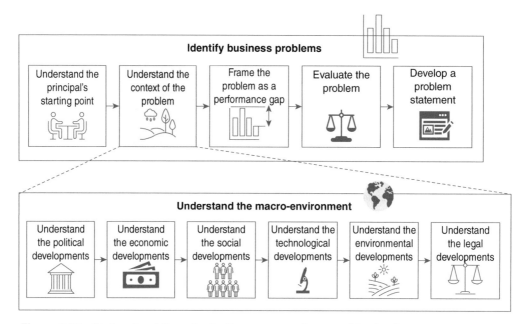

Figure 2.18   Understand the principal's macro-environment in six steps

Frame the problem as a performance gap

Define the problem in terms of performance

If the 'why-why-why' questioning leads to the performance objectives of a company, then there is a *real* rather than a perceived business problem. We define real business problems in relation to a company's performance. If there is no relation between a perceived problem and a company's performance, we do not consider it a real business problem.

'Problem' is a common word that we all understand. But for this method we define problem in a particular way. We define a problem as *a gap between a performance objective and an actual or realized, lower performance*. We illustrate it with a simple example. A person experiences a problem. She is dissatisfied with something, for example her income. The person experiences a gap between the situation that she desires (a desired income or income objective) and the actual undesired situation (the actual, lower income). There is a gap between the desired result and the actual, undesired result regarding something (income). The person does not get what she wants.

Define business problems

A business problem is about the performance of a company. Performance can refer to the company's *processes*. Process performance can be the quality of the process output, the quantity of the process output, the speed of a process, and the costs of a process. The principal perceives that a business process is not running according to the plan, target, or budget. The actual performance of that process is below the desired level. For example, the actual number of goods produced is below the desired number. We can distinguish between the problems of internal and external-facing processes.

- An internal process like manufacturing is not running according to the budget. For example, the actual manufacturing costs of a company's factory are above the budgeted costs.
- An external-facing process like selling is not running according to the sales target. For example, the actual number of product sales of a company's sales force is below the target.

Distinguish between different levels

A problem can be company-wide, departmental, at the level of a business process, or individual.

- Company-wide problem: a company does not meet its performance objectives. For example, a company fails to achieve its profit objective.
- Departmental problem: a department does not meet its performance objectives. For example, a sales department does not reach its sales target.
- Process-level problem: a process does not meet its performance objectives. For example, a marketing process does not generate the required number of leads.
- Individual-level problem: an individual does not meet her performance objectives. For example, an account manager does not reach her personal sales target.

Identify the performance objective

We must understand the principal's key performance indicator (KPI) tree (see Figure 2.20). Production performance indicators are

- the quality of the process output
- the quantity of output or process volume
- the speed of production
- the costs of production

Ask the principal: Why is low quality, low quantity, or low speed relevant to the company? If you continue to ask why, the principal will eventually answer that these indicators influence profit, which is the highest-level financial performance objective of a company.

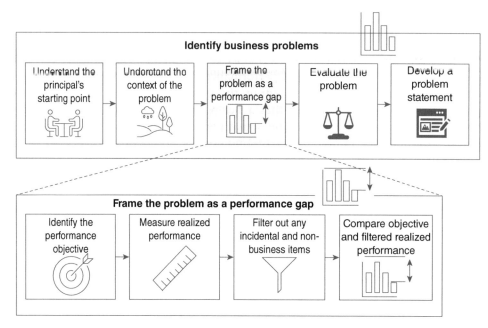

Figure 2.19   Frame the principal's problem as a performance gap in four steps

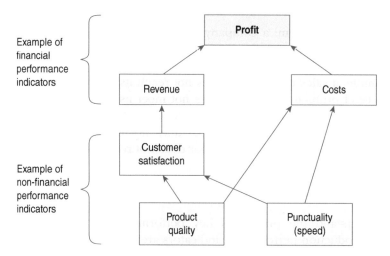

Figure 2.20   A simplified example of a key performance indicator tree

How To Do It?

First, ask the principal whether the company has a KPI tree. Do not reinvent the wheel. If there is no KPI tree, then create a tree yourself. Interview knowledgeable persons, such as a business controller, to identify the KPI. Chapter 4 will explain how to put the indicators into a logical structure.

Identify the right performance indicator for the principal

Identify the right performance indicator for the principal. What is right depends on the hierarchical level of the principal. General managers are responsible for profit. Sales manager will have sales targets. Targets for the production manager will be about production volume, production costs, and product quality. Objectives should be SMART: Specific, Measurable, Achievable, Relevant, and Time-bound.

How To Do It?

Ask the principal: What are your performance objectives? On what performance indicator(s) will your superior judge you?

Measure the realized performance

Having identified the principal's performance indicator, we can collect data about the actual or realized performance. In the case of profit, the financial department of the principal's company can provide us with the data. The principal must ensure that the data owner, such as the financial manager, gives us access to the necessary data.

Filter out any incidental and non-business items

Figure 2.21 shows the development of a performance gap over time. A real problem of a company implies a gap of a relevant performance indicator. The importance of a gap increases with its size, growth, and duration. We do not limit ourselves to one moment in time but choose a period. The minimum length of the measurement period depends on the type of process. Processes that take more time require a longer measurement period than shorter processes. We distinguish between a *one-time* or incidental gap and a structural or permanent gap. An example of a cause of an incidental gap is the costs of a one-time reorganization.

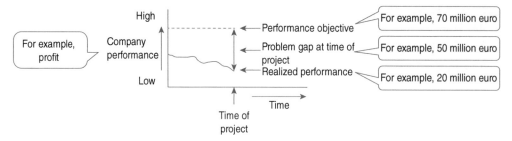

Figure 2.21   An example of the development of a performance gap over time

This book is about *business* solutions for *business* problems. In the case of profit, we look at the *operating* profit, which is the profit from the business operations: sales minus operating costs. We acknowledge the importance of interest and tax for net profit. But interest and tax are non-operating items. Interest and tax problems require, respectively, financial and fiscal knowledge and skills, which are outside the scope of this book.

────────────────   **Running Case RobotCo**   ────────────────

Tara has measured the gap between the waiting time objective and the longer realized time. Recall that RobotCo's highest financial performance objective is profit. RobotCo looks for solutions that close the waiting time gap *in order to* close the profit gap. Solutions for the time problem that do not close the profit gap are outside the scope of this project.

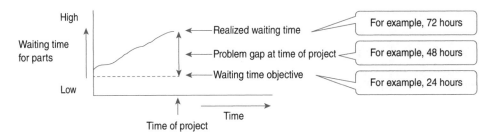

Figure 2.22   A waiting time gap

Account for other objectives besides profit

We have focused on profit as a company's highest financial performance objective. But companies also have a corporate social responsibility (CSR). The so-called '*triple bottom line*' means that companies also have objectives about the well-being of people and the planet.

Multiple objectives can mean multiple performance gaps. We may measure the performance of a business process along three dimensions: profit, impact on people, and impact on the planet (see Figure 2.23).

- 'Profit performance' is about the efficiency (costs), effectiveness, and speed of a business process.
- 'People performance' includes well-being, employee satisfaction, fair pay, fair working hours, safe and healthy working conditions, non-discrimination, job security, insurance, and pension plan. People-related 'Grand Challenges' (a term of the United Nations) are about inequality, injustice, corruption, poverty, and discrimination in society.
- 'Planet performance' is, among others, no greenhouse gas emission and other pollution, no waste, no exhaustion of rare materials, and recycling. Planet-related 'Grand Challenges' are about environmental pollution, climate change, and the exhaustion of natural resources, including drinkable water.

Compare the objective and the realized performance

With the objective and the realized performance, we can identify the performance gap. We compare the performance objective with the realized performance. If the realized performance is lower than the objective, then the principal has a problem. But the realized performance may also exceed the objective.

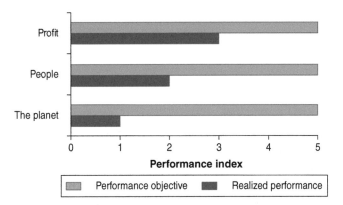

Figure 2.23 An example of multiple performance gaps

Note: The performance index is a composite of indicators. The people performance index is a composite of, for example, well-being, health and safety conditions, and living wages. The planet performance index is a composite of, for example, greenhouse gas emission, percentage recycling, and usage of rare materials.

Running Case RobotCo

Tara discusses with the GM what RobotCo's other objectives besides profit are. The GM mentions that RobotCo aims to improve employee well-being and reduce emissions resulting

(Continued)

from production. Figure 2.24 shows RobotCo's simultaneous gaps for profit, people, and the planet.

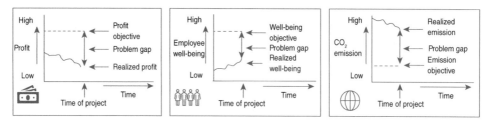

Figure 2.24   Examples of triple performance gaps

   **How To Do It?**

Identify the company's people and planet performance indicators. If they are not available, develop indicators together with the principal and any other knowledgeable persons. Identify the objectives. Measure the actual performances and compare them to the objectives.

Evaluate the problem

Is the problem worth solving?

If a problem is real, there is a performance gap. Next, we must consider whether the problem is worth solving. Therefore, we do a cost–benefit analysis. The larger the gap, the larger the benefits of problem-solving are. Therefore, we need to assess the size, duration, and any growth over time of the performance gap. We cannot predict the future of the gap, but we can make an educated guess of how a gap may evolve over time. Next to sizing the gap, we need to make a rough estimate of the costs of solving the problem.

Running Case RobotCo

Tara discusses with the business controller the impact of the late deliveries on RobotCo's profit. Currently, lost orders and cancellations due to late deliveries cost RobotCo around 30 million euro of revenue. At a 50 per cent profit margin, the resulting profit impact is 15 million euro. The controller predicts that the profit gap will grow if RobotCo lets this delivery problem run its course. Tara discusses that problem with the GM. The GM concludes: "Solving the late delivery problem is our number one priority!"

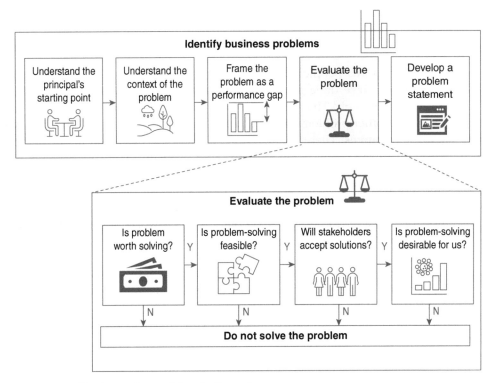

Figure 2.25   **Evaluate the problem in four steps**

Is problem-solving feasible?

The problem may be worth solving, but *can* the principal's company solve it? Therefore, we need to answer the following questions:

- Is the problem familiar to us?
- Have we or others solved the same or a similar problem before?
- Does the principal's company have the resources and capabilities for solving this problem?

If the principal thinks the company can solve the problem, then ask: "How much confidence do you have that the company can solve the problem?" Have the principal name a percentage between zero and one hundred.

Will the stakeholders accept the solution?

We may be able to solve the problem for the principal. However, can the principal implement the solution if some powerful stakeholders inside or outside the company do not approve or accept that solution? We need to ask ourselves: "Are there any stakeholders that probably will block solutions to this problem?" Chapters 3 and 6 will outline how to answer that important question.

Is problem-solving desirable for us?

Problem-solving requires people and other resources. The use of resources entails costs. Therefore, we have done a cost–benefit analysis (step 1). But a positive net result may not be enough. The (human) resources of a company are scarce. The company may face other problems and opportunities that also require the company's scarce (human) resources. Therefore, we need to compare the result of solving the 'focal' problem with the results of addressing other problems and opportunities. We must also consider the level of urgency of the various problems and opportunities. We rank the alternative problems and opportunities that are in search of solutions. The ranking allows us to prioritise these problems and opportunities.

We must also consider the *ethics*. A problem may be worth solving and solving may be feasible, but is it ethical to solve the problem? We ask ourselves:

- "Is the problem ethical?" For example, the principal's problem is about the low production of a factory with unsafe and unhealthy labour conditions and the principal does not want to improve these conditions.
- "Can a solution have (unintended) unethical consequences for some stakeholders?" For example, a solution for a cost problem will increase environmental pollution.
- If we are external consultants, we may ask ourselves: "Is the client's business ethical?" For example, the client sells products or services that are harmful for society, such as tobacco and gambling. Should we solve problems for such a company?

 How To Do It?

What to do if you have too many problems that qualify for solving? You do not have enough resources to solve these problems at the same time. In this case, you can use a priority matrix to rank them in terms of their importance and urgency (see Figure 2.26).

- Importance is about the size of a problem's impact on the principal's performance.
- Urgency is about the time for a problem to significantly impact performance.

You begin with the problems that are most important and most urgent.

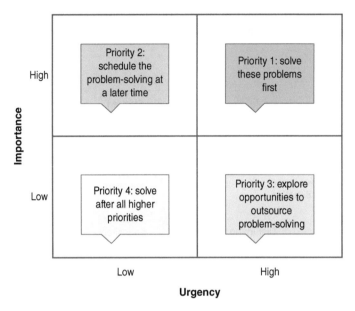

Figure 2.26   **A priority matrix**

Develop a problem statement

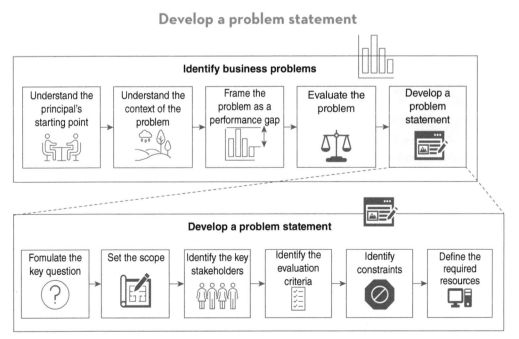

Figure 2.27   **Develop a problem statement in six steps**

Formulate the key question

We define the problem as a question. For that purpose, we use the situation–complication–question framework by Minto (2003) (see Figure 2.28).

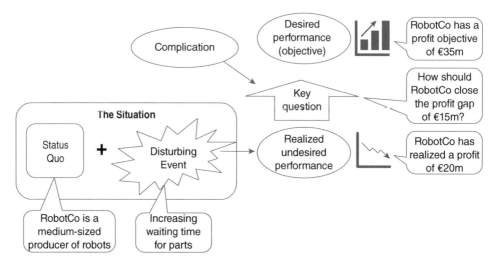

Figure 2.28   The situation–complication–question framework

Note: Author's interpretation based on Minto (2003)

- The *situation* refers to the point of departure of the principal's company. Some event or development disturbed the status quo of that company.
- The *disturbing event* caused the principal's realized performance to be below the objective.
- The *complication* is the aspect that complicates the problem-solving.
  - The complication can be that we do not know whether we have an undesired performance. The corresponding question is: "Do we have a problem?" For example, the principal has realized 10 per cent revenue growth. If the market grew by up to 10 per cent, the principal has done well. But if the market grew by over 10 per cent, the principal has done relatively poorly.
  - The complication can be that we do not know whether the performance objective is correct. The corresponding question is: "What is the performance potential?" For example, the board of the principal's company has set a profit objective of 10 million euro. The management team complains that the target is unattainably high. Who is right: the board or the team?
  - The complication can be that we do not know what the disturbing event is. The corresponding question is: "What has caused the performance gap?" For example, RobotCo knows that the waiting time gap caused a profit gap. But the company does not know what caused the waiting time gap.

- ○ The complication can be that we do not know *how* to close the gap. The corresponding question is: "How should we close the gap?" For example, RobotCo does not know how to close the profit gap.
- We formulate the problem as a single question: *the key question*. It is a prescriptive question. *How should the principal's company close the performance gap?*
  - ○ The question focuses on a SMART objective.
  - ○ The question is action-oriented: How *should* the company...? Note the use of the verb 'should'. The principal does not want to know what *can* be done but what *should* be done. The principal is not looking for a *possible* solution, but for the *best* solution.

──────────── **Running Case RobotCo** ────────────

Tara discusses the delivery problem with the GM. The problem is that actual time is double the objective. The GM wants to close that gap within one (1) year. Therefore, the GM formulates the following key question: "How should RobotCo halve the waiting time for parts within one year?" Tara disagrees with this formulation of the key question. Waiting time is not Robotco's highest objective; the highest financial objective is profit. Tara has estimated the impact of the waiting time problem on profit to be around 15 million euro. A solution to the waiting time problem should close the 15 million euro profit gap. This solution should *not* come at the expense of profit. Such a solution may be attractive for field engineering, but is bad for the company. Therefore, Tara formulates the key question at the highest performance level: *"How should RobotCo respond to the problem of the late delivery of parts to increase its profit by 15 million euro in one year?"*

What to do with multiple simultaneous problems

The company may have multiple problems. Figure 2.29 shows how various problems influence RobotCo's performance.

The complexity of problem-solving increases with the number of problems. Therefore, we try to reduce the number of problems.

1. We *rank* the problems in terms of importance and urgency. How important and urgent are the problems? We plot the performance impact and urgency of the problems in a priority matrix (see Figure 2.26). We prioritise the most important and most urgent problems.
2. We *group* these prioritised problems. Are these problems related to each other? If they are related, then we group them together. For example, a company has a gap for employee absenteeism (actual absenteeism exceeds the objective, or the maximum allowable absenteeism) and a gap for voluntary turnover of employees (actual turnover exceeds the objective, or the maximum allowable turnover). The company may group these two problems as employee-related problems. We create a relatively small number of groups.

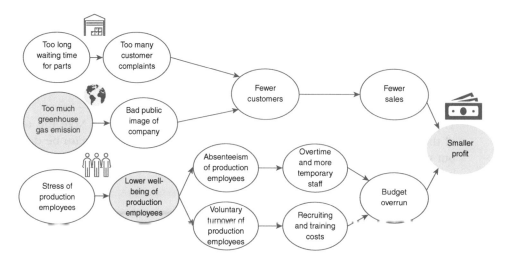

Figure 2.29   A stylized example of how problems influence performance

What to do when one problem causes multiple gaps

One problem may cause multiple performance gaps. For example, outdated production technology leads to:

- high production costs (at the expense of profit)
- health problems for the production personnel
- and pollution of the environment

But multiple gaps may also arise from *different* problem causes. Figure 2.30 provides a stylized example of the assessment of the multiple performance impacts. Multiple gaps for multiple objectives, not only profit but also people and the planet, complicate the problem-solving. Solutions must meet various performance objectives, not only profit but also people and the planet. Therefore, a problem statement must distinguish between the relevant performance indicators.

	Performance indicator	Profit	People	Planet	Overall
	Weight of indicator	+++	+	+	
Problem	Too long waiting time for parts	High	Low	Low	High
	Too much greenhouse gas emission	Low	Low	High	Low
	Stress of production employees	Medium	High	Low	Medium

Figure 2.30   A stylized example of an assessment of the impact of three different problems on various performance indicators

Set the scope

We should agree with the principal on the scope of the project. What is 'in-scope' and what is 'out-scope'? What does the principal expect from us?

- It is obvious that we need to provide a problem analysis. But what should be the level of accuracy, detail, and depth of the analysis?
- Does the principal want one (1) recommended solution or a set of alternative solutions from which she can choose? How detailed should the solutions be?
- Do we also need to create an implementation plan for the recommended solution? If so, how concrete should such a plan be?

Scope creep

'Scope creep' means the unauthorized and uncontrolled expansion or other changes in the scope of the project, leading to extra work for us. We distinguish between five possible sources of scope creep:

- *Underestimation*: We may underestimate the project challenges.
- *Opportunism*: Opportunistic principals try to expand the project and thus give us more work.
- *Misunderstanding*: Stakeholders may not understand or may misinterpret the project scope because of a lack of communication and the absence of a project charter.
- *Unforeseen events and developments*: Even if the project preparation is thorough, we cannot wholly avoid scope creep. Unexpected events and developments can cause scope creep.
- *Change of priorities*: The priorities and wishes of the principal may change. As a result, we must now carry out actions that were previously irrelevant or unimportant to the principal.

──────── Running Case RobotCo ────────

Tara discusses the project scope with the GM. The GM wants Tara to investigate the waiting time problem and develop a recommendation. The GM thinks that Tara should focus on the logistics process. Tara responds: "I would be happy to *start* with logistics but if the problem is not there, then we should look elsewhere." The GM agrees.

Identify the stakeholders

Stakeholders are vital for problem-solving. That is why we devote two chapters to stakeholders. Chapter 3 is about identifying stakeholders. In Chapter 6 we describe how we can best deal with different types of stakeholders.

Identify the evaluation criteria

We must know how the principal will evaluate the recommended solution. Solutions should close the performance gap. But when will the principal be happy with a solution? What evaluation criteria will the principal apply? Without criteria we can only guess what the principal wants. We may assume that we know what the principal is looking for, but we face an unpleasant surprise if it turns out that we were wrong. If we do not know how the principal will evaluate our recommendation, how can we develop one? If we do not know when the principal will be satisfied, then problem-solving becomes a gamble. Then we need luck. We should know upfront (before solution development) how the principal will evaluate our solution. The principal may not have thought about criteria. She may be used to making intuitive decisions. In that case, we must encourage the principal to make the evaluation criteria explicit.

Identify the constraints

What solutions will the principal *not* accept? What are the constraints to the solution space: the space within which we may seek solutions? Sources of constraints are resource limitations, values, or company strategy.

- If the principal has limited financial resources, then we should not propose solutions requiring massive investments.
- The solution should not conflict with the company values. For example, a company has a full employment policy. Solutions involving mass layoffs will not be acceptable.
- There should be no conflict with the company strategy. For example, if the strategy is cost leadership, then we should not propose solutions that lead to costs that are higher than those of competitors.

Define the required resources

We need to define what resources we need for the problem-solving. We need to know how to approach problem analysis and solution development. This book follows the structured problem-solving method. The resources for the problem-solving are mainly about people, data, facilities (such as an office and office equipment), and budget. We need people who:

- have insights into the problem and ideas for solutions
- own data or can collect data
- can analyse data
- can provide project support, such as, planning, organizing, and facilitating meetings, project-related communication, and administrative support

Running Case RobotCo

Figure 2.31 shows the main parts of Tara's problem statement. Due to a lack of space, we omit the details.

Situation	Disturbing event	Key question
Description of status before complication *RobotCo is a medium-sized producer of robots*	The problem trigger *Increasing waiting time for parts*	Problem definition question *How should RobotCo respond to the late parts deliveries problem to increase its profit by 15 million euro in one year?*

Key stakeholders
Influential people who can support or oppose problem-solving
- *Field engineers*
- *Warehouse manager*

Scope of project
What activities are in and what are out?
- *In: Problem diagnosis and solution development*
- *Out: Customer research and solution implementation*

Deliverable of project
- Expected output?
  - o *written report*
  - o *oral presentation with PowerPoints*
- Accuracy level
- Deadline

Evaluation criteria for solution
How will principal evaluate recommendation?
- *Performance impact (profit, people, and the planet)*
- *Ease of implementation*

Solution constraints
What solutions are not feasible or desirable for principal?
- *Large layoffs of employees*
- *Product changes*

Key resources of project
Sources of insights and other support
- *Field engineers*
- *Warehouse manager*

Figure 2.31   An example of a problem statement

Ask the principal to approve the problem statement

We present the problem statement to the principal and answer any questions the principal may have. We may have to incorporate the principal's feedback in the problem statement. If the principal agrees with the (updated) statement, she should formally approve it. We ask her to sign the problem statement document. The problem statement serves as a memorandum of understanding and as a contract for the problem-solving project.

Design the project proposal

The problem statement is about *what* we will do. After the sign-off by the principal, we design *how* we will do the problem-solving. We combine the 'what' and the 'how' into a project proposal. The 'how' is about choosing methods and techniques for problem-solving. We make an educated guesstimate of the required number of interviews, observations, workshops, surveys, and any expenses for external reports and research. We also need to identify the required resources in more detail. We sketch the profile of the required people: the '*who*'. What knowledge, skills, mindset, experience, and personal networks do we need for the problem-solving? Then we prepare a budget. We also make a meeting and communication schedule. A Gantt chart outlines the '*when*' of the project activities. Figure 2.32 shows an example of a project proposal. We present the proposal to the principal for approval. A principal's commitment to a proposal is a critical success factor. After approval, we can start the project.

Problem statement
(Situation, disturbing event, key question, key stakeholders, evaluation criteria, constraints, scope, deliverables, and key resources)

Methods and data	**People and budget**	**Planning**

• Desk research
  ◦ Company studies and financial reporting
  ◦ External research reports
• Field research
  ◦ Interviews
  ◦ Workshops
  ◦ Observations
	• Project team
	  ◦ Member profiles
	• Steering committee
	  ◦ Member profiles
	• Budget
	  ◦ People
	  ◦ Expenses
		Gantt chart
		• Project milestones
		• Meeting and communication schedule

Figure 2.32   **An example of a project proposal**

— **Mini Exercise** —

Think of a recent problem of a well-known company of your choice and use Internet research to frame that problem as a performance gap.

— **Pause and Reflect** —

Use your own experience of a recent project from your study or work. Did you ask yourself: Will the principal really support me with the project or is he only paying lip service?

PART 2: IDENTIFY BUSINESS OPPORTUNITIES

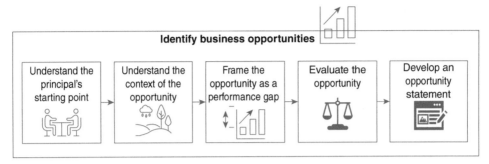

Figure 2.33   Identify business opportunities in five steps

Understand the principal's starting point

Principals may also see opportunities. A principal perceives positive events or developments inside or outside the company that allow the company to raise her performance objective.

- An example of a positive *internal* development is the development of a break-through new product or service by the company's R&D department.
- A positive *external* development is, for example, the opening-up of new geographic markets due to international trade agreements.

But even in the absence of positive events and developments, and in the *absence* of performance gaps, a principal may *believe* that the company can do better. For example, the company is achieving its performance objectives, but the principal believes that the company is not fully utilizing its capabilities, patents, or other assets.

We distinguish between two main types of opportunities:

- *Revenue* opportunities: the principal expects that a revenue increase is possible
- *Cost* opportunities: the principal expects that a cost decrease is possible

Like problems, we define opportunities in performance terms. A problem is a gap between the realized performance and the *current* performance objective. We define an opportunity as a gap between the current performance objective and a higher *new* objective (see Figure 2.34).

How opportunities differ from problems

We distinguish between problems and opportunities because they require a different analysis (see Figure 2.35).

Figure 2.34   An opportunity gap is the difference between a current objective and a higher new objective

	Question	Performance gap	Nature of gap
Problem	Will a (negative) event or development lower the principal's realized performance?	Gap between the realized performance and the current performance objective	Objective gap (the lower realized performance is a fact)
Opportunity	Will a (positive) event or development allow the principal to raise her performance objective?	Gap between the current performance objective and the higher new objective	Subjective gap (the higher performance objective is an expectation)

Figure 2.35   A comparison of a problem and an opportunity

How principals may respond to opportunities

Principals may respond in various ways to opportunities. We distinguish between the following situations:

- The principal believes she already knows the solution for seizing an opportunity
- The principal believes she already has alternative solutions for seizing an opportunity
- The principal does not yet know the solution, but she believes that she knows the opportunity
- The principal believes she has an opportunity, but she is not sure
- The principal only has feelings and hunches about an opportunity

Running Case ConsultCo

ConsultCo is a small management consultancy, consisting of three founders, six consultants, and a secretary. The office is a stately villa in an expensive area of the capital city. In 2003, three young project managers from a large international consultancy firm resigned to start their own consultancy. The three partners focused on digital transformation of medium-sized and large organizations, which was a growth market at that time.

After building up the national practice, they want to develop business abroad as well. The partners want to open new offices in at least three different countries within the next five years. The managing partner (MP) has asked one of the consultants, Arpit, for this internationalization project. Arpit recently graduated from a business school with a specialization in international business. He must investigate the most suitable countries in which ConsultCo can establish itself. The MP has already drawn up a long list of countries and has determined the evaluation criteria, such as:

- the size and growth of the national economy
- the number of medium-sized and large companies in the country
- the number of established rival management consultancies in the country

Respond critically to a principal's opportunity

How to respond to a principal's questions and instructions about *perceived* opportunities? We should not take those questions and instructions blindly. The principal may be overambitious or underestimate the challenges. The opportunity may be about a principal's pet project. For example, a company's GM is an engineer who still enjoys designing new products. He sees opportunities for new products everywhere. The principal may also identify opportunities out of boredom or because she has a large budget that needs to be spent. You need to find out whether the principal is right about the opportunity. Is it a *real* opportunity? Will this opportunity really allow a higher performance? We ask the principal: "*Why* is this relevant for the company?" We continue to ask 'Why?' until we know how this opportunity can allow a higher objective.

If the principal already has a solution, we ask: "For what opportunity is this a solution?" After clarification of the opportunity, we ask:

- "Why is this an opportunity for the company?"
- "How will this opportunity contribute to the company's performance?"

We must avoid getting an overly optimistic view of the opportunity. Let the principal also look at the opportunity with a pessimistic view:

- "Why may this *not* be an opportunity for the company?"
- "Why may this solution fail?"

We can also ask these latter two questions to people who are critical of this opportunity. Chapter 4 will outline an opportunity analysis. If there is a real opportunity, we formulate a key question: *How should the company seize this opportunity to achieve a higher performance objective?* Subsequently, we design an opportunity statement and a project proposal.

An opportunity does not have to be new

An opportunity for the principal does not have to be new to the world or even new to the principal's industry. But it should be new to the principal's company. If other companies have already seized this opportunity, we can use their case to build an argument for the opportunity. But we must be aware of the trap of comparing apples and oranges. Is the opportunity of the other company comparable to the principal's opportunity?

Create an opportunity

We have discussed opportunities that exist 'out there'. The principal identifies something that already exists or is happening, but the principal may also create something new that did not yet exist. Then the principal needs *creative thinking*. We provide some examples of how the principal may create an opportunity:

- The principal develops a new product that fulfils *latent* customer needs. An example is the Apple smartphone. We may use design thinking to discover the unfulfilled customer needs and design an innovative product.
- The principal develops a new business *process*. An example is Toyota, which invented a new, high-quality production process. The digitization of processes is also an example of process innovation.
- The principal develops a new *market* or innovates a market. An example is Amazon, which revolutionized retail with its digital platform.

 Pause and Reflect

Use your own experience of a recent project from your study or work. Did you ask yourself: Is this opportunity not too good to be true?

Understand the context of an opportunity

It is vital to understand the context of an opportunity. We refer to the text about a problem context.

Running Case ConsultCo

Arpit asks the MP: "Could you perhaps tell me a little more about the background of this internationalisation project? What do you see as the main reasons for internationalisation?" The MP is a little surprised: "We see good opportunities for internationalisation." Arpit responds: "What specific opportunities do you see? Could you say a bit more about that?" The MP replies: "That is your assignment. You must assess the market growth and competitive pressure in the selected foreign countries. A large and growing demand for consultancy and relatively little competition make a country an attractive place for us to enter." Arpit formulates the following key question: *How should ConsultCo seize the internationalisation opportunity to increase its profit?* Arpit is aware that this question supposes there is an internationalisation opportunity for ConsultCo. Arpit has no evidence yet that the opportunity exists, but he also has no evidence that there is no opportunity. He leaves the sensitive question about the existence of an opportunity aside for now. In the opportunity analysis, this question will come up automatically. Then Arpit will find the evidence for the opportunity, or he will conclude that there is a lack of evidence. The analysis outcome makes the discussion with the GM a lot easier.

Frame the opportunity as a performance gap

We frame an opportunity as a performance gap. Such a performance gap is not about realized performance. It is a gap between the *current* performance objective and the higher *new* objective. Unlike a problem gap, we cannot measure an opportunity gap at the start. We need to analyse the opportunity before we can *assess* the higher new objective.

Evaluate the opportunity

- Is the opportunity *worthwhile*? We do a cost–benefit analysis of the opportunity. The difference between the current and the higher new objective indicates the potential benefits. Next, we need to assess the costs of seizing the opportunity.
- Is seizing the opportunity *feasible*? We distinguish between a *market* opportunity and a *company* opportunity. A market opportunity is an opportunity for all companies in a market. We define it in general terms. A company opportunity is an opportunity for a specific company. The principal's company has a company-specific opportunity because it has the resources to seize the opportunity. If the principal lacks the requisite resources, then there still is a market opportunity but it is not an opportunity for the principal's company.
- Will stakeholders *accept* that we seize the opportunity? Can the principal seize the solution opportunity if some powerful internal or external stakeholders do not approve or accept that solution? We need to ask: "Are there any stakeholders that will probably block solutions to this opportunity?"
- Is it *desirable* to seize the opportunity?
  - How does the return on the opportunity project compare to other opportunities and problems of the principal's company? Seizing opportunities requires the resources of the principal's company. Different opportunities and problems compete for scarce resources.

    ○   Are the opportunity and the solution ethical? An example of an unethical *opportunity* is the export of goods to a dictatorship that will use these goods to suppress its own population. An example of an unethical *solution* is that a company realizes an apparently ethical growth opportunity by exploiting cheap labour in countries where workers' rights are limited.

Develop an opportunity statement

How should the principal's company deal with an opportunity? An opportunity gap is subjective. We know the current objective and we *expect* that the new performance objective can be higher, but we do not yet know how much higher. We need to analyse the opportunity before we can create a new SMART objective.

 **Mini Exercise**

Think of a recent opportunity of a well-known company of your choice and use Internet research to frame the opportunity as a performance gap.

I can never do that!

In later chapters, we will show the analyses and solutions. When you see the cases, you might think that the work is too complicated. "I can never do that!" To reassure you, you do not have to do all that on your own.

The starting point of this book's method is that you solve the problems together with those involved: the stakeholders. *Together* is the key word. You do not have to have all the knowledge, data, insight, and creativity required for problem-solving. But you need to identify the individuals who have the knowledge, data, insight, and creativity. Then you must engage them in the problem-solving process. Problem-solving is teamwork. Communication and collaboration with stakeholders are therefore essential skills.

Additionally, you must have knowledge of the structured problem-solving method. Introducing the method to your team and motivating the team to follow this process are your most important duties. The discipline to follow this method is a critical success factor. In some cases, you or others may think you already understand the problem or even know the solution. Then it is tempting to deviate from the problem-solving process, skip steps, or do it halfway. Then you run the risk of not finding the *best* solution or not being able to substantiate your recommended solution, thus endangering the acceptance of your recommendation. Since stakeholders play such an important role, we pay a lot of attention to them in this book. In the next chapter you will learn how to identify the stakeholders.

—— **Pause and Reflect** ————————————————

Consider how you may use this technique for identifying real problems and opportunities in your studies, work, and personal life.

SUMMARY

We briefly outline the main takeaways of this chapter.

- Identify a business problem or opportunity
  - understand the principal's starting point in terms of knowledge about a problem (or opportunity)
  - frame a problem as a gap between a current performance objective and a lower realized or actual performance
  - frame an opportunity as a gap between a current performance objective and a higher new objective
- Verify a business problem
  - ask *why* a problem is relevant for the company
  - verify a problem by measuring the performance gap
- Evaluate the suitability of solving a business problem or opportunity
  - Is problem-solving worthwhile?
  - Is problem-solving feasible?
  - Will stakeholders accept the solution?
  - Is problem-solving desirable for us?
- Assess the context of a problem or opportunity
  - the principal's company
  - the company's industry environment
  - the macro-environment
- Formulate a key question about a problem or opportunity
  - key question: How should the principal close the performance gap?
- Appreciate critical thinking
  - do not accept a principal's problem or opportunity definition at face value but ask for a substantiation

 —— **Mini Exercise** ————————————————

Identify the key concepts and terms in this chapter, define them briefly, and compile your own glossary.

REFERENCES AND FURTHER READING

Minto, B. (2003). *The Minto Pyramid Principle: Logic in Writing, Thinking and Problem Solving*. London: Minto International.

Osterwalder, A., & Pigneur, Y. (2010). *Business Model Generation: A Handbook for Visionaries, Game Changers, and Challengers* (Vol. 1). Hoboken, NJ: John Wiley & Sons.

Porter, M. E. (1980). *Competitive Strategy: Techniques for Analyzing Industries and Competitors*. New York: Free Press.

Analyse Stakeholders of Problems and Opportunities

3

INTRODUCTION

Why we prefer to focus on problems rather than people

We have defined a problem and we are fully committed to solving it. It is a complex problem that requires all our brainpower. We do not have time to communicate with those involved, let alone involve them in the problem-solving process. Spending time on communication is something that we cannot afford to do. We are already too busy solving the intellectual puzzle.

After weeks of brain-teasing, we have finally found the solution to that challenging problem, and we are immensely proud of our intellectual accomplishment! All the greater is our disappointment when we do not receive the appreciation that we so deserve. Others are not impressed by our work and do not want to implement or even support our solution. *Why* is that?

- We have missed essential perspectives and ideas
- There is no support for our solution – those involved do not regard it as *their* solution, but as something that is imposed from outside

Many people fall into the trap of focusing on the intellectual challenge of problem-solving at the expense of paying attention to the *people* involved in the problem. It is an understandable tendency to focus on the problem, but we cannot separate the problem from those involved. For the best results, we must engage those involved in the problem-solving to achieve success.

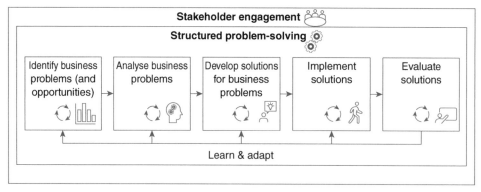

Iterative process of developing and testing hypotheses about problems, solutions, and implementation

Figure 3.1 Structured problem-solving is embedded through stakeholder engagement

We assume business problem-solving is team-based. Either we or the principal form a team. Because of the aforementioned problem-focus, all team members are tempted to get to work immediately. This is a trap and team problems will inevitably arise. Therefore, we must first get to know each other. We should understand ourselves and our team members. It is about personalities, cultural backgrounds, skills, and wills (ambition).

This chapter shows you how to identify and analyse the relevant stakeholders for engagement (see Figure 3.2). It outlines how to identify and map stakeholders, and Chapter 6 describes how to engage stakeholders.

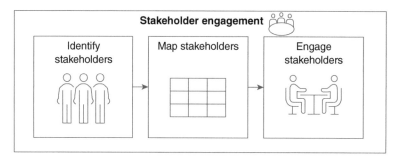

Figure 3.2 Engage stakeholders in three steps

The chapter considers the following elements (see Figure 3.3).

Figure 3.3 Chapter overview

MAIN LEARNING OBJECTIVES

After studying this chapter, you should be able to:

- identify a stakeholder in a problem or opportunity
- explain the relevance of a stakeholder to a principal
- assess the power of a stakeholder over the principal's company
- assess the alignment of the interests of a stakeholder with the principal's company
- create a power-alignment map

IDENTIFY STAKEHOLDERS

Stakeholders have an interest in a problem

Stakeholders in a company are any individuals or groups who can affect or are affected by the achievement of that company's objectives (Freeman, 1984). When we write about stakeholders in problems, it also applies to opportunities. Our focus is on stakeholders in a problem. These individuals or groups have a stake in a problem. Stakes are about interests. The problem affects the stakeholders' interests. Figure 3.4 shows how to identify stakeholders.

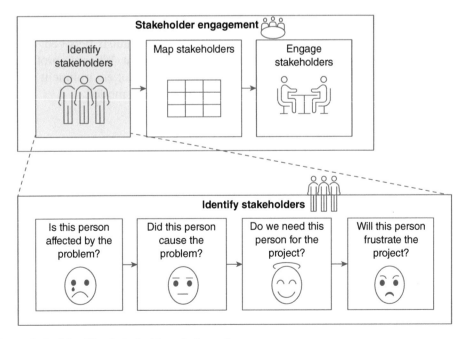

Figure 3.4   Identify stakeholders in four steps

People who are affected by a problem or cause a problem

People who are *affected* by a problem are stakeholders. For example, if the principal's company suffers a loss, then the employees' jobs may be at stake. Stakeholders may also *cause* a problem. For example, a manager underestimates the customers' price sensitivity and therefore raises product prices so much that demand and revenue decline.

People who are needed for the problem-solving project and who may frustrate it

Stakeholders can also *influence* the problem-solving because they have resources, such as knowledge and data, that we need for the problem-solving. These people can have a *positive* influence: they may help to solve a problem. But these people can also *negatively* influence the problem-solving: they may resist, frustrate, manipulate, and sabotage the problem-solving. Whether stakeholders will use their resources positively or negatively depends on their interest. If their interest is aligned with the principal, they will support the solving of the principal's problem. But if their interest conflicts with the principal, they will undermine the problem-solving.

Stakeholders with critical resources can make or break problem-solving. Therefore, we must account for these stakeholders. Engaging stakeholders requires effort, but the benefits of engagement outweigh the costs.

Distinguish between internal and external stakeholders

Internal stakeholders are stakeholders inside the principal's company. External stakeholders are outside that organization. We also distinguish between external stakeholders in the market and the non-market environment. Whereas profit is the leading motivation in the market environment, the non-market environment is about people and the planet. Figure 3.5 shows the so-called 'onion model'.

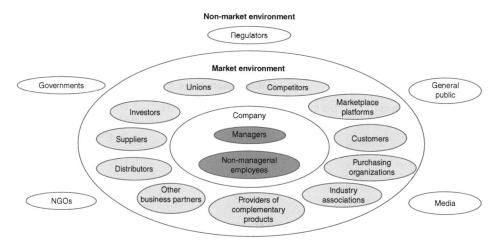

Figure 3.5   An 'onion model' of internal and external stakeholders

Running Case RobotCo[2]

Tara sits down with the general manager (GM) and asks, "Which stakeholders should we consider in this project?" The GM does not seem to understand, and Tara clarifies her question: "Is the analysis of the late deliveries problem dependent on the data and insights of certain individuals inside or outside RobotCo? Are there persons who participate in the decision-making about the solution to the deliveries problem or are there persons who can influence this decision? Which individuals do you need for solution implementation?" The GM thinks about Tara's questions and then lists the names of relevant people inside and outside RobotCo.

 ## How To Do It?

Ask the principal to identify the stakeholders in the problem. Use the following questions (you do not have to follow this exact wording):

- Who causes or contributes to the problem?
- Who suffers from the problem and who benefits?
- Who can affect the problem-solving process?
  - Who can contribute to the process?
  - Who can frustrate, manipulate, or even prevent the process?
- Who will be involved in the problem-solving process, actively or passively?
  - Active involvement: people must contribute.
  - Passive involvement: people must approve or accept the process and/or the solution.
- Who will be affected by the solution? Who will suffer from the solution and who will benefit?

 ## Pause and Reflect

Use your own experience of a recent project from your study or work and identify the stakeholders in this project. Ask yourself: Is this an *objective* identification or is it my *subjective* view?

---

[2]This chapter presents only one case because the techniques for the stakeholder analysis of RobotCo do not differ much from ConsultCo. In subsequent chapters, we only include ConsultCo if it leads to different insights.

MAP STAKEHOLDERS

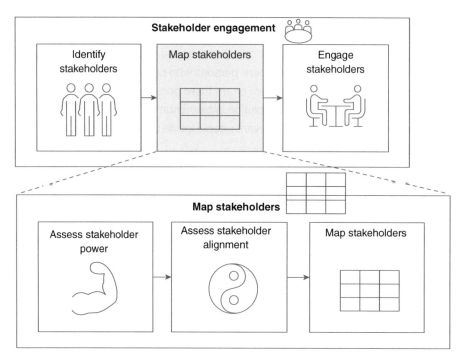

Figure 3.6 Map stakeholders in three steps

Assess stakeholder power

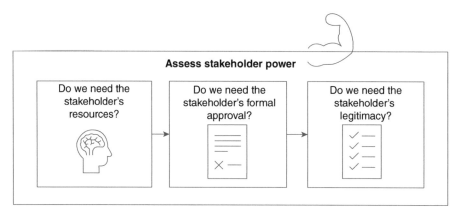

Figure 3.7 Assess stakeholder power in three steps

Sources of power

We start the power assessment with the principal's needs. What does the principal need for problem-solving? We distinguish between three main needs.

- *Need for resources for problem-solving*, such as data, knowledge, people, and budget.
- *Need for formal approval* by decision-makers in the principal's company and by external stakeholders with political or legal authority, such as governments and regulators
  - approval for starting a problem-solving process
  - approval of the problem analysis
  - approval of the solution
  - approval for implementing a solution.
- *Need for legitimacy*, which is the popular belief or acceptance that someone has the right and the justification to do something. This person's actions are widely recognized and accepted as proper and right. We acknowledge that formal approval may grant legitimacy to the principal's problem-solving project. Here we focus on *informal* approval, acceptance, support, recommendation, and support for the problem-solving. Informal leaders in the principal's company may provide legitimacy, but legitimacy may also come from external stakeholders, such as influencers in society. An example is opinion leaders in social media. Influential individuals and organizations, such as some non-governmental organizations (NGOs), may provide the principal with a so-called 'societal licence' to solve the problem.

A critical question is: How *powerful* is the principal? The more resources, the more authority, and the more legitimacy a principal has, the less a principal depends on the stakeholders. The less powerful the principal, the more important the stakeholders become. We distinguish between three main bases of power (see Figure 3.8).

Basis of stakeholder power	Examples	Use of power by stakeholder	
		Positive for principal	*Negative* for principal
Ownership of critical resources	Data, knowledge, insights, capabilities, capital, and other assets	Provide the resources to the principal, or use them to support the principal	Withold the resources from the principal, or use the resources against the principal
Authority	Hierarchical (managerial), legal, or political position	Allow or approve	Forbid or disapprove
Legitimacy	Social capital or network of social relations	Like or accept	Dislike or reject

Figure 3.8   **Three bases of stakeholder power**

How To Do It?

Ask the principal to identify the stakeholders in the problem. Do not accept the principal's answers at face value but be critical. Ask the principal for a substantiation:

- Why do you think this person is a stakeholder in this problem?
- Why do you think this person has power over your company regarding this problem?
- What kind of power is that (what power base)?
- What evidence is there for this kind of power?
- How much power do you think this stakeholder has?
- What evidence is there for this magnitude of power?

To reduce subjectivity, you can interview several people. Choose people who understand the problem and the context, but be careful because these people can also be stakeholders. Their self-interest may colour their opinion about other stakeholders. Therefore, look critically at what they tell you about other stakeholders. Inquire about underlying motives and evidence for their opinions.

Very important: *Only* discuss the outcome of the stakeholder analysis with the principal. Do *not* share your analysis widely as it is politically sensitive. For example, you have identified manager X as a powerful stakeholder whose interests conflict with the principal. Imagine X getting hold of your analysis.

Rank stakeholders

When the principal comes up with a *long* list of stakeholders then we need to evaluate that list. We must ask ourselves: Are all stakeholders equally powerful? There may be listed stakeholders who are not that powerful and who therefore require less time and attention. We rank the stakeholders from the most powerful to the least powerful.

 How To Do It?

Stakeholder assessments are subjective. If you have multiple sources, the assessments of the same stakeholder may vary across sources. Consider the quality and the degree of bias of your sources when weighing up their assessments. A quantification of power (for example, a 5-point scale) suggests exactness but recall that any assessment is subjective. It is important to mention this subjectivity when presenting the assessments to the principal.

════════════ **Running Case RobotCo** ════════════

Tara sits down with the GM to investigate the amount of power held by the various stakeholders.

1. They determine what RobotCo needs for solving the deliveries problem: resources and approval and acceptance of solutions.
2. They determine RobotCo's dependencies on stakeholders with regard to the company's needs for the problem-solving. Figure 3.9 shows examples of power assessment.

Stakeholder	Basis of stakeholder power			Overall assesment
	Critical resources	Authority	Legitimacy	
General manager	+ (managerial knowhow)	+++ (managerial)	++ (formal leader)	++++
Product manager robots	+ (managerial knowhow)	+ (managerial)	+ (informal leader)	+++
Customers	+++ (financial: purchases)			+++
Shareholders	++ (financial: investments)			++
R&D engineers	++ (technical cababilites)			++

Figure 3.9   Examples of power assessment

 ════════ **Pause and Reflect** ════════

Use your own experience of a recent project from your study or work and assess the power of the stakeholders.

Assess stakeholder alignment

Stakeholders in problems

Problems are annoying for most stakeholders, except for those stakeholders, such as competitors, who may benefit from the principal's problems. No stakeholder wants to be blamed for problems. Troublemakers who are opportunistic will try to blame other stakeholders if they can. The troublemakers may also deny problems. A problem analysis can easily end in a political fight where the stakeholders accuse each other of causing the problem. The problem analysis is therefore a sensitive subject.

The solutions to problems are also sensitive. Solutions mean changes and most people do not like changes because changes may:

- cause inconvenience (if people must leave their comfort zone)
- require effort (to learn new ways of working or to work with different people)
- create uncertainty (will people remain successful after the changes?)

Solutions can also mean that managers lose part of their budget or that people lose their jobs.

Stakeholders in opportunities

Unlike problems, opportunities do not induce denial and do not lead to accusations that others are to blame, but opportunities may lead to fights between stakeholders over who discovered the opportunities and deserves credits. Identifying opportunities can also be a game for stakeholders in a company to draw the attention of higher managers and to increase the budget and other resources to capitalize on these opportunities. For example, the head of production wants an investment in new machines because she perceives a big opportunity to increase quality. At the same time, the head of sales wants more account managers because he perceives a substantial market opportunity to sell more. In the analysis of opportunities, the discoverers of these opportunities may be tempted to look for confirmation of their opportunities: the confirmation bias. Finally, solutions for seizing opportunities mean change, which most people do not like.

Prioritise

Whether stakeholders will support or oppose the principal's company depends on their alignment with the principal. Are the stakeholder's interests aligned with those of the principal's company? How to assess the alignment? We distinguish between three main bases of alignment:

- *Objectives*: what does the stakeholder want to achieve? Does the stakeholder have
  - the same or similar objectives as the principal's company?
  - independent, non-conflicting objectives?
  - conflicting objectives?
- *Values*: how does the stakeholder want to achieve her objectives? What is right and proper in her opinion? Does the stakeholder have
  - the same or similar values as the principal's company?
  - independent, non-conflicting values?
  - conflicting values?

- *Views*: how does the stakeholder see the problem and possible solutions? What is the stakeholder's worldview, mental model, or reference frame? What are the stakeholder's assumptions about how things work? Does the stakeholder have
  - the same or similar views as the principal's company?
  - independent, non-conflicting views?
  - conflicting views?

We provide some examples.

- An example of conflicting objectives: the head of sales wants multiple product variants to meet the different needs of different types of customers, but the head of production wants only one variant to keep production simple and efficient.
- An example of conflicting values: the financial manager focuses on profit, whereas the head of HR emphasizes the personnel's well-being.
- An example of conflicting views: the new CEO comes from outside the company and is convinced that AI is the future for the company's services. However, according to the company's veterans, success is about personal service, that is not suitable to automation with smart machines.

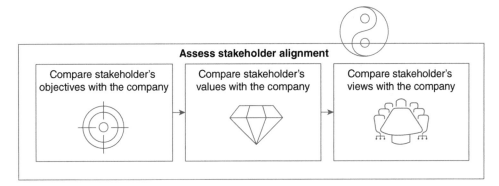

Figure 3.10   Assess stakeholder alignment in three steps

Alignment refers to the principal's company.

1. Assess the company's objectives and values.
2. Assess the principal's view on the problem and the possible solutions. An organization does not have a view but the organization's people do. We assume that the principal's view is representative for the company. Self-assessment by the principal is a good starting point but it is not enough. We need to verify the principal's self-assessment with at least a second opinion.
3. Assess the interests (objectives, values, and views) of the most powerful stakeholders. Weaker stakeholders are less relevant.

Be aware of any hidden agendas when asking stakeholders about their interests. These people may provide politically correct answers and keep their cards close. For example: the head of R&D gives a politically correct answer that innovations for the company are his objective, but in practice he prioritises hobby projects for his own interest. Figure 3.11 shows the three bases of alignment.

Basis of stakeholder alignment	Examples	Relationship between interests of stakeholder and the principal's company	
		Alignment	Conflict
Objectives	• Organizational objectives, such as profit, people, and the planet • Personal objectives, such as career, income, status, power, and work–life balance	Same or congruent objectives	Conflicting objectives
Values	Moral principles: what is good and bad for individuals and society	Same or congruent values	Conflicting values
Views	View of the: • business • problem • possible solutions	Same or congruent values	Conflicting views

Figure 3.11   **Three bases of alignment**

How To Do It?

If a stakeholder is an organization, then it may have defined and published its objectives and values. Do desk research to find such publications. If the stakeholder is an individual, you may have to interview this person and other people who know that individual well. Do not rely on a single assessment of a stakeholder, especially if it is a self-assessment by that person. Use the following questions (you do not have to follow this exact wording):

- Objectives. Relate the objectives to the problem at hand.
  - What should the best solution achieve?
  - What performance outcome should the best solution achieve?

- Values. Relate the values to the problem.

    ○ What should the problem-solving process look like?

    ○ What is a right and proper problem-solving process?

    ○ What should the solution look like?

    ○ What is a right and proper solution?

- Views. Relate the views to the problem. How do you view the problem?

Quantify an alignment score for each dimension: objectives, values, and views. For example, you may consider a 5-point scale: fully aligned (+2), neither aligned nor conflicting (0), and fully conflicting (–2). Numbers suggest exactness but remember that any assessment is subjective.

 Pause and Reflect ────────────────

Use your own experience of a recent project from your study or work, and ask yourself: Would the stakeholders be willing to reveal their true interests to me?

──────────── **Running Case RobotCo** ────────────

Tara continues her conversation with the GM: "Which stakeholders will support the solving of the deliveries problem?" The GM thinks about Tara's question and then gives the names of stakeholders from whom he expects collaboration. Tara asks him: "*Why* do you think these stakeholders will support the problem-solving? What are their reasons for collaborating? How will they benefit?" After checking the motivations of the supporting stakeholders, Tara turns to the other stakeholders: "Which stakeholders will *not* support the solving of the deliveries problem? Which stakeholders have conflicting objectives, values, or views of the delivery problem?"

1. The GM defines RobotCo's objectives, values, and views regarding the late deliveries problem.
2. He assesses any conflicts of objectives, values, or views between RobotCo and its stakeholders. Figure 3.12 shows examples of the interest alignment assessment.

(Continued)

Stakeholder	Basis of alignment			Overall assessment
	Objectives regarding the problem	Values regarding the problem	Views of the problem	
Principal's company	Solve late deliveries to gain €15m profit	Solution should fit with corporate social responsibility	Late deliveries are a business problem: inefficiency or ineffectiveness of processes	
General manager	Profit-based pay: +	Personal values: +/–	Personal view on causes and solutions: +	++
Product manager robots	Solve late deliveries of robots: +/–	Personal values: +	Narrow view on robots: –	ı/
Customers	Timely deliveries, whatever the costs to RobotCo: +/–	Customers' values: –	Late deliveries are lack of customer service: +/–	+/–
Shareholders	Shareholder value: +/–	Primary responsibility of company is to create shareholder value: –	Late deliveries are financial performance problem: +/–	+/–
R&D engineers	Solve late deliveries: +/–	Technical quality of solution: –	Technical perspective:- +/–	+/–

Figure 3.12   Examples of interest alignment

Notes: + = degree of alignment; – = degree of conflict; +/– = mixed

Increasing diversity of stakeholders

The diversity of stakeholders in problems tend to increase because of the following main reasons:

- *Globalisation*: International connectivity has increased, both physical (air, sea, road, and rail transportation) and virtual (digital communication and electronic data transfer). We can connect with stakeholders at increasingly greater distances.
- *Inclusion*: We also note the increasing importance of inclusion of people who differ in terms of, among others, cultural background, ethnic group, race, gender, sexual orientation, and age.
- *Corporate social responsibility*: Companies increasingly acknowledge their responsibility to society. This responsibility causes a shift from the traditional bottom line to the 'triple bottom line': profit, people, and the planet. People and planet objectives refer to a wider and more diverse set of stakeholders.

Pause and Reflect

Use your own experience of a recent project from your study or work, and ask yourself:
Did the stakeholders in the project really collaborate or were they just paying lip service?

Create a power-interest map

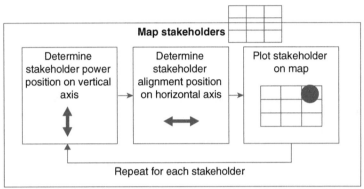

Figure 3.13   Map stakeholders in three steps

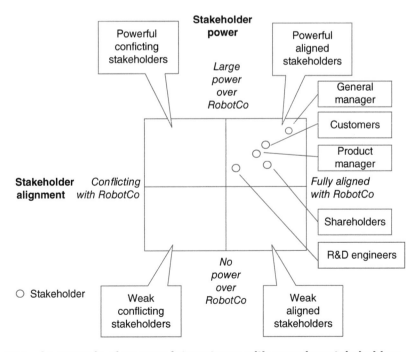

Figure 3.14   An example of a power-interest map with some key stakeholders

Source: Author's interpretation of Mendelow's 'Power-Interest Grid' (Mendelow, 1991)

The combination of power and interest alignment is relevant for stakeholder mapping (see Figure 3.14). Alignment influences *how* stakeholder use their power.

- Alignment contributes to the stakeholders' use of their power for the *benefit* of the principal's company.
- Conflict of interests will induce the stakeholders to use their power *against* the principal's company.

Four quadrants

- *Powerful aligned stakeholders*: They are natural allies or partners of the principal's company. They can provide the most support for problem-solving.
- *Powerful conflicting stakeholders*: These adversaries can pose the largest threat to problem-solving. Conflict arises because of misalignment. Conflict can be about the problem definition, analysis, solutions, and implementation.
- *Weak aligned stakeholders*: They want to help the principal with problem-solving, but they can only help to a limited extent because of their limited power.
- *Weak conflicting stakeholders*: They oppose the principal company's problem-solving, but they can only do so to a limited extent because of their limited power.

Chapter 6 will evaluate the implications of having stakeholders in the four quadrants. We will discuss how to engage stakeholders in the different quadrants.

Running Case RobotCo

Tara looks at the map (see Figure 3.14). Fortunately, there are no powerful conflicting stakeholders who can frustrate the problem-solving. The top-right quadrant is occupied. There are several powerful allies which contribute to the success of the process. However, the alignment assessment shows that there are also tensions in certain areas, such as the relatively poor alignment of the R&D engineers. Tara will have to take that into account.

 ## How To Do It?

The position of a stakeholder on the map should be consistent with the assessment of that stakeholder's power and alignment. If you use quantitative scores for power and alignment, you can more precisely position the stakeholders on the map.

Mini Exercise

Think of a recent strategic product introduction by a well-known company and use Internet research to map the main internal and external stakeholders for this case.

Pause and Reflect

Use your own experience of a recent project from your study or work. After you have created a power-interest map, ask yourself: Am I a neutral arbiter or am I a stakeholder? If I am a stakeholder, where do I fit on the map?

Analyse the project team

The team is a special group of stakeholders. We focus on *team*-based problem-solving because business problem-solving is a collaborative effort. For successful collaboration, team members need to understand each other well. If we need to form a team for a problem-solving project, then we take the following criteria into account.

Skills and knowledge

We ask ourselves: What skills and knowledge does the problem-solving require? Who has the requisite skills and knowledge? We may do a *strengths–weaknesses analysis of candidates*. Additionally, we evaluate our own strengths and weaknesses to see where we need complementing teammates. We also seek diversity of perspectives as it enables the team to look at the problem from different angles.

Personality

To assess team members' personalities, we may use the Myers–Briggs Type Indicator (MBTI) (Myers & McCaulley, 1985). It is a self-report questionnaire for identifying differing psychological preferences in how individuals perceive the world and make decisions. The test distinguishes four dimensions of a personality, each with opposite values (see Figure 3.15).

Dimensions	Values	
Orientation	Extraversion (E)	Introversion (I)
Information-processing	Sensing (S)	Intuition (N)
Decision-making	Thinking (T)	Feeling (F)
Relation to environment	Judging (J)	Perceiving (P)

Figure 3.15   Myers–Briggs Type Indicator personality dimensions and values

We take one letter from each dimension to produce a four-letter personality type, such as 'ESTJ.' In total there are 16 different personality types (see Figure 3.16).

ESTJ	ESFJ	ENFJ	ENTJ
ESTP	ESFP	ENFP	ENTP
ISTJ	ISFJ	INFJ	INTJ
ISTP	ISFP	INFP	INTP

Figure 3.16   Myers–Briggs Type Indicator personalities

You may also use the 'Big Five' personality test. The Big Five refers to five important personality traits. Again, we distinguish between opposite values (see Figure 3.17).

Personality trait	Opposite values	
Openness to experience	Curious/inventive	Cautious/consistent
Conscientiousness	Organized/efficient	Careless/extravagant
Extraversion	Outgoing/energetic	Solitary/reserved
Agreeableness	Compassionate/friendly	Rational/critical
Neuroticism	Nervous/sensitive	Confident/resilient

Figure 3.17   The Big Five personality traits and their values

Working styles

We also need to pay attention to the working styles of team members. These styles may vary along different dimensions (see Figure 3.18).

Working styles	Opposites working styles
Does one task at a time	Multi-tasking
Oriented to detail	Focus on big picture
Avoid risk	Risk prone
Focus on task	Focus on people
Planning	Try, learn and adapt

Figure 3.18 **Some examples of working style dimensions**

Cultural background

Hofstede's cultural dimensions theory is a popular framework for cross-cultural communication (Hofstede, 1984). It shows how the values of six dimensions of a society's culture can differ and so influence behaviour (see Figure 3.19).

Dimension	Value 1	Value 2
Power distance	Low power distance (equal society)	High power distance (hierarchical society)
Individualism	Collectivism	Individualism
Masculinity	Femininity	Masculinity
Long-term orientation	Long-term orientation	Short-term orientation
Uncertainty avoidance	High uncertainty avoidance	Low uncertainty avoidance
Indulgence	Restraint (of needs gratification)	Indulgence (relatively free gratification of needs)

Figure 3.19 **Hofstede's cultural dimensions**

Ambition, motivation, and expectations

We also need to account for the ambition, motivation, and expectations of team members.

- What knowledge and skills does a team member seek to develop in this project?
- What result for the project does a team member aim for? Does the team member want to reach the maximum result, or will he settle for a satisfactory result?
- How much time and effort does a team member *want* to spend on the project? How much *can* a team member spend? How much does a member already have on her plate?
- What does a team member expect from other team members?

An ideal team

What does an ideal team look like? We identify some key success factors.

- *Diversity of personalities*: The personalities complement each other and together form a complete and balanced team. We do not want a team of clones.
- *Diversity of skills and knowledge*: The team members complement each other in terms of knowledge and skills. Moreover, all required knowledge and skills are on board.
- *Alignment of ambitions, motivations, and expectations*: The team has a common purpose and shared values.
- *Small*: The team has the smallest number of people to accomplish the purpose (three to seven persons). This is the core team. There may be other people who contribute to the project from time to time.

Chapter 6 will discuss how to work as a team.

 Pause and Reflect

Consider how you may use this technique for identifying and mapping stakeholders in your studies, work, and personal life.

SUMMARY

We briefly outline the main takeaways of this chapter.

- Identify a stakeholder in a problem (or opportunity)
  - stakeholder can be affected by a problem
  - stakeholder can cause a problem
  - stakeholder can affect the problem-solving
- Explain the relevance of a stakeholder for a principal
  - stakeholder can cause a problem
  - stakeholder can support the problem-solving
  - stakeholder can frustrate the problem-solving
- Assess the power of a stakeholder over the principal's company
  - a powerful stakeholder has critical resources for the problem-solving
  - or a powerful stakeholder must approve the problem-solving and solutions
  - or a powerful stakeholder must legitimize the problem-solving and solutions
- Assess the alignment of the interests of a stakeholder with the principal's company
  - alignment of objectives
  - alignment of values
  - alignment of views on:

- the problem
- the solution
- the company
- the environment

- Create a power-interest map
  - determine a stakeholder's position on the power axis (from no power to great power)
  - determine a stakeholder's position on the alignment axis (from fully aligned to conflicting)

 Mini Exercise

Identify the key concepts and terms in this chapter, define them briefly and compile your own glossary.

REFERENCES AND FURTHER READING

Freeman, R. E. (1984). *Strategic Management: A Stakeholder Approach.* Boston, MA: Pitman.

Hofstede, G. (1984). *Culture's Consequences: International Differences in Work-related Values* (Vol. 5). Newbury Park, CA: Sage.

Mendelow, A. (1991). *Stakeholder mapping.* In Proceedings of the 2nd International Conference on Information Systems (pp. 10–24). Cambridge, MA.

Myers, I. B., & McCaulley, M. H. (1985). *Manual: A Guide to the Development and Use of the Myers–Briggs Type Indicator.* Palo Alto, CA: Consulting Psychologists Press.

Deconstruct Problems and Opportunities

4

INTRODUCTION

Assume that we need to analyse a complex business problem, like the RobotCo example. There are so many elements of the problem to consider, such as the parts inventory, the logistics, the robot diagnostics, the repair process, and customer complaints. We wonder: Where to start? Moreover, everything seems connected to each other. It is an overwhelming challenge to analyse the problem. Some people will experience 'analysis paralysis.' Others may conclude: this problem is too big to analyse. They do not even try to analyse it but they 'just do it': they follow an approach of trial (possible solutions) and error. By learning from their mistakes, they refine their solution until they have solved the problem. We acknowledge that such experimentation may be a way to solve problems. But we do not want to give up analysis too soon. Therefore, we propose a simplification technique for analysis: deconstruction.

We break down a problem into parts. We may compare the problem to a pizza. People (at least civilized persons) do not attempt to swallow a pizza in one go but slice it into eatable parts. Similarly, we slice a problem into analysable parts. At this stage, we do not worry about connections between parts. We take one challenge at a time. First, we look at the parts of a problem individually. Second, we consider any connections between the problem parts. Such sequencing of steps is another simplification technique.

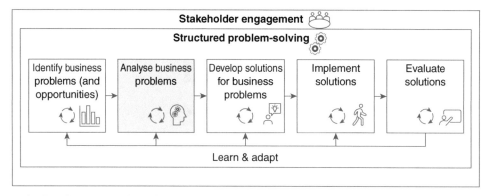

Figure 4.1   **Analysing business problems is the second step of structured problem-solving**

This chapter will outline a relatively simple but effective method for problem analysis: the Sequential Analysis Method (see Figure 4.2).

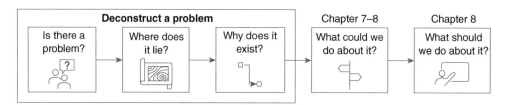

Figure 4.2   **The Sequential Analysis Method**

The chapter is structured as follows (see Figure 4.3).

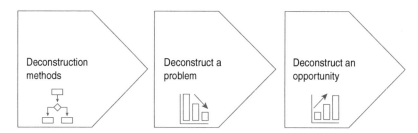

Figure 4.3   **Chapter structure**

MAIN LEARNING OBJECTIVES

After studying this chapter, you should be able to:

- choose from alternative problem-solving methods
  - the Sequential Analysis Method
  - the Issue Tree Method
  - the Hypothesis Tree Method

- analyse a problem (or opportunity) with the Sequential Analysis Method
- deconstruct a performance gap into logical structures of:
  - performance factors
  - segments
  - possible explanations

PART 1: DECONSTRUCTION METHODS

Choose from problem-solving methods

We focus on a few problem-solving methods that have been extensively proven in business practice. These methods are the hallmark of the world's leading management consultants, such as McKinsey & Company, BCG, and Bain & Company. How to select a method? The choice is situational. We distinguish between three situations (see Figure 4.4).

- We *think* we already have an answer to the key question. We have solved this problem before, or we know about solutions in similar cases. Then we can formulate our answer as a hypothesis. We deconstruct our solution hypothesis into a structure of sub-hypotheses for testing. Management consultants call such a structure a 'hypothesis tree' and therefore name it the '*Hypothesis Tree Method*'.
- We do not have a possible answer to the key question, but we can deconstruct the key question into a hierarchy of increasingly small sub-questions or so-called 'issues', and we can develop possible answers. Consultants call such a structure of questions an 'issue tree' and therefore name it the '*Issue Tree Method*'.
- We cannot deconstruct the key questions into an issue tree and develop possible answers because we lack the knowledge. Then we follow what consultants call the '*Sequential Analysis Method*'.

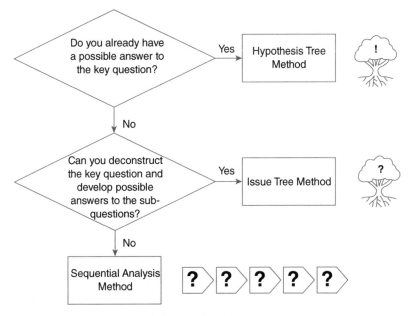

Figure 4.4   Choose a problem-solving method

The Hypothesis Tree Method

If we think we already know the solution, we skip the problem analysis. Figure 4.5 is the author's interpretation of the hypothesis tree approach. Based on research of the literature, we attribute the introduction of this approach in management consultancy to McKinsey & Company. But the use of hypotheses is a hallmark of the scientific method, which goes back to the seventeenth century. The technique of deconstruction also already existed before management consultancy became a profession.

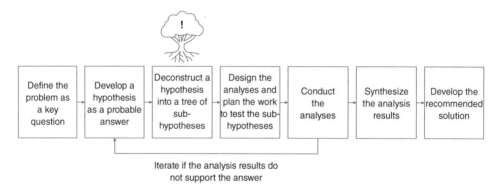

Figure 4.5   The Hypothesis Tree approach

Note: Author's interpretation based on public sources (such as Chevallier, 2016; Conn & McLean, 2018; Garrette et al., 2018; Minto, 2003; Rasiel, 1999; Rasiel et al., 2001)

Chapter 7 outlines the development of a hypothesis tree.

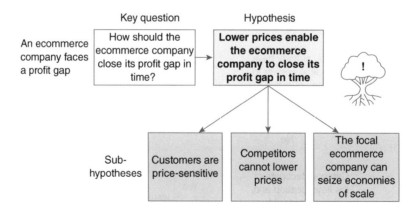

Figure 4.6   An example of a hypothesis tree

The Issue Tree Method

We attribute the introduction of this approach in management consultancy also to McKinsey & Company (see Figure 4.7). This approach also builds on the scientific method.

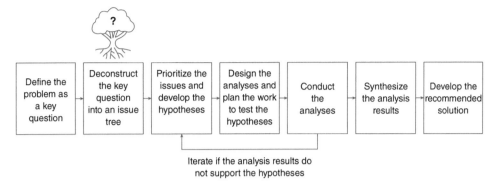

Figure 4.7   The Issue Tree Method

Note: Author's interpretation based on public sources (such as Chevallier, 2016; Conn & McLean, 2018; Garrette et al., 2018; Minto, 2003; Rasiel, 1999; Rasiel et al., 2001)

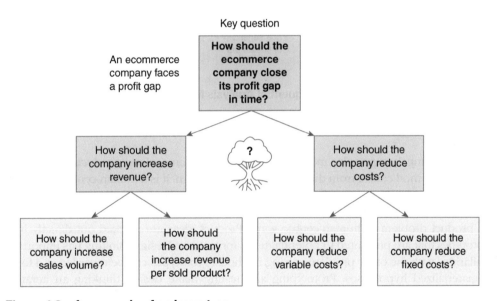

Figure 4.8   An example of an issue tree

The Sequential Analysis Method

We attribute the introduction of this approach in management consultancy also to McKinsey & Company (see Figure 4.9). However, a sequence of questions to explore a problem resembles Socratic questioning and the connected critical thinking. The famous ancient Greek philosopher Socrates (470–399 BC) used thoughtful questions to help people examine ideas.

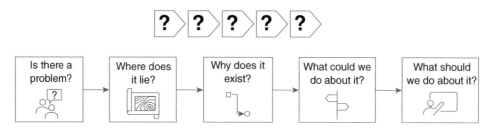

Figure 4.9   The Sequential Analysis Method

Note: Author's interpretation based on Minto (2003)

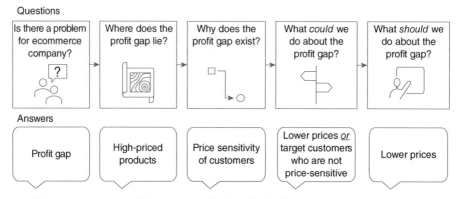

Figure 4.10   An example of the Sequential Analysis Method

Design thinking

Design thinking is a popular method for solving problems *about products* (see Figure 4.11). This method comes from the world of product design. It is a human-centric approach to product development whereby designers and users collaborate. The starting point is an empathic understanding of the human needs regarding products. Design thinkers define the product problem in human-centric ways. Product ideas are worked out directly into prototypes that are presented to potential users for test use. Design thinking has important similarities with the other problem-solving methods. Prototypes can be regarded as a form of materialized hypotheses. Prototyping and testing make design thinking an iterative process, just like the other methods. The collaboration with users is an example of stakeholder engagement that the other methods rely on, but design thinking's scope is limited to products, whereas the other methods can address a wide range of business problems.

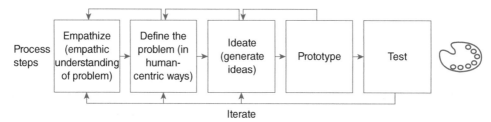

Figure 4.11   Design thinking

Note: The author's interpretation of the Five Stage Design Thinking Model of the Hasso Plattner Institute of Design at Stanford University (Hasso Plattner Institute of Design at Stanford University, 2010)

Data mining

In the twenty-first century, we have enormous amounts of data and the computing power to analyse these data. An example of data analytics is data mining (see Figure 4.12). Data mining and other forms of data analytics may support problem-solving.

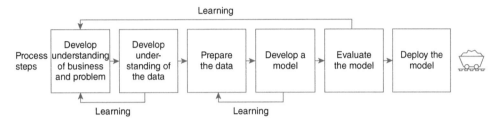

Figure 4.12   **Data mining**

Focus on the Sequential Analysis Method

Design thinking is very suitable for product-related problems. If there is a lot of data, we may use data mining, but for business problems *in general*, we recommend the problem-solving methods of the world's leading management consultancies.

The leading consultancy firms, with their massive knowledge management systems and expert networks, will in many cases already have a pretty good idea of what the solution should look like. Then the Hypothesis Tree Method is the appropriate choice. In other cases, these consultants will revert to the Issue Tree Method. Only if they face truly new-to-the-world problems, will they use the Sequential Analysis Method.

This book focuses on students with limited working experience who cannot tap into massive knowledge management systems and expert networks of the leading consultancy firms. For students, the Sequential Analysis Method is a good starting point. Therefore, we will focus on this method.

Simplify a problem analysis

To simplify solving complex problems, we combine the three simplification techniques (see Figure 4.13):

- *Deconstructing*: do not try to analyse the whole problem, but analyse the parts of the whole
- *Sequencing*: do not try to understand everything at the same time, but take small steps
- *Hypothesizing*: do not try to collect as much data as possible about the problem, but develop *possible* solutions to the problem

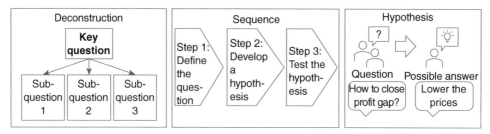

Figure 4.13   Three simplification techniques

Simplify by deconstructing

It is hard to solve a problem if we stay at a high level of abstraction. For example, 'How can the company improve its competitive position?' We need to lower the level of abstraction (see Figure 4.14).

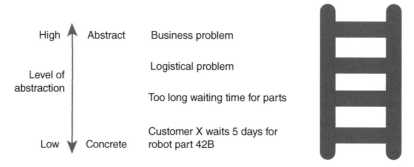

Figure 4.14   A ladder of abstraction

A *complex* problem is hard to analyse because it consists of various related parts. We deconstruct the problem into parts, like slicing a pizza. The deconstruction method is rooted in science and goes back to René Descartes (1596–1650), the French philosopher who was a key figure in the Scientific Revolution. In his book *Discourse on the Method*, Descartes proposed to divide a problem into parts and to start analysing the simplest issues. You may ask: How about the connections between the parts? Our answer: The connections do matter but do not try to do everything (understand the parts and the connections between them) *at the same time*. This brings us to the second simplification technique: sequencing.

Simplify by sequencing

We propose a step-by-step or sequential approach to problem-solving.

1. We *deconstruct* the whole problem into parts to simplify the analysis.
2. We consider any connections between the parts.
3. We combine the insights into the parts *and* their connections to *compose* a solution for the whole problem.

This process of deconstruction and composition resembles a bathtub (seen from a side view) and is named Coleman's bathtub after its creator (Coleman, 1994; see Figure 4.15).

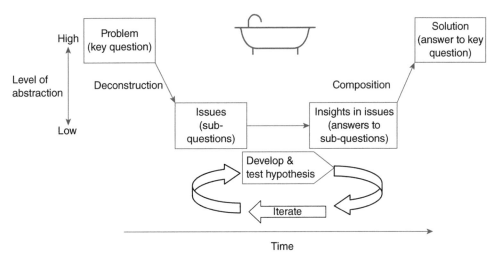

Figure 4.15   Coleman's bathtub of problem-solving

Source: Author's interpretation of Coleman (1994)

Simplify by hypothesizing

We formulate a problem as a single question. The solution is an answer to that question. We propose not to begin problem-solving with collecting and analysing data, but with developing possible answers to:

- the key question (the Hypothesis Tree Method)
- the sub-questions (the Issue Tree Method)
- a series of questions (the Sequential Analysis Method)

Unless the problem is new-to-the-world, there will be people inside or outside the principal's company who have experience on how to solve it. Developing possible answers, or hypotheses, is vital to the scientific method (see Figure 4.16).

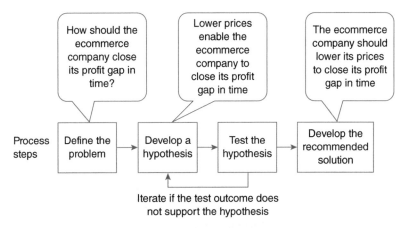

Figure 4.16   The scientific method uses hypotheses

PART 2: DECONSTRUCT A PROBLEM

We discuss two ways to *deconstruct* a problem:

- One way is the Issue Tree Method. We deconstruct the key question into an issue tree.
- The other way is the Sequential Analysis Method. We deconstruct the problem-solving into a sequence of steps. The first step is a deconstruction of the performance gap (see Figure 4.17).

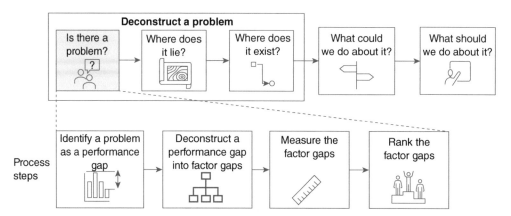

Figure 4.17   The first step of the Sequential Analysis Method

Is there a problem?

The principal wants a reorganization of the company, and we must implement a new organizational structure. During the implementation employees constantly ask us the question: "Why do we have to reorganize?" We must avoid such a situation and ask ourselves: "What is the problem that this reorganization should solve? What goes wrong because of the current organizational structure?"

What can be the problem? Something may have happened to the principal's company. There may have been a negative event or a development inside *or* outside that company. But is it a problem for the company? It is a problem if it negatively impacts the company's performance. We define problems in terms of a performance gap (see Figure 4.18).

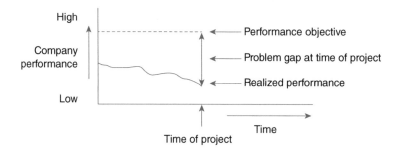

Figure 4.18   An example of a performance gap

What indicates a business process problem?

We can distinguish between different types of business problems, from operational to strategic. Here we focus on operational problems about business processes. We can define several performance indicators for business process problems, such as the following:

- Process output *quality* is too low. Too many products or services do not meet the principal's quality standards.
- Process output *quantity* is too low. The process does not produce enough products to meet the production volume target.
- Process output *flexibility* is too low (if the process can produce a variety of products). The process cannot switch quickly or easily to alternative product variants.
- Process output *speed* is too low. The process delivers the products after the promised delivery date.
- Process output *costs* are too high. The costs of producing the products exceed the budget.

Measure a performance gap

We define a performance gap as the difference between the realized performance and a performance objective. If the realized performance is below the objective, the company has a problem. In the opposite case, if the realized performance exceeds the objective, then the company has a windfall, or the objective is too low.

We measure the size of the gap. The size of the gap defines the size of the problem. The larger the gap is, the larger the problem is. We also look at the duration of a gap. Has the gap existed for a long time? If so, is the gap increasing, is it stable, or is it decreasing? If the gap is already narrowing, we must judge whether the problem may disappear without us solving it. If it is a new problem, we ask ourselves if it may be a one-time problem, an incident, or a more structural problem. We prioritise structural, lasting problems over temporary ones.

════════════ **Running Case RobotCo** ════════════

As a refresher: The project focus is on the waiting time for parts (see Figure 4.19). The general manager (GM) wants to close that gap within one year. Tara formulates the following key question: "How should RobotCo respond to the problem of the late delivery of parts to increase its profit by 15 million euro in one year?"

(Continued)

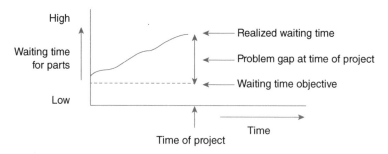

Figure 4.19   RobotCo's performance gap

Deconstruct a performance gap

If applicable, we deconstruct a performance gap into sub-gaps. For example, in the case of a 'process output quality' problem, we can deconstruct the total number of product defects into the number of defect products and the average number of defects per product. One (1) product can have multiple defects. For example, a car has a defect in the braking system and a defect in the air conditioning. It is a formula:

> *Total number of defects = number of defect products × average number of defects per product*

Another example: we can split a 'process output delay' into the number of products overdue and the length of the average delay per product overdue (number of minutes or other time units, such as days). For example, five hundred products with an average delay of half an hour result in a total delay of two hundred and fifty hours. The formula is:

> *Total delay (minutes) = number of products overdue × average delay per product overdue (minutes)*

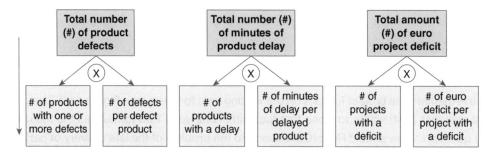

Figure 4.20   Examples of performance deconstructions

Logic trees

We want to deconstruct a performance gap into simpler parts. We start with a performance indicator. The indicator is a formula of factors. For example: profit = revenue – costs. We use the formula to deconstruct the indicator into its factors These structures of factors are called *logic trees* because they look like a tree with the roots visible.

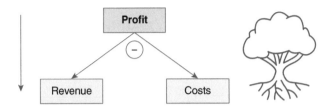

Figure 4.21   An example of a deconstruction of a performance indicator

The visual presentation of deconstructions may differ. We use a *vertical* presentation, with the high-level indicator at the top and the lower-level factors at the bottom. However, some people use *horizontal* presentation, with the whole to the left and the parts to the right (see Figure 4.22).

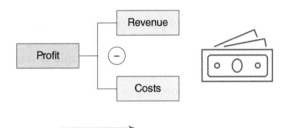

Figure 4.22   Example of a horizontal presentation of a deconstruction

We can also use other formulas to deconstruct profit:

- Profit = contribution margin – fixed costs
  - contribution margin = (price – variable cost per product) × sales volume
- Profit = (price – variable cost per unit) × sales volume – fixed costs
- Profit = revenue × profit margin

Gap analysis

We deconstruct a profit *gap* into a revenue gap and a cost gap (see Figure 4.23). As profit equals revenue minus costs, a profit gap equals a revenue gap *minus* a cost gap.

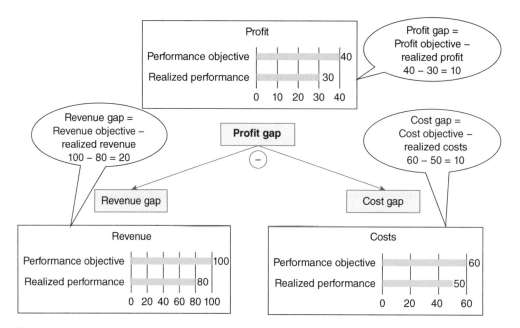

Figure 4.23   An example of a performance gap analysis

Note: A positive cost gap (cost below objective or budget) reduces a profit gap

Use the Minto Pyramid Principle

We may ask ourselves: What is a *good* deconstruction? The 'Minto Pyramid Principle' of deconstruction is the gold standard of the world's leading management consultancies for structured thinking and writing. This principle is named after its creator, Barbara Minto, who is the first female consultant of McKinsey & Company. Minto compares the hierarchical presentation of the parts with the side of a pyramid (see Figure 4.24) (Minto, 2003). Minto's Pyramid Principle is that these parts should be mutually exclusive and collectively exhaustive (MECE).

- *Mutual exclusiveness* of parts means that the parts do not overlap. For example, revenue and costs are mutually exclusive factors of profit. An amount of money is either revenue or costs. It cannot be both.
- *Collectively exhaustive* means that the set of parts should be complete. There should be no missing parts. Revenue and costs form a collectively exhaustive set of profit factors. There are no other factors of profit (at least not at the same level as revenue and costs).

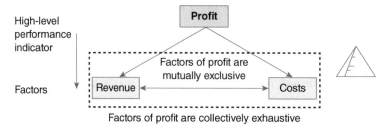

Figure 4.24   An example of the Minto Pyramid Principle

Note: author's interpretation based on Minto (2003)

Overlapping parts cause problems

Overlapping parts are problematic for two reasons:

- Overlapping parts may lead to *errors*. If we measure the values of overlapping parts, the sum of the parts will be greater than the whole. For example, we deconstruct profit into revenue, sales volume, and costs. Revenue overlaps with sales volume as revenue equals sales volume times price. Our deconstruction no longer adds up. The revenue gap, the volume gap, and the cost gap do not add up to the profit gap.
- Overlapping parts may cause *duplicate work*. In the example, if we delegate the measure of revenue to team member A and the measure of sales volume to member B, then their work will overlap. They will do duplicate work, which is inefficient.

Levels of deconstruction

We deconstruct a high-level performance indicator into factors. The factors are the first level of deconstruction. However, we may also deconstruct each factor into sub-factors, which are the second level of deconstruction (see Figure 4.25).

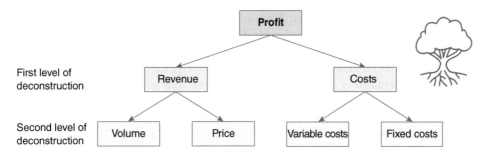

Figure 4.25   An example of two levels of deconstruction

We may follow different ways to deconstruct a performance indicator. Figure 4.26 provides an alternative deconstruction based on another formula:

Profit = contribution margin − fixed costs

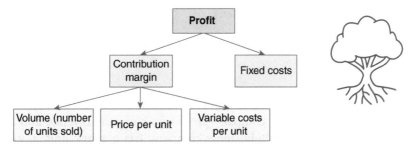

Figure 4.26   An alternative deconstruction of profit

A third deconstruction of profit uses the activity-based costing approach. We deconstruct total costs into the various categories of value-adding activities (see Figure 4.27).

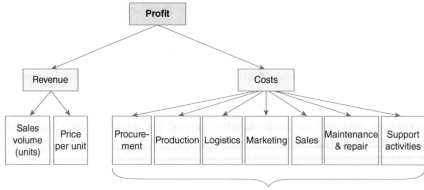

Figure 4.27   Another deconstruction of profit

Categorization and causality

We distinguish between the categorization of parts and the causal relations between parts. Overlap is about categories. Parts may not overlap but they may have causal relations. For example, revenue and costs do not overlap but they are causally related (see Figure 4.28). High revenue can cause lower costs if there are economies of scale or experience effects. Lower costs can allow lower prices and so stimulate higher revenue (if the demand is price-elastic). Please note that volume and price also have causal relations. Price increases generally decrease demand.

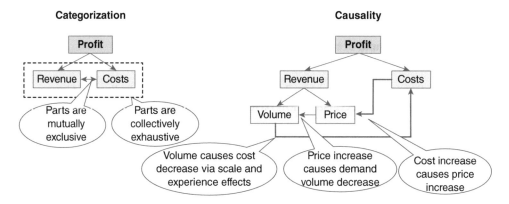

Figure 4.28   A comparison of categorization and causality

Complex cases

A company may hold multiple business units that each have a profit-and-loss account. Then we cannot deconstruct the company profit into company revenue and company costs. For example, a fictive multi-business company has a snack unit, a sodas unit, and a fast-food restaurant unit. We cannot add snack revenue, soda revenue, and fast-food restaurant revenue as these are different revenue streams. The same applies to the multi-business company costs. We cannot add the costs of the snack, soda, and fast-food units. Instead, we deconstruct the profit of a multi-business company into business units' profits (see Figure 4.29). Subsequently, for each business unit, we deconstruct the unit's profit into the unit's revenue and the unit's costs.

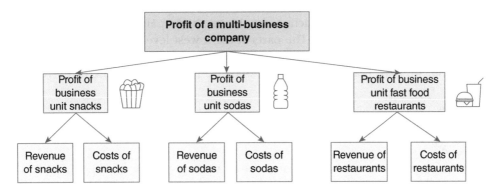

Figure 4.29   An example of deconstructing the profit of a multi-business company

Insightful deconstruction

MECE is necessary but not sufficient for deconstruction. The deconstruction should also be insightful to help the principal understand the problem. We prefer a tailor-made, specific deconstruction over a theoretical, generic deconstruction. A deconstruction should be tailored to the specific situation of the principal's company. For example, we can deconstruct the profit of a restaurant into revenue and costs, but we can also make the deconstruction more specific for a restaurant (see Figure 4.30).

Revenue (per day) = number of tables × number of visits per table (per day) × revenue per visit

A deconstruction of costs into restaurant-specific cost categories provides more insight than a split into variable and fixed costs.

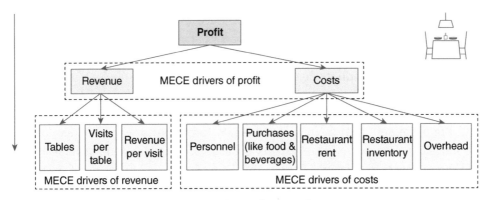

Figure 4.30   An example of a tailor-made profit tree of a restaurant

Number of parts and levels in a deconstruction

We may ask: How many parts should a deconstruction consist of? There should be least two parts, otherwise it is not a deconstruction. We limit a deconstruction to maximally seven parts to keep the structure comprehensible. If we end up with more than seven parts, then we group some parts together and create another level for deconstructing that group into parts.

How many levels of deconstruction should we aim for? How long should we continue to deconstruct something? The parts at the lowest level of the structure should be concrete enough for observation and measurement. Then we can collect facts about them. We have reached the bottom once we have arrived at the fact level.

 How To Do it?

- We use one criterion for deconstruction at a time. Do not deconstruct using two or more criteria at the same time. If we have multiple criteria, we will deconstruct for each criterion at a time. For example, we first deconstruct sales of a business-to-business company by country, then we deconstruct the country sales by the customer's industry, and subsequently we deconstruct industry sales by the customer's order size.

- We do not reinvent the wheel if we face a familiar problem, such as a performance deconstruction. In such cases, we consider standard analytical frameworks, such as KPI trees.

- We avoid endless searching for the *perfect* deconstruction. We try out different deconstructions and see which structure creates most insights into the problem.

- We look for an insightful deconstruction. For example, a deconstruction of costs into fixed and variable costs is probably not the most insightful structure. We ask ourselves: How does this company make money? If the business model is about capacity utilization, like an airline, a hotel, a restaurant, or a battery plant, then consider the following deconstruction of production volume: production capacity × capacity utilization rate.

- We do not try to deconstruct without engaging knowledgeable people. We may achieve mutual exclusiveness, but collective exhaustiveness is hard to realize without a sounding board. We do not know what we do not know. Therefore, we ask knowledgeable others to help us develop a deconstruction, or at least we let these people provide feedback on our work.

- If there are too many parts, then we may group all small parts. We may use a garbage can by labelling that group 'Other parts'.

- We make sure that we give clear labels to the parts. For example, the label 'customers' is clearer than 'markets' because some people understand markets as both supply and demand.

Measure gaps

We define a problem at the highest level of performance objectives: profit, people, or the planet. This way we know that we have the most important consequences in view. For the problem *analysis*, however, we descend to lower performance levels. For example, we deconstruct a profit gap into revenue and cost sub-gaps. The sub-gaps can be unequal. A specific sub-gap can be much larger than the rest. We do not want to divide our limited time and resources equally among unequal sub-gaps. Instead, we prioritise the sub-gap that matters most. We analyse other sub-gaps in order of diminishing importance. It is perfectly acceptable to limit our analysis to one or more relatively large sub-gaps if we clearly communicate this to our principal.

Rank the factor gaps

We compare the impact of the various sub-gaps on the overall gap. If the impacts of the sub-gaps are (almost) equal, we need to investigate them all. But if the impacts are (highly) unequal, then we focus on the sub-gap(s) with the largest impact. We rank the sub-gaps according to their impact.

 How To Do It?

We use Figure 4.31 to illustrate measuring the impact of sub-gaps on a higher gap.

	Realized performance	Performance objective	Performance gap		Realized performance	Performance objective	Performance gap
Price	4.5	5	−0.5	Revenue	90	125	−35
Volume	20	25	−5	Variable costs	45	50	−5
Variable cost per unit	2.25	2	0.25	Fixed costs	5	10	−5
Fixed costs	5	10	−5	Profit	40	65	−25

Figure 4.31   An example of performance gaps

Abbreviations

Profit Realized: PR; Profit Objective: PO; Profit Gap: PG
Revenue Realized: RR; Revenue Objective: RO; Revenue Gap: RG
Variable Costs Realized: VCR; Variable Costs Objective: VCO; Variable Cost Gap: VCG
Fixed Costs Realized: FCR; Fixed Costs Objective: FCO; Fixed Cost Gap: FCG

Formulas

Profit gap: $PG = PR - PO$
$PG = (RR - VCR - FCR) - (RO - VCO - FCO)$

(Continued)

PG = (RR – RO) – (VCR – VCO) – (FCR – FCO)
PG = (90 – 125) – (45 – 50) – (5 – 10)
PG = (–35) – (–5) – (–5) = –25

Please note that a *negative* cost gap (realized costs are smaller than the cost objective or budget) contributes to profit. In Figure 4.31, both the variable cost and the fixed cost gaps are negative. Therefore, both contribute to profit. We conclude that the revenue gap causes the profit gap.

  We prioritise the revenue gap and deconstruct it into a price gap and a volume gap.

price realized: pr; price objective: po; price gap: pg
volume realized: vr; volume objective: vo; volume gap: vg

Revenue gap: RG = RR – RO = 90 – 125 = –35
RG = (pr × vr) – (po × vo)
RG = (pr – po) × vr + (vr – vo) × po
Impact of the price gap on the revenue gap: (pr – po) × vr = –0.5 × 20 = –10
Impact of the volume gap on the revenue gap: (vr – vo) × po = –5 × 5 = –25

Please note that we can also use the following alternative formula:

RG = (pr – po) × vo + (vr – vo) × pr
Impact of the price gap: (pr – po) × vo = –0.5 × 25 = –12.5
Impact of the volume gap: (vr – vo) × pr = –5 × 4.5 = –22.5

Although the outcomes differ, the volume gap has the largest impact on the revenue gap according to both formulas.

Compare the *relative* price gap with the *relative* volume gap.
The relative price gap: (pr – po) / po = –0.5 / 5 = –0.1
The relative volume gap: (vr – vo) / vo = –5 / 25 = –0.2

We prioritise the revenue gap as it is the largest factor gap for profit. Within the revenue gap we prioritise the volume gap as it is the largest factor gap for revenue.
  As an example, we deconstruct the variable cost gap:

Abbreviations

variable cost per unit realized: ur; variable cost per unit objective: uo; variable cost per unit gap: ug
volume realized: vr; volume objective: vo; volume gap: vg

  Variable Cost Gap: VCG = VCR – VCO = 45 – 50 = –5
  VCG = (ur × vr) – (uo × vo)

VCG = (ur – uo) × vr + (vr – vo) × uo

Impact of variable cost per unit gap on the variable cost gap: (ur – uo) × vr = 0.25 × 20 = 5

Impact of volume gap: (vr – vo) × uo = –5 × 2 = –10

The variable cost per unit gap is positive. The impact of the variable cost per unit gap on *profit* is negative because a positive cost gap lowers profit.

The volume gap is a double-edged sword. The lower realized volume (compared to the objective) lowers revenue by 25, but it also lowers variable costs by 10.

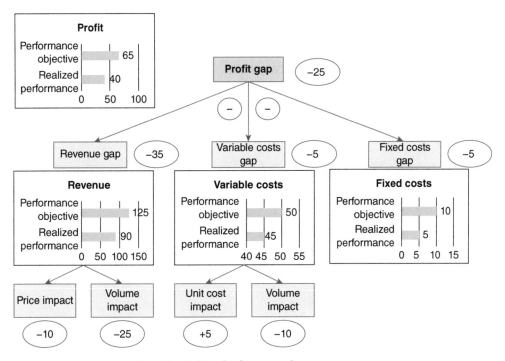

Figure 4.32   An example of isolating the impact of gaps

 **Pause and Reflect**

Use your own experience of a recent project from your study or work and identify the gap in this project.

Where does the problem lie?

Segment the prioritised sub-gap

Suppose the principal's business-to-business (B2B) company suffers a large revenue loss. The revenue gap has the highest priority. We have interviewed the purchasing managers of the principal's 100 customers. It turns out that 20 customers account for the principal's revenue loss. The other 80 customers have remained loyal to the principal. Business problems can be concentrated in one segment. Another example: some suppliers cause a disproportionate share of input quality issues. A third example: some employees cause a disproportionate share of errors. We want to avoid spending valuable research time on customers, suppliers, or employees who did not cause (many or large) problems. Therefore, we need to answer the question: *Where does the problem lie?*

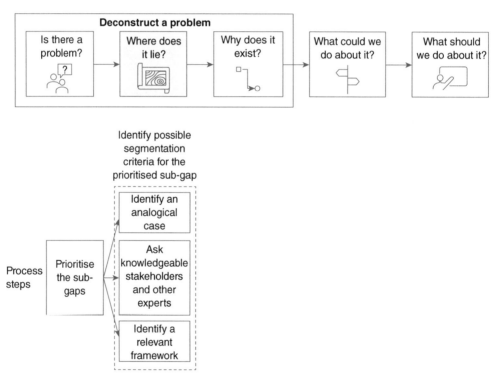

Figure 4.33   Three alternative approaches for segmenting a sub-gap

We have compared the sizes of all sub-gaps and prioritised the largest one. Figure 4.33 shows the process for segmenting that sub-gap.

We need to think about the possible criteria for segmenting the sub-gap. For example, shall we segment the revenue gap by customers, distribution channels, or countries? We may ask: How do we find these criteria? We distinguish between three alternative approaches.

- We ask ourselves: Are there *analogical cases*? There may have been identical or similar problems in the past, inside or outside the principal's company. Consider the criteria that people used to segment these cases.
- We ask ourselves: Are there *knowledgeable stakeholders and other experts*? If these people are close to the problem or have experience with this type of problem, they may have ideas how to segment the gap.
- We ask ourselves: Are there *relevant frameworks*? A framework may provide a MECE overview of all relevant aspects of a problem. These aspects may be segmentation criteria. For example, the value chain provides a way to segment a cost gap by activity.

Each of these approaches may generate alternative criteria for segmenting the sub-gap.

Prioritise the segments

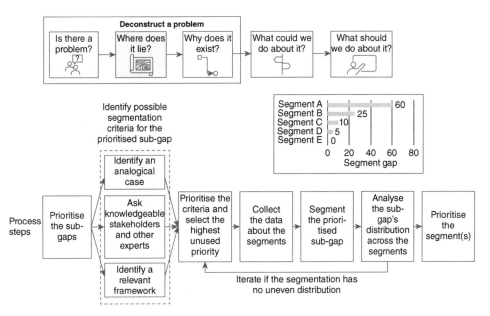

Figure 4.34   A process for prioritising segments

1. We evaluate the possible segmentation criteria and ask ourselves: Which criterion leads to the most skewed gap distribution? Ideally, a criterion shows an 80–20 or even more skewed distribution. Twenty per cent of the segments represent 80 per cent of the sub-gap. Before we measure segments, we can only form expectations about the distribution of the sub-gap across segments. We use our expectations and the expectations of knowledgeable stakeholders and other experts to rank the segmentation criteria based on the *expected* skewness of the distribution.
2. After we have chosen a criterion, we will collect the required data. For example, if we decide to segment a revenue gap by customers, we need revenue data per customer.

3. We segment the gap based on our chosen criterion.
4. We analyse the distribution of the gap across the segments. If the distribution is not skewed, we choose the highest ranked criterion that has not yet been used and repeat the prior steps (2 to 4).
5. If the distribution is skewed, then we prioritise the segment with the disproportionate share of the sub-gap. This segment will be the priority for the root cause analysis.

We distinguish between different criteria to segment a factor gap (see Figure 4.35).

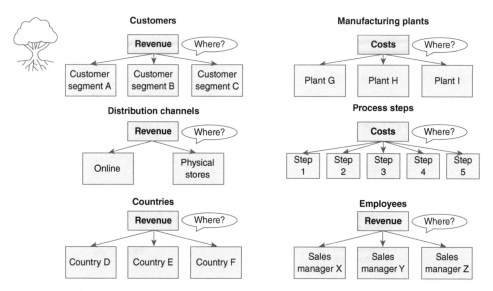

Figure 4.35   **Some criteria for segmenting revenue and cost gaps**

Check the MECE-ness of a segmentation

Figure 4.36 shows two examples of segmentations that are not MECE.

Figure 4.36   **Two examples of segmentations that are not MECE**

Venn diagrams and matrices visualize mutual exclusiveness of segments (see Figure 4.37).

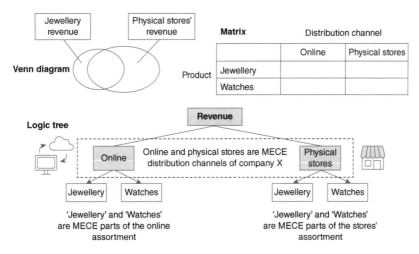

Figure 4.37   Visualisations of mutual exclusiveness

	Overlap of segments	Mutual exclusiveness of segments
Collective exhaustiveness of segments	• Watches revenue • Online watches revenue — Not MECE • Jewellery revenue	• Online jewellery revenue • Stores' jewellery revenue — MECE • Online watches revenue • Stores' watches revenue
Incomplete set of segments	• Watches revenue • Online watches revenue — Not MECE	• Online jewellery revenue • Stores' jewellery revenue — Not MECE

Figure 4.38   MECE versus non-MECE segmentations

Analyse and prioritise the segments

We analyse the distribution of the sub-gap across segments. We prioritise the segment with the largest gap (see Figure 4.39). This segment's gap is the priority requiring explanation.

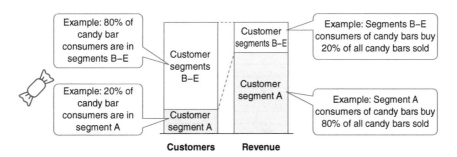

Figure 4.39   An example of an 80–20 distribution

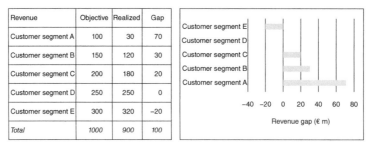

Revenue	Objective	Realized	Gap
Customer segment A	100	30	70
Customer segment B	150	120	30
Customer segment C	200	180	20
Customer segment D	250	250	0
Customer segment E	300	320	−20
Total	*1000*	*900*	*100*

Figure 4.40   An example of an uneven distribution

——————————— **Running Case RobotCo** ———————————

Where is the waiting time problem for parts? Does the waiting time vary by parts and by customers? How is the waiting time distributed by steps of the shipping process? Knowledgeable stakeholders think that the process is the most relevant criterion for segmenting waiting time. A waiting time problem arises when a part is not in the warehouse. The extra process steps to ship parts from the factory take time (see Figure 4.41).

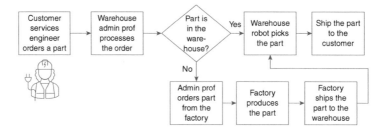

Figure 4.41   The process for shipping parts
Note: 'Admin prof' means administrative professional

Figure 4.42 shows the waiting time segmentation by process step.

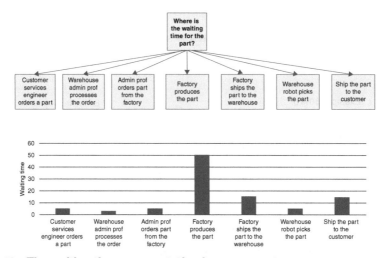

Figure 4.42   The waiting time segmentation by process step

Pause and Reflect

Use your own experience of a recent project from your study or work and segment the gap in this project.

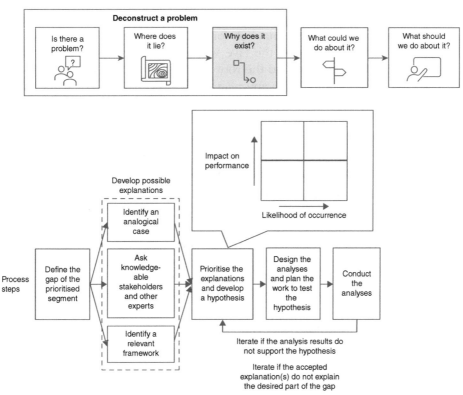

Figure 4.43 A process for explaining a segment of a factor gap

Assume that the principal in our example believes that the 20 customers who caused the revenue loss should receive discounts to win back the business. The principal asks us what the optimal discount is. When we talk with these 20 customers, we discover that they are *not* dissatisfied with the price. The unsatisfactory after-sales services caused the problem. Before we can solve a problem, we must first understand the problem cause. Therefore, we need to answer the question: *Why* does the problem exist?

Develop possible explanations

We have prioritised the segment with the largest gap. Figure 4.43 shows the process for explaining that gap.

1. We need to think about the *possible* causes for the gap. For example, is the revenue loss due to high prices or low-quality after-sales services? We may ask ourselves: How do we find these possible causes? We distinguish between three alternative approaches:

    a. We ask ourselves: Are there *analogical cases*? There may have been identical or similar problems in the past, inside or outside the principal's company. Consider the explanations of these cases.

    b. We ask ourselves: Are there any *knowledgeable stakeholders and other experts*? If these people are close to the problem or have experience with this type of problem, they may have ideas for how to explain that problem. We ask them: "Why does the problem exist?" When they provide a possible cause of the problem, we may ask for the cause of the cause: "Why does this cause exist?" According to the Five Whys technique (Ohno, 1988), we must ask 'why?' five times to find the root cause. Figure 4.44 shows three whys.

    c. We ask ourselves: Are there any *relevant frameworks*? A framework may provide a MECE overview of all relevant aspects of a problem. We can consider these aspects as possible explanations. For example, the Ishikawa or Fishbone diagram provides an overview of possible causes of process problems.

2. Each of the three approaches may generate possible causes of the gap. We evaluate our list of candidate explanations and ask ourselves two questions:

    a. How much of the gap can this cause explain? Can it explain the gap fully, for a large part, or only for a small part? We judge the explanatory power or impact of this possible cause.

    b. How likely is this cause for this specific problem case? Is it a likely cause or is it only theoretical? We judge the likelihood of this possible cause.

    c. We use our judgment and the judgment of knowledgeable stakeholders and other experts to rank the possible causes based on their expected impact and likelihood.

3. After ranking the possible explanations, we will develop a hypothesis about the prioritised possible explanation. The hypothesis looks like this: *'This cause contributes to the segment gap'*.

4. We plan the analyses and the work for testing the hypothesis. The work comprises the collection of the data, the analyses, and the presentation of the analysis results.

5. We collect the required data, conduct the analyses, and present the analysis results:

    a. If the analysis results do not support the hypothesis, we reject the hypothesis and select the next highest-ranked cause. We iterate, or repeat, the prior steps of hypothesis development and testing.

    b. If the analysis results support the hypothesis, we accept the hypothesis.

        -   If the cause explains the complete gap or at least the desired part of that gap (the minimum share of the gap that the principal desires to be explained), then we have a supported explanation of the gap. We have completed the analyses.

        -   If the cause explains a smaller part of the gap (smaller than the desired part), we select the next possible cause on the priority list. We iterate the prior steps of hypothesis development and testing until we can explain the desired part of the gap.

6. If we have multiple, small causes, we combine them for a complete explanation.

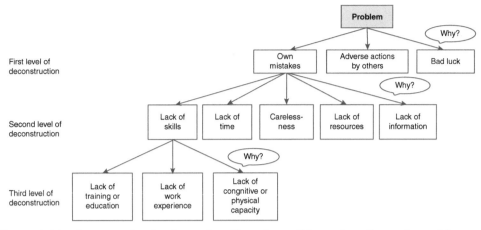

First level of
deconstruction

Second level of
deconstruction

Third level of
deconstruction

Figure 4.44 **An example of a deconstruction of possible explanations of a problem**

Question	Unit of analysis	Examples of frameworks
Is there a problem?	Performance	KPI tree, for example, a profit tree DuPont formula of return on assets
Where does the problem lie?	Segments	Value system Value chain SIPOC Congruence model
Why does the problem exit?	Explanations in general	SWOT PESTEL Ishikawa/fishbone diagram 7S
Why does the revenue problem exist?	Explanations of revenue gaps	3C Competitive forces Value-based Strategy Blue Ocean Canvas Sales funnel S-curve Network effects Market size – market share Porter's drivers of differentiation
Why does the cost problem exist?	Explanations of cost gaps	Porter's drivers of costs Economics of scale and scope Experience effects Break-even analysis

Figure 4.45 **Some examples of frameworks for answering questions**

Notes to Figure 4.45

KPI: Key Performance Indicator

SIPOC: Suppliers, Inputs, Process, Outputs, and Customers

Congruence model: processes, resources & capabilities, structure & systems, culture (Nadler & Tushman, 1980)

SWOT: Strengths, Weaknesses, Opportunities, and Threats

PESTEL: Political, Economic, Social, Technological, Environmental, and Legal factors in the macro-environment

7S: Strategy, Structure, Systems, Staff, Skills, Style, and Superordinate goals or shared values (Peters & Waterman, 1982)

3C: Customers, Competitors, and Company (Ohmae, 1982)

Value-based Strategy: Willingness To Pay (WTP) and Willingness To Sell (WTS) (Oberholzer-Gee, 2021).

Identify a relevant framework

A framework may help knowledgeable stakeholders and other experts to identify possible causes. We may use a framework to develop an interview guide or a workshop agenda. We can also use frameworks *after* developing possible explanations. Then we may use the framework to put the possible explanations in a logical structure. Figure 4.45 provides some examples of popular frameworks.

 How To Do It?

- To generate possible explanations of a problem, we may organize a brainstorming workshop with our project team and with knowledgeable stakeholders and other experts. People may write their explanations on post-it notes and put them on a whiteboard. If applicable, we may also consider role playing. Workshop participants can play the roles of stakeholders. For example, they put themselves in the shoes of a customer. This may help us to explore several stakeholder perspectives on the problem.
- After collecting the ideas, we may confront every idea about a problem explanation with its opposite. We can ask ourselves: "Why would it not be the other way around?" For example, stakeholders point to a decline of customer demand as an explanation of a revenue gap. We can ask: "Why would the principal's company not be the cause of the revenue gap?"
- We can force ourselves to consider alternative explanations.
- We may also ask ourselves and stakeholders questions about the possible explanations: "What would we have to know or believe to accept this explanation of the problem?"
- If stakeholders have given their explanation, we may ask them about alternative explanations. We can ask: "What else may have caused the gap?"
- Ask knowledgeable stakeholders and other experts who have given their explanations *how* these specific causes contribute to the problem. For example, a sales representative of the principal's company points to high inflation as the explanation for the company's revenue gap. We can ask: "How does high inflation cause the revenue gap?" Let these people explain the logic or relationship between their cause and the performance gap.
- We also ask them for empirical proof for this cause. We need facts to support an explanation.
- Instead of a workshop, we may also consider (online) surveys among knowledgeable stakeholders to collect ideas about possible causes.

Put the possible explanations in a logical structure

We have a long list of possible causes of the problem. To get the big picture, we develop a logical structure of these possible causes. We want these explanations to be mutually exclusive. It may surprise you, but collective exhaustiveness of explanations is nice to have but not necessary. We do not want to spend time analysing possible causes that have little explanatory power or impact on the gap. We are also not interested in theoretical explanations that are highly unlikely. But we must be certain to identify the most important possible causes in terms of explanatory power and likelihood.

As an illustration of how this structuring of causes works, Figure 4.46 presents a logical structuring of the possible causes of a revenue gap. To keep the figure clear, we limit the revenue deconstruction to four levels, and we do not show the cost explanations.

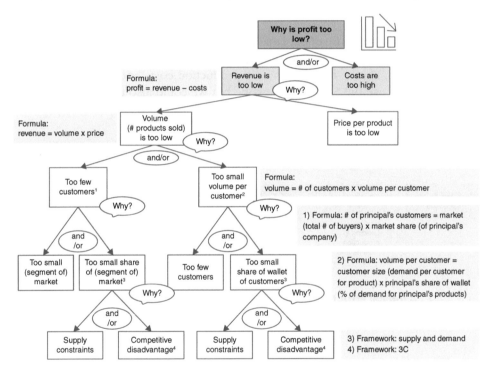

Figure 4.46   An example of a logical structure of possible explanations of a profit gap

Note: 'And/or' means that both explanations may be true, but one explanation would be enough

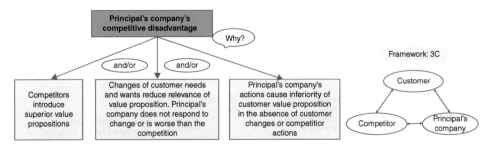

Figure 4.47   An example of a logical structure of possible explanations for a competitive disadvantage

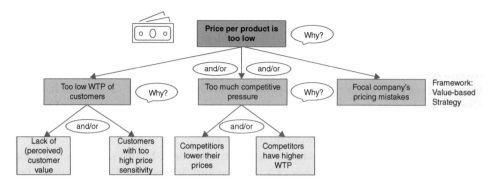

Figure 4.48   An example of a logical structure of possible explanations for a price gap

Note: WTP means Willingness To Pay

We also provide a structure of explanations of cost overruns. Because the costs come from a wide range of different value-adding activities, we segment the costs by activity. For clarity reasons, Figure 4.49 shows only production costs and one level of deconstruction. Here we use the SIPOC framework, but we could also use other structures.

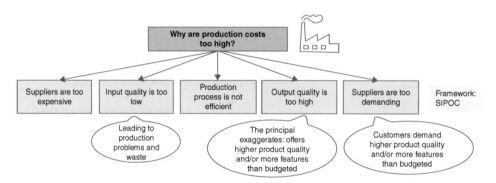

Figure 4.49   A logical structure of possible explanations for a production cost problem

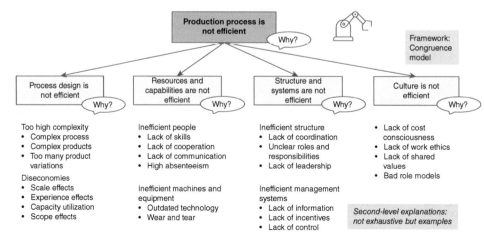

Figure 4.50   A logical structure of possible explanations for production process inefficiency

In Figure 4.50, we deconstruct one possible explanation from Figure 4.49. Here we use the congruence model to identify possible explanations for production process inefficiency.

How To Do It?

When we have identified a possible cause, we can ask ourselves and knowledgeable stakeholders and other experts: *Why* does this cause exist? We continuously ask 'Why?' So, we deconstruct the problem into a hierarchy of increasingly fundamental causes. We stop asking why when we can no longer answer the question. Then we have found the root cause. Asking why the root cause exists does not make sense. There is no cause of a root cause.

Running Case RobotCo

"*Why* are the needed parts not in the warehouse?" Tara asks that question to several stakeholders and receives many answers (see Figure 4.51). Young engineers blame the robots: "These machines are so hard to analyse." Older engineers criticize the human resource policy: "Nowadays people are promoted to full engineer way too soon and work independently for their own clients. In the past, we had to stay as an assistant much longer to develop experience."

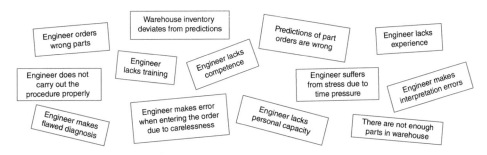

Figure 4.51   Examples of the answers

How to deal with all these answers? Tara puts them in a logical structure (see Figure 4.52). Next, she judges, together with selected knowledgeable stakeholders, the explanatory power or impact and the likelihood of the lowest-level explanations. Then Tara can prioritise the explanations.

(Continued)

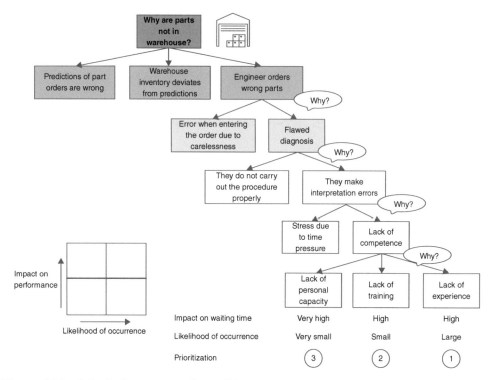

Figure 4.52   A logical structure of possible explanations for missing parts

Pause and Reflect

Use your own experience of a recent project from your study or work and develop a logical structure of possible explanations for the problem.

Discuss the objective

A performance gap is the difference between the performance objective and the realized performance. So far, we have explained a gap by a low realized performance. We *assume* that the performance objective is correct. But the objective might be too high (or too low). Figure 4.53 provides some explanations for a too high profit objective. If we suspect that the objective is too high (or too low), we may ask the principal: "How did you formulate the objective? Based on what data and what analysis did you decide on the objective?"

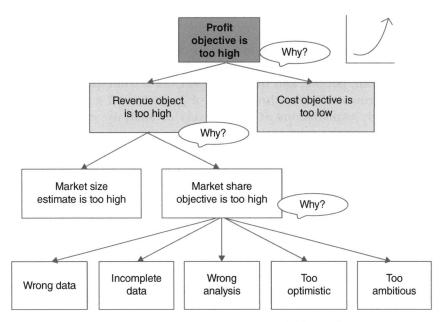

Figure 4.53 Some examples of explanations for a too high profit objective

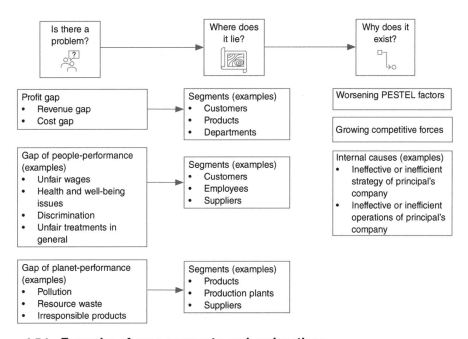

Figure 4.54 Examples of gaps, segments, and explanations

Wrap-up

Figure 4.54 provides an overview of a sequential analysis. We address the first question with the 'triple bottom line' model. The principal may have simultaneous gaps for profit, people, and the planet. For the second question, we provide examples of segments for the three types of gaps. For all gaps, we distinguish between possible explanations at three levels of analysis: macro-environment, industry, and company.

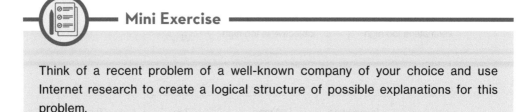

Mini Exercise

Think of a recent problem of a well-known company of your choice and use Internet research to create a logical structure of possible explanations for this problem.

PART 3: DECONSTRUCT AN OPPORTUNITY

Assume the principal, a director of a training company, perceives a great opportunity in online training. The principal instructs us to develop an online training offer. Together with a team of trainers, we produce the first online course. To the principal's great surprise, the students are dissatisfied with this online offering. They would much rather meet in a classroom with a trainer and fellow students. This example illustrates that we need to be sure that the perceived opportunity really exists. We must systematically analyse a perceived opportunity before we develop a solution (see Figure 4.55).

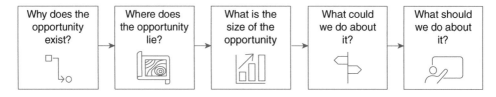

Figure 4.55   The Sequential Analysis Method applied to an opportunity

An opportunity analysis differs from a problem analysis because opportunities differ from problems (see Figure 4.56). A problem gap is a fact. In contrast, an opportunity gap is an expectation. An opportunity gap cannot be the starting point for an analysis. We first must validate the expectation before we can assess the gap.

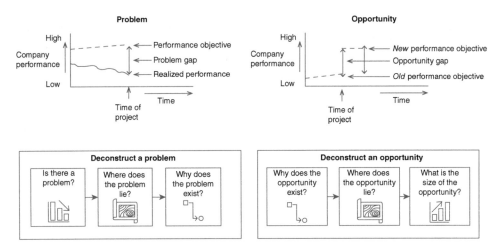

Figure 4.56   Different sequences for problem and opportunity analyses

Why does the opportunity exist?

The first question in an opportunity analysis is: "*Why* does the opportunity exist?" We identify the *possible* explanations of the *perceived* opportunity. What drives this opportunity? In the case of revenue opportunities, we may ask: "Why would customers prefer this [new product, service, sales channel, etc.]?" For cost opportunities, we could ask: "Why would this [new input, process, equipment, etc.] reduce costs?"

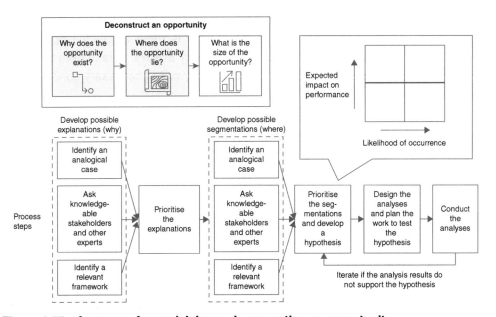

Figure 4.57   A process for explaining and segmenting an opportunity

Figure 4.57 combines the processes for explaining (why) and segmenting (where) opportunities. We combine the 'why' and the 'where' because we can only test hypotheses about opportunities in specific segments. We cannot test opportunity explanations (the why) without segments (the where) because explanations without segments are abstract. The segments (where) make the explanations (why) testable. As with problem analysis, we start by collecting all possible explanations and segmentations and then prioritise them based on their expected impact and likelihood.

How To Do It?

Preferably approach a wider group of knowledgeable stakeholders and other experts, including people outside the principal's company. If some stakeholders disagree with, or even deny, the perceived opportunity, then ask: "Why does the opportunity *not* exist?" If critics recognize the opportunity but believe that the principal's company is unable to seize this opportunity, ask the following question: "What barriers keep the principal's company from taking advantage of this opportunity?"

Running Case ConsultCo

We repeat the key question: "How should ConsultCo seize the opportunity to internationalize to increase its profit?" To analyse this perceived opportunity, Arpit first asks the partners and knowledgeable stakeholders: "*Why* is there a revenue opportunity abroad?" Figure 4.58 shows the first-level opportunity drivers. Please note the ovals with 'and': driver 1 *and* 2 *and* 3 must be present. They are *all* necessary conditions for this opportunity.

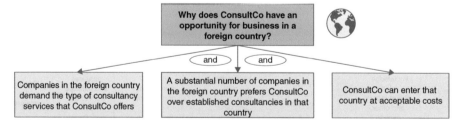

Figure 4.58   A logical structure of the drivers of an opportunity

Arpit continues to ask 'why?' to identify lower-level drivers. Figure 4.59 presents a deconstruction of the first first-level driver 'customer demand'.

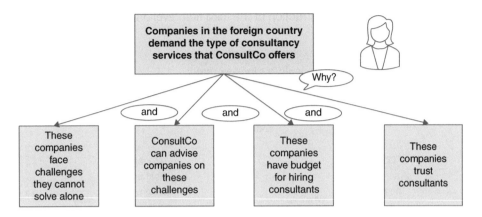

Figure 4.59   A logical structure of the drivers of customer demand

Figure 4.60 presents a deconstruction of the first-level driver 'customer preferences'. Please note that we only prioritise drivers if they are substitutes ('or- logic'). If drivers are necessary conditions for an opportunity ('and- logic'), then we should examine them all. 'Impact' of a driver is about the driver's explanatory power or importance for the opportunity. To what extent can this driver explain the opportunity?

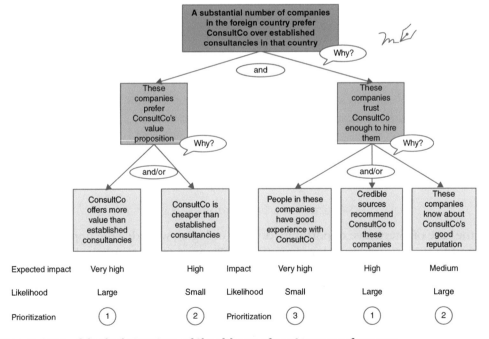

Figure 4.60   A logical structure of the drivers of customer preferences

(Continued)

Figure 4.61 presents a deconstruction of the third first-level driver 'entry costs'.

Figure 4.61 A logical structure of the drivers of entry costs

---

Pause and Reflect

Use your own experience of a recent project from your study or work and develop a logical structure of possible explanations for the opportunity.

Where does the opportunity lie?

In the case of alternative opportunity drivers (or-logic), we judge the impact and likelihood to prioritise drivers (for example, see Figure 4.60). Regarding the prioritised drivers, we ask: Where, in what segment, are these drivers strongest? As with problem analysis, we segment the opportunity. We must find a relevant way to segment the opportunity. Examples of revenue opportunity segments are products, customers, geographies, and distribution channels. Segmentation criteria for cost opportunities are, among others, processes, suppliers, and departments. As with problems, we look for a segmentation that reveals a skewed distribution of an opportunity across segments. For example, the 20 per cent 'category A users' will account for 80 per cent of the demand for a new consumer product.

Running Case ConsultCo

Where is the international opportunity? Arpit needs to segment the revenue opportunity. ConsultCo's MP wants Arpit to identify the most attractive countries. But Arpit needs a more fine-grained segmentation, namely 'prospects', which are potential customers. The reason is that countries do not hire consultants, but customers do. Therefore, customers are the relevant level of analysis. The question arises: "Where are these prospects?" Based on discussions with the MP and other knowledgeable stakeholders, Arpit distinguishes two groups of prospects. One group is prior customers who have had a good experience with ConsultCo. The other group consists of companies that are open to recommendations from others to hire ConsultCo.

Pause and Reflect

Use your own experience of a recent project from your study or work and segment the opportunity.

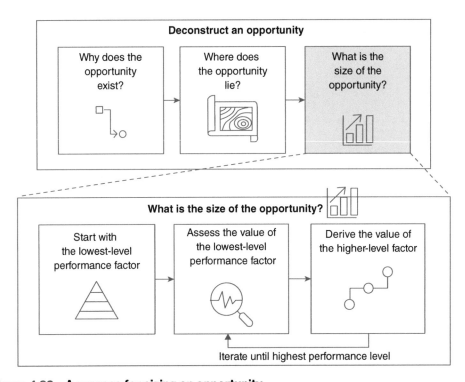

Figure 4.62　A process for sizing an opportunity

What is the size of the opportunity?

If there is proof of an opportunity hypothesis (see Chapter 5 for hypothesis testing), we estimate the size of that opportunity. The size of the opportunity is the opportunity gap, which is the difference between the current and the new higher performance objective. The new objective is an expectation. Unlike a problem gap, we cannot *measure* an opportunity gap. We can only *estimate* how much the objective may increase because of the opportunity. The new objective is about the expected performance impact of seizing the opportunity. If the objective is profit, then we can monetize the impact of the opportunity. We quantify how much more profit is possible. Sizing an opportunity is a bottom-up process that starts with the profit factors (see Figure 4.62).

──────── **Running case ConsultCo** ────────

Arpit estimates the size of the opportunity gap through a bottom-up approach (see Figure 4.63). Arpit can build up the profit estimate from the profit factors.

- How many additional customers abroad will ConsultCo be able to serve per year if the firm internationalizes?
- Per international customer, how many projects will they give to ConsultCo?
- What will be the revenue of these projects?
- What will be the associated costs?

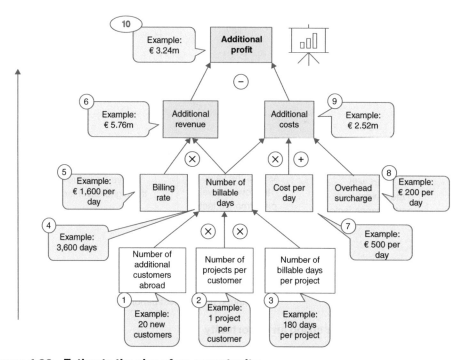

Figure 4.63 Estimate the size of an opportunity

Arpit estimates the project revenue in terms of the number of days that ConsultCo can bill to the customer (number of consultants on the project × number of billable days per consultant).

 Pause and Reflect

Use your own experience of a recent project from your study or work and estimate the size of the opportunity.

 How To Do It?

How do we estimate the revenue opportunity for a new product?

- The quick way to do it is a *top-down approach*.
  - We start with the size of the total market for the focal product (or service). We use public data, or we estimate the market size. Assume the market is 500 million euro.
  - The next step is to estimate the principal's market share. We estimate that the principal can get a 5 per cent share. Therefore, the revenue opportunity is 25 million euro. This looks straightforward but the share estimate can be a challenge. What is the argumentation for 5 per cent? We can base ourselves on the judgment of knowledgeable stakeholders and other experts or on analogical cases.
- The systematic way is a *bottom-up approach*.
  - We start with an individual customer of the focal product. Who will buy how much and why? The 'who' and the 'why' refer to our analysis of segments and opportunity drivers.
  - Based on the opportunity analysis, we estimate the size of the revenue of the opportunity: number of customers × number of products per customer per year × price of product. For example: 1 million customers × 10 products per customer × 2.50 euro per product = 25 million euro.

 Mini Exercise

Think of a recent opportunity taken by a well-known company of your choice and use Internet research to create a logical structure of the possible drivers of this opportunity.

Pause and Reflect

Consider how you may use this technique for deconstructing problems and opportunities in your studies, work, and personal life.

SUMMARY

We briefly outline the main takeaways of this chapter.

- Choose from alternative problem-solving methods
  - the Sequential Analysis Method: answers a series of questions
  - the Issue Tree Method: deconstructs the key question into a tree of sub-questions (issues)
  - the Hypothesis Tree Method: deconstructs a solution hypothesis (the probable answer to the key question) into a tree of sub-hypotheses
- Analyse a problem with the Sequential Analysis Method
  1. Is there a problem?
  2. Where does the problem lie?
  3. Why does the problem exist?
  4. What could we do about the problem?
  5. What should we do about the problem?
- Deconstruct a performance gap into logical structures of:
  - performance factors: isolate the impact of factors on a performance gap
  - segments: search for an uneven or skewed distribution of a gap across segments (using the 80/20 rule)
  - possible explanations: continue to ask 'why' to identify the gap's root cause(s)

 Mini Exercise

Identify the key concepts and terms in this chapter, define them briefly and compile your own glossary.

REFERENCES AND FURTHER READING

Chevallier, A. (2016). *Strategic Thinking in Complex Problem Solving*. Oxford: Oxford University Press.

Coleman, J. S. (1994). *Foundations of Social Theory*. Cambridge, MA: Harvard University Press.

Conn, C., & McLean, R. (2018). *Bulletproof Problem Solving: The One Skill that Changes Everything*. Hoboken, NJ: John Wiley & Sons.

Descartes, R. (2008). *A Discourse on the Method*. Translated by I. Maclean. Oxford: Oxford University Press.

Garrette, B., Phelps, C., & Sibony, O. (2018). *Cracked It! How to Solve Big Problems and Sell Solutions Like Top Strategy Consultants*. London: Palgrave Macmillan.

Hasso Plattner Institute of Design at Stanford University (2010). *An Introduction to Design Thinking: PROCESS GUIDE*. Retrieved from: https://web.stanford.edu (accessed 19 July 2023).

Minto, B. (2003). *The Minto Pyramid Principle: Logic in Writing, Thinking and Problem Solving*. London: Minto International.

Minto interview. McKinsey website. Retrieved on November 30, 2020, from www.mckinsey.com/alumni/news-and-insights/global-news/alumni-news/barbara-minto-mece-i-invented-it-so-i-get-to-say-how-to-pronounce-it

Nadler, D. A., & Tushman, M. L. (1980). A model for diagnosing organizational behavior. *Organizational Dynamics*, *9*(2), 35–51.

Oberholzer-Gee, F. (2021). *Better Simpler Strategy*. Boston, MA: Harvard Business Review Press.

Ohmae, K. (1982). *The Mind of the Strategist: The Art of Japanese Management*. New York: McGraw-Hill.

Ohno, T. (1988). *Toyota Production System: Beyond Large-Scale Production*. New York: Productivity Press.

Peters, T. J., & Waterman Jr, R. H. (1982). *In Search of Excellence*. London: Harper & Row.

Rasiel, E. M. (1999). *The McKinsey Way: Using the Techniques of the World's Top Strategic Consultants to Help You and Your Business*. New York: McGraw-Hill.

Rasiel, E. M., Friga, P. N., & Enriquez, J. (2001). *The McKinsey Mind: Understanding and Implementing the Problem-Solving Tools and Management Techniques of the World's Top Strategic Consulting Firm*. New York: McGraw-Hill.

Develop and Conduct Relevant Analyses

5

INTRODUCTION

The first progress meeting of the project will be in two weeks and the principal has high expectations. We work hard because we must show something good in two weeks. We collect data but the more data we collect, the more we become aware of other relevant data. All data seem important to us, but time is running out. Now we quickly perform the well-known analyses. During the progress meeting we present all the results to the principal. We hope for a compliment, but the principal says: "You clearly worked hard, but what should I do with these analyses?" This chapter will outline a more effective approach to analysis.

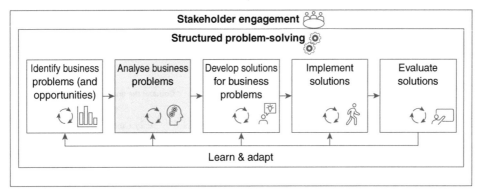

Figure 5.1 **Analysing business problems is the second step of structured problem-solving**

Here we follow the Sequential Analysis Method to analyse problems (see Figure 5.2).

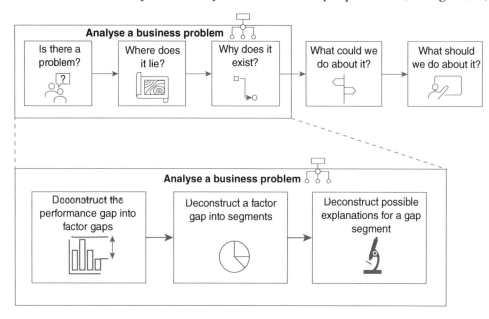

Figure 5.2   The Sequential Analysis Method for analysing a business problem

The chapter follows the process for explaining a business problem (see Figure 5.3). The chapter is structured into two parts: develop analyses and conduct analyses.

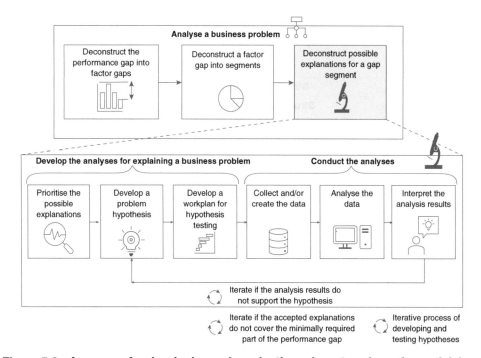

Figure 5.3   A process for developing and conducting relevant analyses for explaining a business problem

MAIN LEARNING OBJECTIVES

After studying this chapter, you should be able to:

- evaluate alternative possible explanations of a problem
- develop a problem hypothesis
- select a proper analytical framework for testing a problem hypothesis
- design an analysis if no proper framework is available
- develop a workplan for testing a problem hypothesis
- select appropriate data collection methods
- select appropriate data creation methods

PART 1: DEVELOP RELEVANT ANALYSES

Prioritise the possible explanations

A trap with data collection is that we cannot stop collecting data. We discover new data every time and everything seems relevant. Plus, the more data we have, the more confident we feel. But how can we distinguish between data that are relevant and data that are irrelevant for problem-solving? We can use hypotheses about possible explanations of the problem. These hypotheses determine which data are relevant. Working with hypotheses avoids the pitfall of endless data collection.

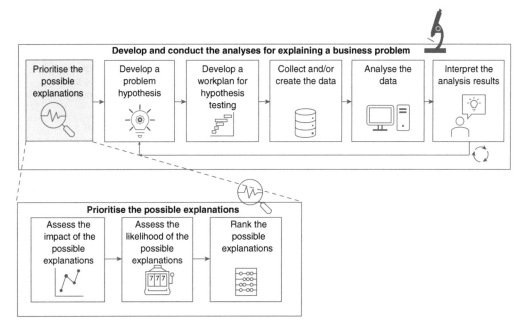

Figure 5.4 Prioritisation of possible explanations is the first step in explaining a business problem

The previous chapter showed how to generate possible answers to the why-question: Why does the problem exist? We need to verify these possible answers before we can accept them. Hypothesis testing is crucial, but it means collecting and analysing data, which are time-consuming and costly. Do we need to test *all* possible answers to the why-question? We want to avoid wasting time and effort on testing unimportant or unlikely answers. Instead, we focus our time and effort on the most important and likely possible explanations. Therefore, we need to rank the possible answers on the basis of their importance and likelihood.

- The *importance* or *impact* of a possible answer is about the effect on the performance gap. Note that it is *expected* impact. Before the test, we do not know whether the answer is true, and if so, what part of the gap it explains.
- The *likelihood* of occurrence of a possible answer is the chance of that answer being true. We ask ourselves: Is this a realistic or a theoretical answer? How likely is it that this answer, this explanation, applies to the principal's problem? For example, in *theory*, this explanation can play a role in explaining the problem. But this is very unlikely in the principal's case because there is no condition for this explanation.

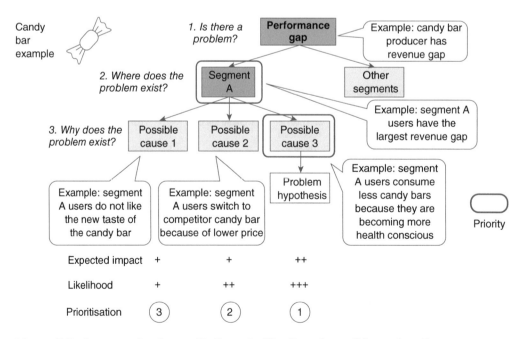

Figure 5.5   An example of a qualitative prioritisation of possible explanations

Possible explanation	Expected impact on performance gap (€ m)	Expected likelihood (or confidence)	Overall (expectancy value in € m)
1: segment A users do not like the new taste of the candy bar	50	10%	5
2: segment A users switch to competitor candy bar because of lower price	60	33%	20
3: segment A users consume less candy bars because they are becoming more health conscious	100	50%	50

Figure 5.6   An example of a quantitative prioritisation

Running Case RobotCo

Recall the key question: "How should RobotCo respond to the problem of the late delivery of parts to increase its profit by 15 million euro in one year?" The waiting time for parts increases when they are not in the warehouse. Unavailability contributes to *excess* waiting time: the time exceeds the service-level agreement with customers. Figure 5.7 shows a logical structure of three possible reasons why parts are not in the warehouse. Tara, together with knowledgeable stakeholders, judges the impact and likelihood of each explanation. Wrong predictions by the software are a theoretical answer. The programmers have extensively tested their software. Therefore, it is very unlikely that the software fails.

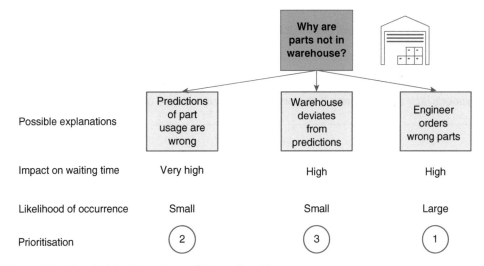

Figure 5.7   A prioritisation of possible explanations

(Continued)

Tara dives deeper into the prioritised explanation to make it more specific.

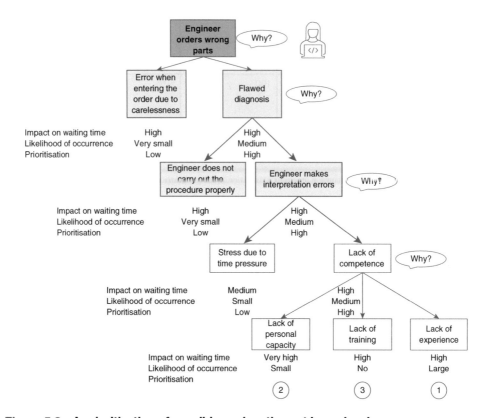

Figure 5.8   A prioritisation of possible explanations at lower levels

Together with the principal and knowledgeable stakeholders, Tara concludes that an engineer's lack of experience is the prioritised possible cause of wrong orders.

 **How To Do It?**

How can we assess the impact and likelihood of possible explanations *before* testing? Before the test, we judge the impact and likelihood. An exception is explanations based on analogical cases, where data are available. In other cases we use our own experience for the judgment. Besides, we may consult knowledgeable stakeholders and other experts for their judgment. We may use project team voting:

1. Every team member receives several votes: they can give votes to one or more possible answers.
2. We compare the judged impact and likelihood of the alternative possible explanations.

 Pause and Reflect

Use your own experience of a recent project from your study or work and prioritise the possible explanations of the problem or opportunity.

Develop a problem hypothesis

We prioritise the possible explanations that are most impactful and most likely. The prioritised explanations become our problem hypotheses. We formulate hypotheses as a relationship between the cause (the possible explanation) and the effect (the performance gap).

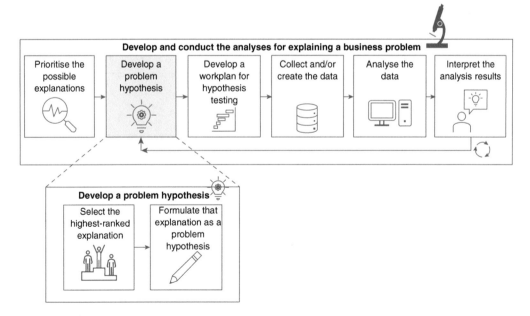

Figure 5.9   Hypothesis development is the second step in explaining a business problem

Hypothesis: This specific possible explanation contributes to this specific performance gap.

Example of a hypothesis: The product recall contributes to the revenue gap.

We use the verb 'contributes' instead of 'causes' because we do not want to exclude other explanations before we have tested our hypothesis. For example, we find that the product recall cannot fully explain that gap. Another explanation is a sales promotion campaign of the most important competitor.

Running Case RobotCo

An engineer's lack of experience contributes to wrong orders. These ordered parts are not available in the warehouse because the inventory is based on software that assumes that all orders are correct. Tara formulates the following initial problem hypothesis: *An engineer's lack of experience contributes to excess waiting time for parts.*

Running Case ConsultCo

The key question for ConsultCo is: How should ConsultCo seize the internationalisation opportunity to increase its profit? Based on the opportunity analysis, Arpit creates the following opportunity hypothesis: *ConsultCo's entry into country B adds 3 million euro to profit within two years.*

 ## Pause and Reflect

Use your own experience of a recent project from your study or work and develop a hypothesis about the problem or opportunity.

Develop a workplan for hypothesis testing

Determine the required proof for the hypotheses

We resist the temptation to immediately dive into the data. Instead, we start with the end in mind, which is the hypothesis test. The data is a means to test a hypothesis. Before we collect the data, we need to know what data the test requires. A test is an analysis that may prove the hypothesized explanation. We need to identify the type of proof that the principal and any other relevant stakeholders need in order to accept the hypothesis.

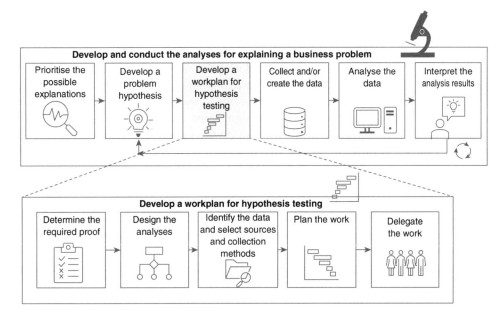

Figure 5.10   Workplan development is the third step in explaining a business problem

Distinguishing between types of proof

Take the hypothesis: The product recall contributes to the revenue gap. We distinguish between three types of proof.

- *Quantitative facts*: we have collected facts about the product recall and revenue. A statistical analysis reveals that the recall explains 50 per cent of the revenue gap.
- *Qualitative facts*: we have interviewed a couple of former customers who stopped purchasing after the recall. These interviews tell us that the recall was a decisive factor in stopping purchases.
- *Judgment*: we ask an industry expert for her opinion on the impact of the recall.

Deciding on the type of proof

We must make a trade-off between the quality of the proof and the costs of realizing this proof. The quality is about the level of accuracy and reliability. Accuracy is the precision or validity of the proof, whereas reliability refers to the amount of evidence. If we spend more time, we can reach higher levels of accuracy and reliability. For example, compare the following three efforts:

- 'Day one' proof: there is limited data (low or very low reliability) that is readily available on the first day of the hypothesis testing (probably low accuracy)
- Proof after one week of work: the right data (high accuracy) is found but there is relatively little data (low- or intermediate-level reliability)
- Proof after three weeks of work: the right data (high accuracy) is found and there is now relatively a lot of data (high reliability)

The proof determines whether the principal and any other relevant stakeholders will accept the explanation of the problem. This explanation influences the development of the solution as the solution should address the cause(s) of the problem. Therefore, the definition of the required proof has significant implications for the problem-solving project. We ask ourselves: What proof do the principal and any other relevant stakeholders need in order to accept an explanation of the problem? We may use the following questions to determine the proof.

- *Nature of explanation*: How controversial is the explanation of the problem? If a cause of the problem is logical and intuitive, the principal and the relevant stakeholders will require less proof than if an answer is against their intuitive understanding of the problem.
- *Risk attitude*: How risk-averse are the principal and the relevant stakeholders? Risk-averse people want more proof than less risk-averse ones.
- *Type of decision influence*:
  - How much accuracy do the principal and the relevant stakeholders need to decide? Does the proof have to be very accurate, or is a rough approximation enough? In some cases, people want very precise proof while in other situations a ballpark range is sufficient. In the example of the product recall, a rough estimate of the revenue impact may be enough. In another example about excess manufacturing costs, the principal may require very precise proof about which machines contribute to what extent to the cost overrun.
  - How much value is at stake for the principal and relevant stakeholders? With increasing stakes, these people want more proof.

If we think we know what the required proof is, we still must check it with the principal. We should not assume that we know what the principal wants. Therefore, we present our proposal for proof to the principal and ask whether this information is sufficient proof for accepting the problem hypothesis. If the principal rejects our proposal, we should ask what the sufficient proof should look like. We should never test a problem hypothesis without knowing the required level of proof.

Running Case RobotCo

We repeat the hypothesis for your convenience: An engineer's lack of experience contributes to excess waiting time for parts due to wrong orders. The question arises: *How* should Tara test this hypothesis?

Tara operationalizes the variables in the hypothesis.

- *An engineer's experience.* How to measure experience? Tara uses the number of years of relevant working experience.
- *Waiting time for parts.* How to measure waiting time? Tara chooses the number of hours between order and delivery.

Tara asks herself: How to identify the wrong orders? Is waiting time for ordered parts the answer? Tara thinks about it and concludes that waiting time is not the answer. She reasons as follows: if some engineers place wrong orders, then these mistaken engineers may take the parts that other engineers later really need (see 'a' in Figure 5.11). If these other engineers place their correct orders *after* the wrong orders of their mistaken colleagues, these right engineers will face out-of-stock situations (see 'b'). Out-of-stock and waiting time for engineers can result from their own wrong orders (see 'c'), but also from wrong orders by other engineers.

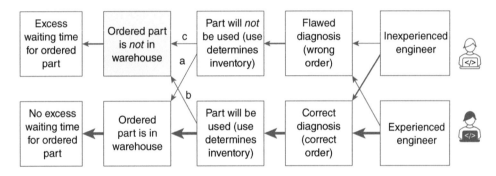

Figure 5.11   A drawing of the process

Therefore, Tara focuses on the number of *unused* parts per engineer (the engineer does not need the parts because the diagnosis was wrong). Tara does not focus on the absolute number of unused parts per engineer. To correct for any differences in the number of orders per engineer, Tara uses *the percentage of unused ordered parts*: the number of unused parts/the total number of ordered parts × 100 per cent.

Visualise the proof

How will we present the proof to the principal? We do not do an analysis and afterwards start to think about the presentation of the analysis results. *Before* the data collection, we visualise the proof. What graphical presentation of the proof will convince the principal? We think in advance about a convincing way to present the proof. Typically, we make PowerPoint slides with figures or tables. At this stage we use dummy data because we do not yet have the results.

━━━━━ Running Case RobotCo ━━━━━

Tara defines the following convincing proof for the hypothesis: the relationship between an engineer's years of relevant working experience and the percentage of unused ordered parts. If Tara can collect a sufficiently large number of observations, she can conduct inferential statistics, such as a regression analysis. If she does not have enough observations for inferential statistics, then she may use descriptive statistics to do a so-called 'eyeball test'.

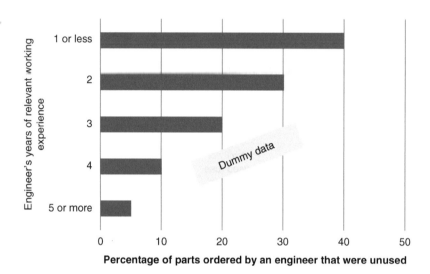

Figure 5.12   A presentation with dummy data

Design the analyses

What kind of analysis can provide the required proof? We distinguish between two basic forms: comparison and deconstruction analysis.

- *Comparison analysis*: This is the comparison of a principal's problem with a comparable problem of another company. We may call the comparison analysis a '*benchmark analysis*'. Comparing the principal's problem with an analogical case can explain a principal's problem. We can use the problem causes of the other company to clarify a principal's problem. But we can also compare the principal's company with a 'best practice' company to identify opportunities. The differences between the principal and the best practice may indicate opportunities for performance improvement.
  - ○ We can put a principal's company side by side with a comparable company. This is an *external* comparison. For example, Tara can benchmark RobotCo's waiting time against a comparable competitor. Next, she can analyse the differences between RobotCo and that company to explain RobotCo's undesired performance.

○ But we can also do an *internal* comparison of various parts of a principal's company. We may compare departments, factories, offices, stores, teams, or individuals. For example, Tara can compare the waiting time figures of the various engineers.

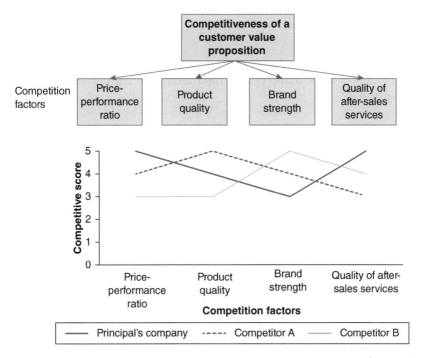

Figure 5.13   An example of a deconstruction analysis of competitiveness based on the Blue Ocean Canvas framework

• *Deconstruction analysis*: If the unit of analysis is complex, we can deconstruct that unit into its parts. It is easier to analyse the parts than the whole unit. For example, we need to analyse the market size. We can deconstruct the market into segments. Subsequently, we can analyse the size of a segment by analysing the drivers of segment size. Examples of segment size drivers are the number of customers in the segment and the demand per customer. We can deconstruct these high-level drivers into a hierarchy of drivers at increasingly low levels. We stop deconstruction when we can relatively easily measure or assess the value of the lowest-level drivers. As we use drivers, we call a deconstruction analysis also a 'driver analysis'. We distinguish between three approaches to identify drivers:

○ *Experience*: we use our own experience and the experience of a principal, any knowledgeable stakeholders, and other experts.

○ *Analogical or comparable cases*: we use a deconstruction analysis of a comparable problem.

○ *Frameworks*: we use a deconstruction presented by a framework. A framework of something is a logical structuring of that something. For example, the Competitive Forces framework of an industry (Porter, 1980) is a logical structuring of the drivers of industry attractiveness. Another example, the Blue Ocean Canvas framework (Kim & Mauborgne, 2004), is a logical structuring of the competition factors, or the criteria that customers use to choose between competitors (see Figure 5.13). The Blue Ocean Canvas is a deconstruction of competitiveness into factors.

Examples of framework analyses

Figure 5.14 provides some examples of popular frameworks. Sufficient information about these analyses is available on the Internet and in textbooks. We will therefore not go into it further.

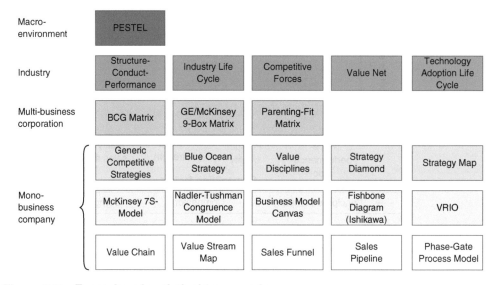

Figure 5.14   Examples of analytical frameworks

—————————— **Running Case ConsultCo** ——————————

Opportunity hypothesis: ConsultCo's entry into country B adds 3 million euro to profit within two years. Arpit deconstructs profit into revenue and costs. He also deconstructs revenue and costs. Figure 5.15 shows Arpit's revenue deconstruction. The first level is a segmentation: different streams of revenue. The second level is a deconstruction into drivers. We only show a deconstruction of the repeat business, or business from returning customers. The 'win rate' is the odds of ConsultCo's success in acquiring business or ConsultCo's share of the subsidiaries' business. For example, a 25 per cent win rate suggests that ConsultCo will get 25 per cent of the money that the subsidiaries spend on consulting.

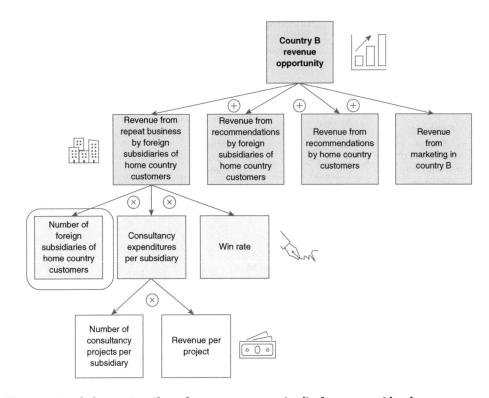

Figure 5.15   A deconstruction of a revenue opportunity from repeat business

Arpit prioritises the analyses for testing the 'repeat business opportunity'. He does the so-called 'knock-out' analyses first. These are about the variables that are 'show-stoppers'. In the left branch of Figure 5.15 (revenue from repeat business by foreign subsidiaries), a knock-out analysis is about the number of foreign subsidiaries. If that number is low, then the other two factors are no longer relevant as the outcome of the multiplication will be small. Arpit also deconstructs the revenue opportunity from recommendations (see Figure 5.16). The business partners of a subsidiary are the parties to whom that subsidiary can recommend ConsultCo.

Arpit also wants to deconstruct the opportunity from marketing. He uses a sales funnel framework to deconstruct marketing (see Figure 5.17). Targets are all companies in foreign country B that demand the type of consultancy services that ConsultCo offers.

(Continued)

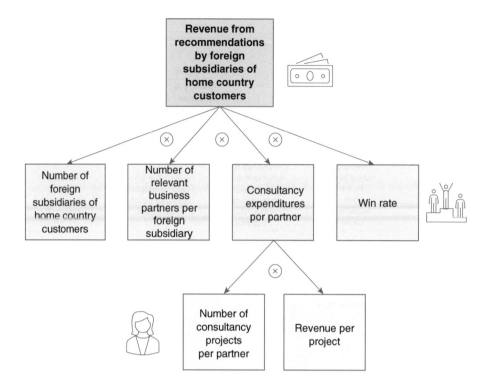

Figure 5.16   A deconstruction of a revenue opportunity from recommendations

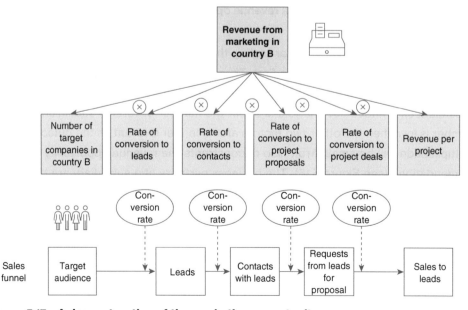

Figure 5.17   A deconstruction of the marketing opportunity

Mini Exercise

Think of a recent strategic product introduction by a well-known company and use Internet research to deconstruct the revenue opportunity for this case.

Identify the data

Analyses require data. Data are the fuel of the so-called 'analysis engine'. Based on the analysis design, the team identifies the required data. After identifying the data, the team locates the sources of these data. Next, the team decides on the best method for collecting the data from these sources. The second part of this chapter will elaborate on data sources and data collection methods.

Plan the work

The team has designed the analyses and goes to work. But at the next team meeting, there are surprises. Team members question each other as follow: "Did you do the revenue analysis as well? I also did it. Did you not do that cost analysis? I did not do that analysis either because I thought you would. Did you perform the analysis *this* way? That was not what I had in mind." The conversation continues. We do not want such unpleasant surprises. Therefore, we carefully need to prepare and plan the hypothesis testing work.

Follow a logical sequence

We do not do analysis for the sake of analysis. An analysis is about testing a hypothesis leading to proof or rejection. Therefore, we design an analysis that can prove *and* reject the hypothesis. The analysis design defines the relevant variables that determine the data requirements. The data in their turn point to the appropriate data sources. The sources influence the choice of data collection methods (see Figure 5.18).

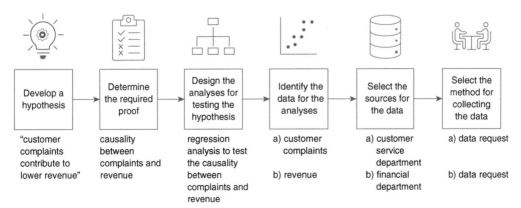

Figure 5.18 A logical sequence for preparing a hypothesis test

Write clear and concrete instructions

Workplans are a means to divide the project work among the team members. Plans allow project managers to delegate the project work. It is the job of project managers to draw up a workplan for the project team members. Workplans outline *how* to test a problem hypothesis. These plans specify analysis designs, data sources, and appropriate data collection methods. Moreover, project managers set due dates for the analyses, and assign responsibilities to team members. To do their work correctly, team members need instructions.

Workplans are the instructions. Therefore, these plans should be clear and concrete. Team members should understand what to do, when to do it, and how to do it. Ideally, the team members should understand the plan without a verbal explanation from their manager. The ideal workplan is self-explanatory.

Therefore, project managers must clearly define analyses, data, and data sources. They should not assume that team members already share the project manager's interpretations of analyses, data, sources, and other relevant subjects. The members cannot see what is in the manager's mind. They can only read what managers write in the workplan.

For example, how do we interpret the 'market'? Is the market only the demand side: the total set of customers? Or do we define a market as the meeting of supply and demand? Is the market a combination of all customers and suppliers of a product? If we do not know what a market is, how can we analyse the attractiveness of a market? As another example, what do we mean by 'sales'?

- Is it revenue or sales volume, i.e. the number of products sold?
- What is the geographic scope of sales? Is it worldwide sales, sales in a country, sales in a province, or a smaller scope?
- What is the time scale of sales? Is it annual sales, quarterly sales, or something else?
- What is the currency of sales? Is it dollar, euro, renminbi, or another currency?

Project managers must clearly specify the steps that members need to take to conduct the analyses. Managers must make the steps as simple as possible. With large steps, managers are quickly prepared, but the larger the step the more difficult managers make it for the team members to understand the work properly.

Running Case RobotCo

Tara's initial hypothesis is: An engineer's lack of experience contributes to excess waiting time. The logic of the hypothesis is wrong orders. For the hypothesis test, Tara must define *how* to measure wrong orders. She distinguishes two measures.

- Tara measures the number of wrong orders *per engineer* for the consequences of an engineer lacking experience. Experience is about an engineer and therefore wrong orders are also per engineer.
- To explain excess waiting time in a period, Tara measures the wrong orders *in that period*. Waiting time in a period is about the number of wrong orders in that period. Tara does

not measure the waiting time per engineer. As you recall, engineers with correct orders may become victims of wrong orders by mistaken colleagues.

Tara deconstructs the hypothesis into two sub-hypotheses: H1 and H2 (see Figure 5.19).

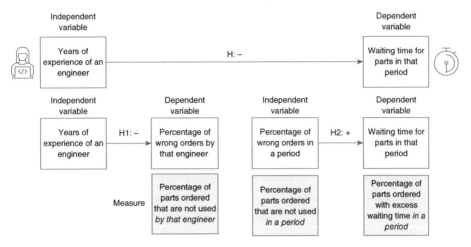

Figure 5.19   A deconstruction of a hypothesis to facilitate testing

Note: 'H' means Hypothesis; 'H: –' means a negative relationship between the independent and the dependent variables. The larger the independent variable (such as experience of an engineer), the smaller the dependent variable (such as waiting time); 'H: +' means a positive relationship. The larger the independent variable (such as percentage wrong orders in a period), the larger the dependent variable (such as waiting time).

Analysis design	Analysis output	Activity	Data	Data source	Data collection method	Responsible team member	Due date
Comparison analysis: Compare all part orders in the past 12 months	Regression statistics	Data collection	Name of engineer who placed order for parts in past 12 months	Warehouse department	Data request	Zhang Wei	March 20
Regression analysis: Assess the extent to which lack of experience causes wrong orders (parts not used in repair)			Engineer's number of years of relevant working experience	HR department	Data request	Milan	
			Usage status of ordered part (used or not used in repair)	Engineer department	Data request	Milan	
		Regression analysis				Tara	March 25

Figure 5.20   An example of a workplan for a hypothesis test

(Continued)

To test a hypothesis, Tara needs sufficient variation in the independent variable. The engineers must differ in experience and the periods must differ in percentage of unused parts. Figure 5.20 shows Tara's workplan for testing sub-hypothesis H1: An engineer's lack of experience contributes to wrong orders.

 Pause and Reflect

Use your own experience of a recent project from your study or work. Did you develop a workplan?

- If so, what was your experience with the plan?
- If not, how would the project have benefited from a plan?

Delegate the work

When project managers schedule the activities, they consider any dependencies between these activities. Analytical activities depend on data. Therefore, data collection precedes data analyses. Some analyses may need to precede others. For example, Tara first analyses the relationship between wrong orders and waiting time before she analyses the relationship between experience and wrong orders. If wrong orders do not explain waiting time, then it does not make sense to analyse the relationship between experience and wrong orders.

Moreover, managers distinguish between activities that are under their own control and actions where they depend on inputs or other support from others. Managers try to carry out these 'dependent' activities as quickly as possible to avoid any delays. For example, if we need interviews, then planning these interviews is a priority. The interviewees' agendas tend to fill up. The longer we wait, the more difficult it becomes to make appointments for interviews within the project's time frame.

Manage the workload

Project managers must ensure that the work is feasible for the team members. There are limits to what project managers can ask from their team. Managers must distinguish between the essential 'need-to-have' analyses and 'nice-to-have' but unnecessary analyses. Team members should do no unnecessary work. Moreover, managers should not go beyond the depth of analysis that principals can understand. Furthermore, managers must, in a diplomatic but firm way, prevent principals from introducing new questions and other requests during projects that fall outside the project's scope: a phenomenon called 'scope creep'.

Work as a team

Team members collect and analyse data, while project managers supervise their work and check the quality of data collection and analyses. Projects are teamwork. Team members should collaborate, act as each other's sounding board, and help each other in other ways. Team members may also collaborate with stakeholders. For example, the team may work with the principal's employees on data collection and analyses. During team meetings, team members provide status updates of their work, discuss any challenges, and exchange feedback and other thoughts.

 Pause and Reflect

Use your own experience of a recent project from your study or work. What is your experience of dividing the work among team members, and working together?

PART 2: CONDUCT RELEVANT ANALYSES

Collect the data

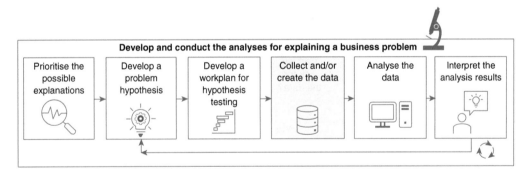

Figure 5.21   Data collection and creation are the fourth step in explaining a business problem

Data sources

Analyses are about data. For example, team members want to analyse the price sensitivity of the principal's customers. The calculation of the price sensitivity variable requires the collection of data about changes of prices and corresponding changes in demand. We distinguish between data collection and creation (see Figure 5.22).

The question arises: When to collect data and when to create data? If the data are 'out there' in the real world, then we may collect the data. Figure 5.23 outlines the questions that we can use to identify the data that are out there to be collected.

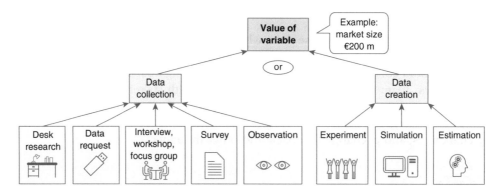

Figure 5.22   Data collection and creation

But if the data do not yet exist because it concerns future developments, then we must create data. An example of future developments is a new opportunity that has not yet been exploited by any company. Therefore, we cannot collect data about how other companies exploited the opportunity. In the absence of analogical cases, we have to create data. If the data already exist out there but collection of that data would be too costly, difficult, or time consuming, then we may also create the data. Moreover, privacy and confidentiality considerations may prevent data collection.

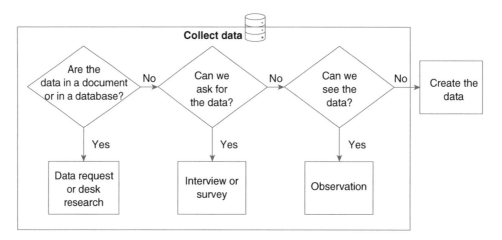

Figure 5.23   A process for selecting a method for collecting data

Running Case RobotCo

The RobotCo example illustrates the data needed for a problem analysis (see Figure 5.24). To keep the figure clear, we focus on the first hypothesis:

The more years of experience an engineer has, the smaller the percentage of wrong orders (unused parts) attributed to that engineer.

Question	Subject	Variable	Measure	Analysis	Data has already been collected	Data can be collected	Data needs to be created
Is there a problem?	Problem identification: Performance gap	Performance (RobotCo: unused parts)	Realized performance versus objective % unused parts	Compare realized and objective	Data request	• Internet • Interview • Survey • Observation	
Where does the problem exist?	Problem segmentation: Gap distribution across segments	Segments (RobotCo: field engineers)	Differences in % unused parts across engineers	Compare segment gaps	Data request	• Internet • Interview • Survey • Observation	
Why does the problem exist?	Problem explanation: Performance impact of cause	Cause (RobotCo: engineer's experience)	Relation between % unused parts per engineer and years of experience	• Simple: data visualization and correlation analysis • Complex: regression analysis	Data request	• Internet • Interview • Survey • Observation	• Expert judgment • Experiment • Simulation

Figure 5.24   An example of data for a problem analysis

Question	Subject	Variable	Measure	Analysis	Data has already been collected	Data can be collected	Data needs to be created
Why does the opportunity exist?	Opportunity explanation: Performance impact of opportunity driver	Opportunity driver (ConsultCo: number of foreign subsidiaries of home country clients)	Relation between performance and driver	• Simple: data visualization and correlation analysis • Complex: regression analysis	Data request	• Internet • Interview • Survey • Observation	• Expert judgment • Experiment • Simulation
Where does the opportunity exist?	Opportunity segmentation: Gap distribution across segments	Segments (ConsultCo: countries)	Differences in driver strength per segment	Compare segments	Use segment-level data about drivers		
What is the size of the opportunity?	Opportunity quantification: Performance gap	Performance (ConsultCo: profit)	Potential *new* performance objective versus *current* performance objective	Model the performance improvement to identify the new objective	Use data about drivers and segments		

Figure 5.25   An example of data for an opportunity analysis

————————— **Running Case ConsultCo** —————————

We illustrate data for an *opportunity* analysis with the ConsultCo example (see Figure 5.25).

Desk research

Team members start to search for data that were collected and published before: desk research. They do not want to reinvent the wheel by going into the field to collect data if they can also find the data via desk research. A good starting point for desk research about the principal's company is that company's own publications, such as annual reports, if the company is listed, and the company website. Other data sources are publications by industry associations and (paid) research reports by market research firms and consultancy firms. Publications by the media (such as papers, magazines, and websites) are another source. Furthermore, publications of (supranational) governmental agencies can provide data about companies, industries, and countries.

Unreliable data

Team members must be careful with Internet searches. There is not only *fake* news on the web, but there are other, unintended, problems with data quality as well. Team members critically look at the data source and ask: Is this resource reliable? One indicator of the quality of web resources is an explanation of the 'production' of the data. Is the web resource transparent about its data methodology and data sources? Government publications are generally reliable unless the governments are not. Team members may also compare data from different sources to check for consistency. Do the data from various sources match, or are there significant differences? If so, can team members explain these differences?

Big data

Before the days of the Internet, team members had much fewer data at their disposal. Due to the Internet, team members have an abundance of data at their disposal. One speaks of big data, data pools, and data lakes.

The Internet of Things

In addition to the Internet of people, there is the Internet *of Things* (IoT), which is the Internet-based network of smart physical devices or things (such as cars, vending machines, and alarm systems) that have sensors and software for exchanging data with other smart things and systems, and which can act autonomously. These intelligent devices allow for remote control of operations, such as the 'smart home' or the remote health monitoring of people. Companies collect data from these intelligent devices. The IoT can be a data source for team members.

Pause and Reflect

Use your own experience of a recent project from your study or work. What is your experience with collecting data on the Internet?

Data requests

Some data are not publicly available because they are owned by people inside or outside the principal's organization, such as a business controller or a human resource manager. Team members may request data from these data owners. Such requests must be very precise and clear. Team members should not ask for 'revenues' but specify their request in detail, such as the period to which the revenue relates, currencies if applicable, and a revenue split by country. Data requests should be 'fool proof', or impossible to misinterpret for the data owners.

To make it easier for data owners to provide the requested data, team members may provide templates with the requested data formats, such as a spreadsheet table whose rows and columns are already titled.

Team members do not expect that data owners understand their requests immediately. Therefore, the members make the same points multiple times, but in various ways. Furthermore, team members send regular reminders to avoid delays. After receiving the data, they send a thank-you note.

Interview, workshop, and focus group

Interview

What team members ask in an interview should not be available through desk research. In the case of *problem*-solving, stakeholders may be suspicious of team members and will not be eager to talk to team members. For example, the principal's employees may ask themselves:

- What are the team members doing here in my department?
- What do they want to change here?
- Are they going to recommend that I am made redundant?

The principal can order that the employees speak to team members, but forcing interviews with external stakeholders, such as customers, is impossible. Team members must convince these external stakeholders of the importance of the interviews. The members can try to convince interview candidates that interviews are also in these persons' interests. Team members may also offer candidates something in return for interviews to create 'win–win' deals. If interview candidates collaborate in the discussions, team members will provide them with relevant information, such as (small) parts of a report. Team members should also send thank-you notes to the interviewees directly after the interviews.

Workshop and focus group

Team members also meet with groups of stakeholders. Such group meetings have the advantage that individual stakeholders can respond to each other. Team members use workshops and focus groups (discussion groups) to brainstorm about the possible explanations of problems and the possible solutions to these problems. Group meetings also lend themselves to reciprocal coordination and the alignment of participants. The participants must take each other into account and coordinate their behaviour. It is in everyone's interest to behave well in such meetings because good relationships are a critical success factor in problem-solving projects. The question arises: How to choose between interviews and workshops? Figure 5.26 compares these two alternatives.

	Interview	Workshop
Objective (why use it)	Diverge: Stimulate diversity of insights and perspectives	Converge: • Build on each other's ideas • Create consensus • Reach agreement
Condition (where to use it)	Political organization or domination by one or a few persons: interview allows people to speak freely	No politics or dominant persons
Advantage	More time and attention for an individual	Interaction: Respond to each other's ideas

Figure 5.26   **Comparing interviews and workshops**

How To Do It?

How to prepare for an interview?

- Team members define their objectives before the interviews. They determine in advance what they want to get out of the interviews.
  - ○ Do they want information from interviewees?
  - ○ Do they want team members to check their findings?
- Team members also think about the interviewee's position. If the interviewee is a stakeholder, team members ask themselves: What are this stakeholder's interests, and how great is her power? Team members must be wary of stakeholders who

have different and even conflicting agendas. These individuals may intentionally misinform team members to lead them astray. Team members must keep asking critical questions and not take these stakeholders' answers for granted.

How to define interview agendas?

- Team members always have plans for interviews. They choose the question form (open or closed) with care. They also ask control questions to check whether interviewees have fully understood the questions.
- Team members start with simple questions that interviewees can and will quickly answer. Team members ask the most difficult and sensitive questions at the end of interviews. If interviewees then no longer want to collaborate, team members already have answers to most of their questions.
- A nice ending of interviews is to ask what we have not asked but what is essential in the interviewee's opinion. Team members may use this question: Have I forgotten to ask for something important?
- Team members ask if they can come back if they unexpectedly have new questions.

We emphasize the importance of sending thank-you notes to interviewees. It is a small effort but can create a lot of good will that we may need later in the problem-solving project.

 Pause and Reflect

Use your own experience of a recent project from your study or work. To what extent did you prepare for interviews?

- If so, what was your experience with the preparation?
- If not, how would the interview have benefited from a preparation?

Survey

Surveys are a suitable tool if the number of people to be questioned is vast. Interviews then become too time-consuming and expensive. Moreover, surveys lend themselves to statistical analysis, which provides convincing proof for the principal. But drawing up good surveys is a craft. The questions must be straightforward because team members are not present when survey participants must answer these questions. Team members must be sure that the questions measure what they want to measure. If survey participants interpret the questions differently, their answers are worthless.

Team members will therefore want to test their surveys in advance among groups of test subjects.

Judgments

Team members ask stakeholders via interview, workshop, or survey, preferably for verifiable, measurable information. These are questions about facts. However, there are also questions about judgment. Examples are:

- What do you think is the most probable cause of the cost overrun?
- What do you think is the probability that this market opportunity will materialize?
- How do you estimate the chance that the principal's organization will be able to develop this new product?

Team members may use judgments of the principal, knowledgeable stakeholders, and other experts. Such expert opinions are subjective and can be intuitive. Experts may not be able to substantiate their views. The persuasiveness of the judgment depends on the expert's reputation. The case becomes stronger if experts confirm each other's judgment. Team members may use a panel of experts to develop a consensus on a matter. A well-known approach is the 'Delphi method'.

Observation

Observation of people's behaviour, such as the principal's employees, can be a valuable data source. Team members may decide not to ask persons questions but to look at what they are doing. People can give socially desirable and politically correct answers, or answers that are convenient for them because of personal agendas. For example, employees will never admit that they sometimes cut corners instead of adhering to the formal work processes. Moreover, individuals may be unable to put something into words. They may not even be aware of specific knowledge. For example, account managers may not know why so many visits to potential customers end in failure. Therefore, team members may use what they call 'day in the life of' (DILO) studies, which means that the team members follow someone during a working day. Such studies answer the question: What does this person's day look like? In the example of RobotCo, Tara may observe engineers in the workplace to answer the question: *How* do these engineers conduct a problem diagnosis? What exactly are they doing?

Team members hope to discover unexpected, surprising behaviour of the observed stakeholders. For example, RobotCo's engineers may use diagnosis routines that are not by the book. Team members can also detect hidden best practices this way. For example, observation may teach Tara what sets the best engineers apart from the rest when it comes to diagnosis. It is vital that the observations do not influence those being observed. When people know that they are being observed, they may behave differently. Team members do not want the observed people to change their behaviour because of the team members' presence.

Competitive intelligence

Desk research

Competitive intelligence is the practice of collecting data about competitors. Team members start with desk research. If the required data is already available, team members do not have to do field research.

- The members check *data published by competitors*, such as company websites and annual reports. The 'about us' page and the 'investor relations' page of a competitor's website can be valuable sources of data.
- Team members may also study documents that *others*, such as *governments*, publish about competitors. Research reports by market researchers, industry experts, and management consultancies can also be valuable information sources.
- Team members may check any *published profiles* of a competitor's top managers or executives.
- Papers, magazines, and websites may publish *interviews* with top competitors' executives that can yield interesting information.
- *Announcements* of significant personnel changes, such as the hiring and departure of top managers, are also relevant.
- *Social media* can contain valuable information about the resumés of competitor managers.
- Finally, team members check any *publicity* about executives' critical decisions, such as market-entries, product development, R&D projects, investments in plants, mass lay-offs, corporate restructuring, mergers and acquisitions, divestments, and the creation and termination of joint ventures.

Observations

After team members have exhausted the opportunities of desk research about competitors, it is time for *field* research.

- *Descriptions of the ingredients or components* of competitors' products are typically available.
- Another opportunity is to do '*reverse engineering*' of competitors' products. Experts can take the competitors' products apart to understand their components and assembly.
- Team members may also analyse competitors' *prices* if they are public.
- Competitors' *promotion and advertisement* activities are also visible.
- Team members may study competitors' *distribution channels*, such as wholesale and retail outlets and websites.
- They may also learn from competitors' *offices* and other buildings:
  - The number and *size* of offices can be proxies for the number of white-collar workers, while the number and size of production plants can serve as proxies for the number of blue-collar workers.
  - Team members may also observe the inbound and outbound *traffic* from the competitors' plants. These observations allow team members to determine which suppliers, distributors, and customers come and go, and how often.

Interviews

- Another competitive intelligence source is interviews with *former employees* of competitors who now work for the principal or business partners. It is crucial to be ethical. We should not pressure or otherwise entice these ex-employees to share any confidential information about their former employer.
- Team members may also interview the principal's *customers* who also buy from competitors (because of a multi-vendor policy) or who bought from competitors in the past.
- Likewise, team members may question the principal's *suppliers, distributors*, and *other business partners* who also work, or who worked in the past, with competitors. Suppliers may inform team members what ingredients, components, materials, machines, and equipment competitors buy.
- Interviews with *stock market analysts, company watchers*, and *industry experts* may also provide valuable information about competitors.

In all these conversations, we should not cross ethical boundaries. The possibilities for competitive analysis are endless, but team members need to distance themselves from illegal and unethical practices, such as industrial espionage.

 Pause and Reflect

Use your own experience of a recent project from your study or work. To what extent did you collect data about competitors? Which approach to competitor analysis was successful and what did not work for you?

Create the data

Team members strive for fact-based analysis. They will use all *legal* and *ethical* possibilities to collect the necessary data. Team members are willing to put in a lot of effort to get the data, but sooner or later, team members will find themselves in situations where not all necessary data are available. Data collection can be too costly, or data can be too time-consuming to collect. Data may not be available or may not be legally and ethically accessible, think of privacy and confidentiality.

If team members cannot find the data, they will *not* give up. Instead, they aim for a second-best solution. If they cannot collect that data, then they *create* the missing data. Please make no mistake about it, creating information is different from making up data. Team members do not fabricate data or dream up data. Here we discuss some responsible approaches to creating data (see Figure 5.27):

- Experiment
- Simulation
- Estimation

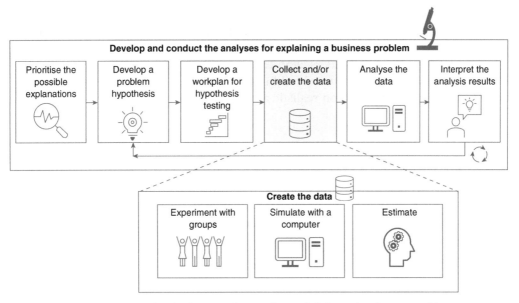

Figure 5.27 Data creation is the fourth step in explaining a business problem

Experiment

Suppose the missing data is about a causal relationship between an independent and a dependent variable, such as the price of a product and the customer demand for that product. In that case, team members can manipulate the independent variable, the price, to see what happens to the dependent variable, the demand. Typically, team members work with two groups: a manipulated group and a control group (no manipulation). In our example, the manipulated group receives a discount whereas the control group must pay the original price. Team members compare the outcomes of the groups.

Simulation

Team members may build computer models about the relationships between known data and the missing data. They can vary the input variables to see how the output variables will change. Team members may also opt for a random variation of inputs, such as 'Monte Carlo' simulations. The availability of big data offers opportunities to create advanced data-analytical models. When modelling gets very complicated, team members outsource the work to data analysts or data scientists.

Estimation

Team members can make estimates of the missing data themselves or ask experts for estimates. But estimating scares many people. Experts may be reluctant to estimate if they perceive estimates as unscientific and manipulative. Moreover, experts may be afraid of critique on their assessment.

But criticism of estimates can be a tool for team members if used at the right time. Criticism during team members' presentation of the recommendation to the principal is too late. Therefore, team members present their estimates to the principal or other knowledgeable stakeholders at an earlier stage. Of course, estimates should be intelligent or educated. Estimates should not be wild guesses without some substantiation; they should be based on realistic assumptions and reasoning.

Communication

We need to be transparent about the uncertainty associated with the created data. Created data are not real-world evidence. To ensure transparency for the principal and other stakeholders it is vital to acknowledge and communicate that some data were created rather than collected. We also document the methodology that we used for creating the data.

 How To Do It?

If knowledgeable stakeholders and other experts are reluctant to make estimates, then we make the estimates ourselves. We present our estimates to these people and ask if they agree. They must consider our methods of assessment. Now the experts must either agree on or criticize our estimates. If they do not agree, we ask for constructive criticism of our estimates. It is much easier and safer for people to criticize another person's estimate. Picking holes in someone else's estimate is more attractive than making an estimate yourself.

If knowledgeable stakeholders and other experts come up with corrections or improvements, we use their feedback to improve our estimates. The estimates get better, and stakeholders feel involved and heard. Our improved estimates will receive more support among stakeholders because we have incorporated the experts' responses. This type of criticism at an *early* point in the project does not detract from the team members' reputation.

Running Case ConsultCo

The availability of staff in a country is one of the criteria for country selection. Arpit may estimate the staff availability. He starts with official statistics about the labour market in a specific country. Preferably, Arpit obtains the number of consultants in a country. There may also be consulting industry data about how long consultants stay with a consultancy firm (tenure) until they change employers. This statistic allows Arpit to calculate how many consultants are available for new jobs (number of consultants divided by the average tenure at one consultancy firm). He also uses public statistics about education, such as the number of graduates from relevant schools. Arpit benefits from statistics about what share of graduates joins consultancy. These data allow him to assess the total annual talent pool in a country: the number of new consultants graduating from school and the number of experienced consultants changing consultancy firms.

 Pause and Reflect

Use your own experience of a recent project from your study or work. To what extent did you estimate data? Which approach to estimation was successful and what did not work for you?

Analyse the data

We deconstruct the analysis of data into three steps (see Figure 5.28):

- Enter the data
- Implement the analysis design
- Check the output

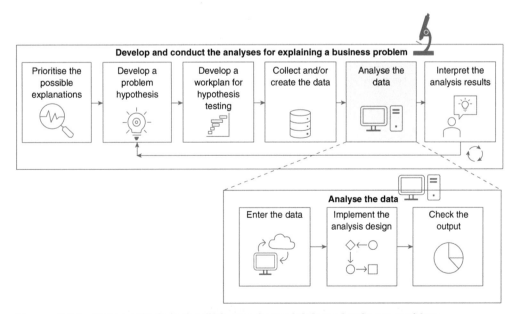

Figure 5.28 Data analysis is the fifth step in explaining a business problem

Analysing compared to cooking

The team members have collected or created the data. Now they are ready to analyse the data. The analysis design is the recipe, the data are the ingredients, and analysing is like cooking. Project managers design the analyses and team members follow the procedure to do the analyses. For simple quantitative analysis, team members use a spreadsheet program. Nowadays, with big data, analyses have become more complicated and sophisticated, and we may use a business intelligence (BI) software package.

It is vital to document the analyses well. If we use spreadsheet models, we add explanations about formulas and calculations. We also list any assumptions that we have used. Qualitative analysis is about text analysis. We analyse the transcripts from interviews and the notes of our observations. If we analyse opinions and judgments, then we prefer confirmation by other, independent, sources.

Interpret the analysis results

We deconstruct the interpretation of analysis results also into three steps (see Figure 5.29):

- Interpret the data
- Interpret the analysis
- Interpret the results

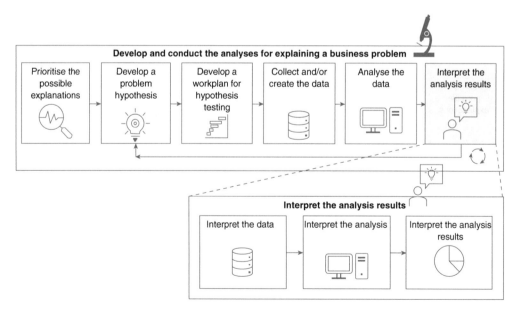

Figure 5.29   **Interpreting the results of the analysis is the sixth step in explaining a business problem**

Interpret the data

The quality of analysis output depends on the quality of analysis input. The saying goes: Garbage in, garbage out. Therefore, project managers should first assess the data that the team members collected. Examples of questions that project managers should ask themselves are:

- What is the quality of the data? Relevant criteria include the accuracy, precision, reliability, and validity of the data.
- What is the quality of the data sources? If it is difficult to assess the quality of the data, we may be able to deduce the quality of the data from the quality of the source. We may take a critical look, among others, at the reputation, independence, and the data collection methodology of the source.
- What is the quantity of the data? Do we have all the requested variables? Do we have enough data points?

A related key question is: Have the data been collected in real-world practice or is it about created data? In the case of created data, we must take a critical look at the underlying assumptions and methodology for data creation.

Interpret the analysis

After checking the quality and the quantity of the data, project managers should assess how team members processed the data. The managers have designed the analyses. Therefore, they do not need to assess the design. But managers need to assess how well team members followed the analysis instructions. To what extent have the team members adhered to the designed analysis procedure? Did some people deviate from the prescribed routines and cut corners?

Interpret the analysis results

After approving the data and the analysis method followed, project managers consider the results of the analysis. *Before* the test, managers, along with the principal's input, have defined the evidence that is required to prove the cause of the problem. *After* the test, managers compare the analysis results to the required proof. Do the results meet or exceed the needed proof?

- If so, managers accept the problem or opportunity hypothesis. They accept the hypothesized explanation of the problem or opportunity. Because the results meet or exceed the principal's requirements, principals will also accept the explanation.
- If the analysis results do *not* match the required proof, managers *reject* the hypothesis. They do not take a rejection as a personal failure because, as a result of the rejection, the managers know what does *not* explain the problem or opportunity. This is a valuable insight if the principal or stakeholders thought that the hypothesized explanation was correct.

If the proof is entirely based on real-world evidence, then we can use evidence-based decision making. But if the proof is partly or entirely based on created data, there is uncertainty associated with that proof. As indicated earlier, data creation is inevitable when we analyse (new) opportunities, but even in the case of problem-analysis, we sometimes cannot avoid data creation. In the case of uncertainty about the proof, we need to *complement* evidence-based decision-making with intuitive decision-making. But intuitive decision-making requires that we have the necessary knowledge and experience with the subject of the decision.

Hypothesis rejection

Rejection of the initial problem hypothesis means that we must develop and test another hypothesis. Therefore, we return to our prioritisation of possible explanations of the problem. We pick the next best answer on our list as our new hypothesis to be tested. We iterate hypothesis development and testing until we have an accepted cause of the problem.

If we run out of explanations before we have an accepted hypothesis, we need to iterate the why-exercise: Why does the problem exist? Then we look again at possible explanations. We broaden our search to look beyond the rejected explanations. We may also use our imagination and think 'outside the box'. To broaden our perspective, we may invite other knowledgeable stakeholders and other experts to share their ideas. Figure 5.30 shows the iteration of hypothesis development and testing.

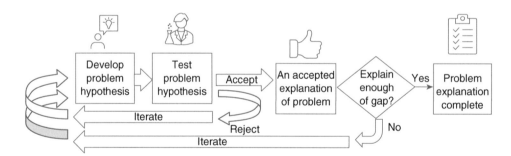

Figure 5.30   Iteration of hypothesis development and testing

Explain at least the minimum part of the gap

Acceptance of our problem hypothesis means we have found *one* cause of the problem. We must ask ourselves: Do we have a *complete* explanation or are there any other causes of the problem? To examine how complete our explanation is, we need to see to what extent the accepted cause explains the problem. To what extent does the accepted cause contribute to the gap between the performance objective and the lower realized performance? If the cause creates the whole gap, then we have a complete explanation. But in other cases, the cause explains only a part of the gap.

How much of the gap should we explain? The minimum extent of the gap we need to explain depends on the principal. One hundred per cent is probably not feasible or necessary. The minimum may be somewhere between 60 per cent and 80 per cent. If one cause explains at least the minimum part of the gap, then we have completed the problem analysis. If not, then we look for more possible explanations, until we can explain the minimum part of the gap.

━━━━━━━━━━ **Running Case RobotCo** ━━━━━━━━━━

The GM has accepted the first hypothesis: An engineer's lack of experience contributes to wrong orders. The percentage of unused orders is an indicator of wrong orders. Figure 5.31 shows excess waiting time is related to unused parts, which point to wrong orders. This is the real data instead of the dummy data of Figure 5.12. Figure 5.31 is a visualisation of data for an 'eye-ball test': you see the relationship between the experience of engineers and the usage status of ordered parts. This picture is clear, but it may not always be the case. If Tara has a large enough data set, then she can do a statistical analysis.

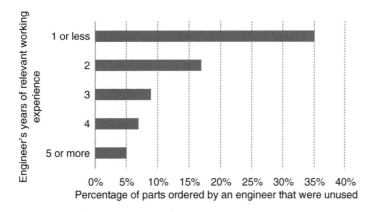

Figure 5.31   A visual presentation of analysis data

Wrong orders by inexperienced engineers may have one or more causes, such as entering errors, not carrying out procedures, stress, lack of personal capacity, and lack of training. If there are many engineers, Tara may conduct a statistical analysis. In the case of small numbers, Tara may check for the presence of these other causes in the cases of wrong orders by inexperienced engineers.

Tara also tests the *second* hypothesis: Wrong orders in a period contribute to waiting time for parts in that period. Note that this hypothesis is not about engineers but about periods. The percentage of unused parts in a period indicates the wrong orders. Tara measures the waiting time in terms of the percentage of parts with excess waiting time in that period. Figure 5.32 is a visualisation of data for an 'eye-ball test'. If Tara has enough data points, she can conduct a statistical analysis.

(Continued)

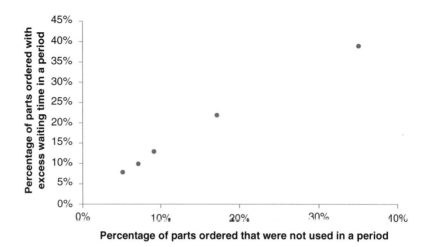

Figure 5.32   A visual presentation of the real data for the second hypothesis

―――――――――― **Running Case ConsultCo** ――――――――――

Arpit assesses the opportunity in country A, country B, and country C. Figure 5.33 shows the countries' scores for the evaluation criteria, which range from 1 (poor) to 5 (excellent). Some criteria are quantitative. Arpit can measure them (such as, the number of subsidiaries) or make estimates (such as, the network of recommenders and the availability of staff). Other criteria are qualitative. Here Arpit uses observations (such as, the ease of travel) and makes judgments (such as, the competitive advantage in a *new* country).

Criteria	Country A	Country B	Country C
Foreign subsidiaries of ConsultCo's customers	2	3	5
Recommenders' networks of ConsultCo	2	2	5
Good reputation of ConsultCo	3	4	5
Competitive advantage of ConsultCo	4	5	4
Ease of travel	2	5	3
Absence of cultural differences	3	3	3
Absence of language barriers	4	5	4
Absence of regulatory barriers	3	3	3
Availability of staff	4	3	4
Average score	3	3,7	4

Figure 5.33   An evaluation of country-opportunities

Pause and Reflect

Use your own experience of a recent project from your study or work. Did you find it difficult to interpret the results of the analysis? If so, what made it difficult? How did you deal with the difficulties?

Data-analytical thinking

What developments drive data-analytical thinking?

This book is an introduction to problem-solving rather than an introduction to data analytics. But problem-solvers need at least some basic understanding of what data-analytical thinking is. Data analytics is the result of two developments: the emergence of big data and the growth of computer power.

1. Companies have increasing opportunities to collect data because of the Internet (including IoT) and the digitization of their business processes. As a result, the principal has big data sets that are too large for traditional statistical analyses.
2. Computer power continues to increase. According to Moore's Law (effective since 1965!), the number of transistors on a microchip doubles every two years, while the computing costs halve. Growing computing power allows for new, more advanced AI-based techniques for analysing data.

Data science, or data-analytical thinking, is about the use of these techniques for extracting valuable knowledge from big data. Data analytics is the examination of (very large) data sets with (AI-based) software tools to identify patterns and draw conclusions about the insights that these patterns may contain. We may use Business Intelligence (BI) software for Extraction, Transformation, and Loading (ETL) of data from multiple sources and consolidate these data for analyses. There are four types of analytics:

- *Descriptive* analytics: identifying and describing what is happening (patterns)
- *Diagnostic* analytics: explaining what is happening
- *Predictive* analytics: predicting what is likely to happen in the future
- *Prescriptive* analytics: prescribing what should be done to realize an objective

A specific form of descriptive analytics is *data mining*. It is about the automated search and discovery of patterns in big data. Figure 5.34 presents the author's interpretation of Shearer's CRoss-Industry Standard Process for Data Mining (CRISP-DM) (Shearer, 2000).

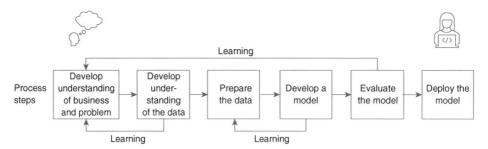

Figure 5.34   A data-analytical thinking process

Process steps of data mining

We briefly touch on the process steps of Figure 5.34.

- Develop an understanding of the business and the problem. For example, the principal cannot realize its profit objective because it has many unprofitable customers. The principal wants to transform these unprofitable customers into profitable customers. Therefore, the principal wants to understand the profitable customers better. A crucial question is: Who are the most profitable customers?
- Develop an understanding of the data. This step is about evaluating the available and accessible data. To what extent do the data match the problem? In the example, does the principal have sufficient data to identify and predict the profitable customers? What are the strengths and limitations of the data?
- Prepare the data. The data may not be in the format that the analytical technologies require. In that case, analysts need to convert the data into the required format.
- Develop the data-analytical model. This is about the choice of analytical modelling technologies. In the example, the model should identify and predict the profitable customers.
- Evaluate the model. In this stage, analysts assess the model's effectiveness: Will the model identify profitable customers and predict what customers will be profitable? Do the analysts have confidence in the model?
- Deploy the model. Analysts apply the model to solve the business problem. In the example, this is to identify profitable customers and to predict what customers will be profitable.

There are several iterations in the model. See the learning loops in Figure 5.34. In subsequent steps, analysts may gain new insights that increase their understanding of the business problem, help them to understand and prepare the data better, or improve the model.

Pause and Reflect ────────────────────

Consider how you may use these techniques for developing and conducting relevant analyses of problems and opportunities in your studies, work, and personal life.

SUMMARY

We briefly outline the main takeaways of this chapter.

- Evaluate alternative possible explanations of a problem
  - assess the importance of possible explanations
  - assess the likelihood of possible explanations
  - rank the possible explanations
- Develop a problem hypothesis
  - select the highest-ranked possible explanation
  - formulate that explanation as a problem hypothesis: this explanation contributes to the performance gap
- Select a proper analytical framework for testing a problem hypothesis
  - determine the required proof of the hypothesis
  - visualize the proof
  - find a matching framework that can produce the proof
- Design an analysis if no proper framework is available
  - deconstruction analysis (driver analysis)
  - comparison analysis (benchmark analysis)
- Develop a workplan for testing a problem hypothesis
  - analysis design
  - data required for analysis
  - data sources
  - data collection method
- Select appropriate data collection methods
  - desk research
  - data request
  - interview
  - workshop
  - focus group
  - survey
  - observation

- Select appropriate data creation methods
  - experiment
  - simulate
  - estimate

Mini Exercise

Identify the key concepts and terms in this chapter, define them briefly and compile your own glossary.

REFERENCES AND FURTHER READING

Kim, W. C., Mauborgne, R. (2004). *Blue Ocean Strategy: How to Create Uncontested Market Space and Make the Competition Irrelevant*. Boston, MA: Harvard Business School Press.

Porter, M. E. (1980). *Competitive Strategy: Techniques for Analyzing Industries and Competitors*. New York: Free Press.

Shearer, C. (2000). The CRISP-DM model: The new blueprint for data mining. *Journal of Data Warehousing*, 5(4), 13–22.

Collaborate with Team Members and Other Relevant Stakeholders

INTRODUCTION

The principal assigns a couple of people to the project. These people do not know each other well and there is no time to get to know each other because the problem is urgent. Everybody quickly gets to work, focusing on their own tasks. But the progress is slow, and the quality of output is low. Then people start blaming each other.

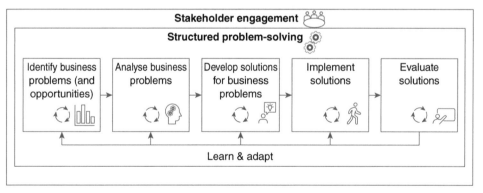

Iterative process of developing and testing hypotheses about problems, solutions, and implementation

Figure 6.1   Structured problem-solving is embedded in stakeholder engagement

We acknowledge that problem-solving is teamwork, but how to form a team and work as a team? We address these questions in this chapter. And yet, collaboration should not stop with the team. Even a perfect team cannot solve a company's problems without the collaboration of relevant stakeholders. The team depends on data, knowledge, and other support from these stakeholders. Engaging relevant stakeholders is a critical condition for successful problem-solving (see Figure 6.1).

This chapter will outline how to engage relevant stakeholders (see Figure 6.2).

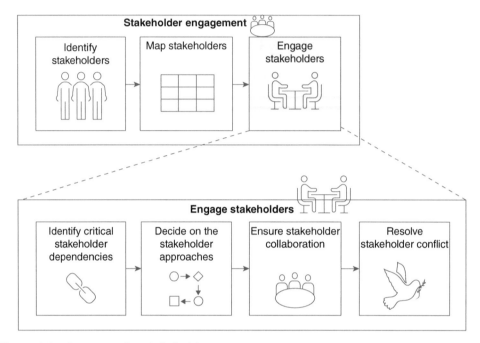

Figure 6.2   **A process for stakeholder engagement**

The chapter is structured as follows (see Figure 6.3).

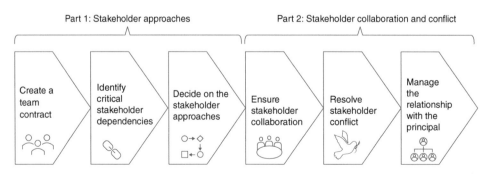

Figure 6.3   **Chapter structure**

MAIN LEARNING OBJECTIVES

After studying this chapter, you should be able to:

- develop a team contract
- identify the critical stakeholder dependencies
- prioritise stakeholder approaches
- select a proper form of resolving a conflict with a particular stakeholder

PART 1: STAKEHOLDER APPROACHES

Create a team contract

The principal will designate several people to solve a problem, but these people are not automatically a team. Forming a team requires an effort from those involved and a team contract is an important technique to form a team. We outline the steps for creating a contract:

1. Develop objectives for the team
2. Identify the values of the team
3. Develop rules for the team
4. Develop roles for the team members

Develop objectives for the team

We ask the team members about their aspirations, hopes, and concerns. By doing so, we distinguish between *task* and *process* objectives.

- *Task* objectives are about *what* we want to accomplish. Tasks include analyse problems, develop a recommended solution, and implement that solution. The project manager designs a workplan for these tasks.
- *Process* objectives are *how* we will collaborate to achieve the task objectives. We collaborate with team members, but we also work with relevant stakeholders outside the team.

Examples of process objectives are:

- Respect for each other: we treat each other with respect, regardless of background, position, race, gender, sexual orientation, and any other differences.
- Trust in each other: the starting point is trust in each other, until the contrary is proven.
- Accountability: individuals have their own responsibilities and may be held accountable for them.

- Innovation: we are open to improvements.
- Conflict resolution: we find it important that conflicts within the team are resolved in a good way.

Identify the values of the team

We identify the *shared* values of the team. What do we value as a team? We identify a couple of trade-offs:

- *Autonomy versus control*: How much do we value the autonomy of team members? How much control are we willing to accept?
- *Accuracy versus speed*: How important is speed? Are we under a significant time pressure and do we have to trade-in accuracy for speed?
- *Commitment to the project versus work–life balance*: How much do we value work–life balance? Should the project always and everywhere take precedence? Does private life have to give way for the successful completion of the project?
- *Collective versus individual achievement*: How important is the collective? Do we want to do this together or is it mainly everyone for themselves?
- *Democratic or hierarchical*: How do we make decisions? Does every team member have a vote (or even a veto) or does the manager determine what happens?
- *Formal or informal*: How do we get along? Are we doing everything according to the procedures and the hierarchy?
- *All-business or also social*: Are the relationships business-like or friendly? Does the team also engage in social activities together?
- *Openness versus confidentiality*: To what extent should we take confidentiality and sensitivity of information into account? Can we speak freely, or should we be careful not to spread confidential information?
- *Risk aversion versus risk acceptance*: To what extent can and will we take risks to solve the company's problem?

We distinguish between, on the one hand, the team's *shared* objectives and values and, on the other hand, a member's *personal* objectives and values. How can we reconcile any conflict between the shared and the personal objectives and values? The boundaries for individual behaviour must be clear from the outset. We clearly indicate what individuals can determine for themselves and what they need the team's permission to do.

Develop rules for the team

Rules of engagement prescribe the desired conduct for achieving the process objectives. We clarify the expectations about team behaviour because we should not assume that everybody knows and shares our expectations. Figure 6.4 shows an example of the rules of engagement (which are not collectively exhaustive).

Tasks	• Take ownership • Consider consequences of actions for others • Take risks but inform or ask for approval if needed • Complete tasks on time
Relations	• Maintain good working relations with other team members • Control own anger and emotions • Respect other members' ways of working, do not impose your own approach on others
Collaboration	• Handle handovers of tasks with care: stay in touch with fellow members until the next task is done • Accept and support team decisions even if you would prefer alternative decisions • When you ask another member for something, always motivate your request (explain why) • When another member asks you something, explain what you will or can do, and what you cannot do • Be flexible, be willing to change your position or compromise • Volunteer to do some extra work if you have time to spare • Do not take an opposing view as a personal attack • Invite constructive dissent, encourage people with dissenting views to explain and motivate • Encourage innovation by delaying evaluation • Give positive feedback and constructive, negative feedback • Accept justified negative feedback and admit mistakes
Conflict resolution	• Assume others have good intention and work in good faith • Discuss conflict first directly with involved member(s) • Resolve conflict in line with objectives and interests of the team • Stay polite and civilized
Communication	• Invite quiet people to speak up • Do not monopolize the discussion, give others room to speak • Listen without drawing conclusions. Ask speaker for clarification and motivation. Keep others informed about progress of your task • Inform about problems that will affect other members as soon as these issues arise. Do not expect problems to go away automatically • Respond to calls and emails in expected time • Share relevant information with parties that need to know • Keep conversations confidential. Do not share confidential and sensitive information with third parties
Meetings	• Attend all required meetings • Prepare • Play an active role and contribute to the meeting

Figure 6.4   An example of the rules of engagement

Develop roles for the team members

We need to divide the work of the team. By doing so, we distinguish between *task* roles and *process* roles. *Task* roles are about *what* a team wants to accomplish (see Figure 6.5).

Project leader	Meeting facilitator	Record keeper	Time keeper	Liaison
Designs project approach and holds members accountable	Facilitates team meetings (agenda, discussion, time keeping)	Records key decisions and all project documents	Monitors progress and holds members accountable	Maintains relationships with the principal and other relevant stakeholders

Figure 6.5   Examples of task roles

Note: Leader applies only to hierarchical teams

Process roles are about *how* team members collaborate (see Figure 6.6). In addition to the devil's advocate, all team members should review each other's work and provide feedback.

Consensus taker	Devil's advocate	Gate keeper	Mediator	Morale manager	Rule keeper
Monitors to what extent team members agree with decisions and to what extent they are commited	Critically challenges the thinking of team members to improve the quality of decisions and work	Monitors during meetings participation of members and encourages any passive members to participate	Mentions problems that members are unaware of or unwilling to mention, and guides conflict resolution	Keeps motivation and morale high by acknowledging achievements and organizing celebrations	Monitors adherence to team rules and facilitates improvement if needed

Figure 6.6   Examples of process roles

An alternative way to look at the division of roles in teams are Belbin's team roles (see Figure 6.7) (Belbin, 1993). Teams should have a mix of nine team roles.

People-oriented	Resource investigator	Team worker	Coordinator
	Finds ideas to bring to the team	Identifies the work and completes it on behalf of the team	Focuses on team objectives, draws out team members, and delegates the work
Thought-oriented	Plant	Monitor evaluator	Specialist
	Solves problems in a highly creative way	Makes impartial judgments and weighs the team's options dispassionately	Brings in-depth expertise of a key area
Action-oriented	Shaper	Implementer	Complete finisher
	Provides the drive to ensure that the team gets things done	Plans a workable approach and carries it out efficiently	Polishes and scrutinizes the team's output for any errors

Figure 6.7   Belbin's team roles

Source: Belbin (1993)

Put everything together in a team contract

We put the objectives, values, rules, and roles together in a team contract (see Figure 6.8). All members must commit to the contract by signing it and each member receives a copy as a reminder.

Items	Details	
Team members	Names	
Objectives	• Task objectives • Process objectives	
Values		
Rules of conduct	• Tasks • Relations • Collaboration • Conflict resolution • Communication • Meetings	
Roles	• Task roles • Process roles	Names of team members
Evaluation	• Metrics for task objectives • Metrics for process objectives	Measurement
Signatures for agreement		

Figure 6.8   An example of a template for a team contract

 Pause and Reflect

Use your own experience of a recent project from your study or work. Have you made a team contract or made agreements in any way?

- If so, what are your experiences?
- If not, how would the project have benefited from a contract?

Steering committees and sounding boards

The project team reports to the principal but if a project is complex, there may be a multi-person steering committee, consisting of the principal and other senior managers. Additionally, there may be a sounding board group or advisory group. A sounding board has no decision-making power, but its members have the right to provide advice or feedback on the team's work.

The challenges for distributed teams

An increasing number of people may work part time, from home, or from remote offices. Distributed or virtual teams present new challenges for projects. There are the technological challenges of computer and network hardware and software problems. But even if technology works smoothly, team members still communicate with relatively blunt tools. Conference calls and video chats cannot match the richness of personal, face-to-face interaction in a room. Online communication is poorer as team members are missing some of the nonverbal communication. They also miss the collegiality and energy that they may experience when they meet in the same physical space. Working from home may also lead to feelings of isolation because people miss the social and spontaneous contacts. Motivation and discipline may suffer as well. Moreover, others, including the principal, will find it hard to monitor the team members' work. Work from home creates flexibility to mix work and home life, but flexible work schedules make communication and collaboration difficult. Problems become even worse when people are in different time zones. Because of all these complications, the importance of clear objectives, values, roles, and rules of engagement is even greater for distributed teams than for teams in the same physical place. Distributed teams must adapt the rules of engagement to the communication technology. For example, when will we use what channel: conference call, video chat, phone call, text messaging, or email? Which etiquette rules ensure that video communication runs as smoothly and politely as possible?

Sometimes team members should meet in a physical space. For example, meeting in person is important if members need to get to know each other. The first meeting is best done in person. Once a relationship of trust has been established, people can communicate online. But for emotionally charged communication, team members may revert to physical meetings.

Identify critical stakeholder dependencies

In this section we refer to stakeholders in general. Stakeholders involve everyone involved in a problem-solving project, including team members. Everything we write about stakeholders also applies to team members.

What do we need from stakeholders for the problem-solving?

A project team needs help from outside to do the problem-solving. Business is about people and problems are about stakeholders. Stakeholders are affected by the problem or the solution (see Chapter 3). They can benefit or suffer from problems and solutions. But stakeholders can also affect the problem or the solution. Stakeholders can cause or contribute to problems. They can create or contribute to solutions, but they may also resist solutions. Stakeholders' importance to the principal increases with their powers. For example, a principal who is the general manager faces a powerful opponent, the financial director, who disagrees with the project objectives, the problem analysis, the recommended solution, and the way of implementation.

- *Problem analysis*: Most-times, a project team does not have all knowledge and information for a perfect analysis of the problem. Even if the analysis is perfect, the team depends on the acceptance and approval by relevant stakeholders.

The stakeholders' acceptance and approval give a team a (social) licence to solve a problem.

- *Solution development*: Most-times, a team lacks part of the necessary knowledge and information to develop a perfect solution. Then a team needs inputs in the form of knowledge and information from well-informed stakeholders to broaden the team's perspective and deepen their insights. Such stakeholders may contribute to the quality of the solution. A project team may also need stakeholders to accept and approve solutions. Again, a team needs a licence to operate.

- *Solution implementation*: In almost every case, a project team cannot implement solutions on its own. A team needs stakeholders to perform the implementation tasks. Stakeholders must accept and approve a team's implementation approach. Again, a team needs a licence to operate. Moreover, stakeholders must be willing and able to participate in the implementation project.

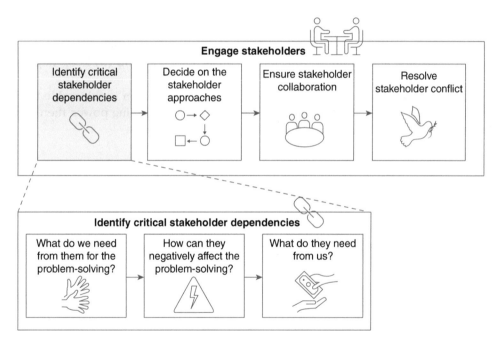

Figure 6.9   Identifying the critical stakeholder dependencies is the first step in engaging stakeholders

How can stakeholders negatively affect the problem-solving?

- *Problem analysis*: Some stakeholders may not accept or approve an explanation of a problem. Some people may even deny a problem exists. They may also manipulate the analysis of the problem by withholding data or providing false information.

- *Solution development*: Some stakeholders may not share their knowledge to develop solutions. They keep essential knowledge to themselves. People may even provide false information to manipulate the development of a solution.

Some stakeholders may not accept or approve solutions. Powerful opposing stakeholders may veto a solution.

- *Solution implementation*: Stakeholders may not accept or approve an implementation approach. These people may have no confidence in the approach or the approach conflicts with their interests, values, or norms. As a result, they may resist or even manipulate the implementation of the solution.

What do stakeholders need from us?

Powerful stakeholders may need something from the principal or the project team. If the principal is the top manager, then internal stakeholders need her approval for their plans and budgets. External stakeholders, such as suppliers and business partners, may also depend on the principal's approval for selling products to the principal's company or for working together with that company. Such dependencies of powerful stakeholders contribute to the project team's bargaining power. The team should use the principal's power wisely to: (a) obtain support from the stakeholders who have critical resources and (b) keep negative stakeholders at bay.

If the team depends on stakeholders' resources or if the team is vulnerable to the negative actions of the stakeholders, and the team lacks bargaining power, then these dependencies and vulnerabilities undermine the team's success.

—————— Running Case RobotCo ——————

When Tara approaches the stakeholders, they immediately demand that their own solutions should be implemented. For example, the engineers complain that:

- robots break down too often
- diagnostic information is too limited
- there is a lot of uncertainty
- inventories at customer sites are too small

According to the engineers, the solution is to hold more inventory at the warehouse, have more warehouses, and develop faster logistics.

But the warehouse manager wants the engineers to pay more attention to order entry. He wants more discipline from the engineers. The engineers should follow the diagnostic procedures more thoroughly.

The engineering manager wants more engineers to manage the heavy workload.

Account managers want the faster delivery of parts.

But the financial director does not want to increase the budget. Figure 6.10 shows an example of a stakeholder assessment.

Stakeholders	What do we need from them?	How can they negatively affect the problem-solving?	What do they need from us?
Field engineers	Information about diagnosis of robot problems	Do not provide information or manipulate information	Solution for waiting-time problem
Warehouse manager	Information about parts inventories	Same as above	Solution for out-of-stock problem
Account managers	Information about customers' complaints about late repairs	Same as above	Solution for customer complaints

Figure 6.10   An example of a stakeholder assessment

Pause and Reflect

Use your own experience of a recent project from your study or work. Do you recall some team members who did not make themselves heard? If so, did you ask them what was on their mind?

Decide on the stakeholder approaches

Map the stakeholders

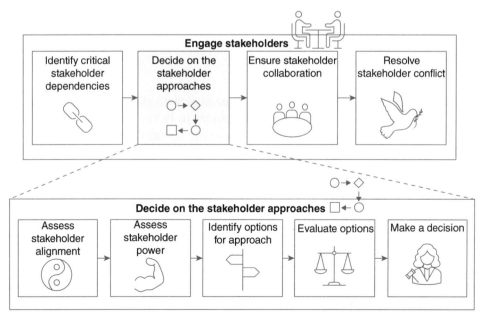

Figure 6.11   Deciding on the stakeholder approaches is the second step in engaging stakeholders

Not all stakeholders are equally powerful. The powerful ones require most attention. We distinguish between powerful stakeholders with conflicting and aligned agendas (see the two top quadrants of Figure 6.12).

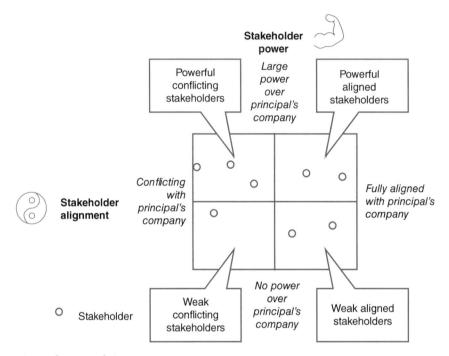

Figure 6.12   A power-interest map

Source: Author's interpretation of Mendelow's 'Power-Interest Grid' (Mendelow, 1991)

Identify the options for the approach

A power-interest map guides us on how to engage with different stakeholders. We must adapt our approach to a specific stakeholder to fit the stakeholder's characteristics. The saying is: 'Different horses for different courses'. Figure 6.13 shows the suitable approaches per quadrant.

1. *Engage powerful aligned stakeholders*: We need the powerful aligned stakeholders for successful problem-solving. Although they are aligned, we should not take their support for granted. These stakeholders may lack understanding or awareness of the problem. They may also have wrong ideas about the causes of the problem. We need to know how the powerful aligned stakeholders think about the problem-solving project. We must communicate with the powerful aligned stakeholders to ensure that they perceive the problem-solving correctly.

2. *Align powerful conflicting stakeholders*:
   a. We must *search* for the common interests of the powerful conflicting stakeholders and the principal. Perhaps there are long-term common interests. Then we

may convince these stakeholders that a solution for a problem is also in their long-term interest. For example, a works council is strongly against a recommendation to dismiss some personnel. We can explain that our advice may reduce jobs in the short term, but will increase employment in the long term.

b. The principal may *change* the powerful conflicting stakeholders' interests by providing them with (financial) incentives to support the problem-solving. For example, an IT department may oppose a change process because of the extra workload. The principal may increase the IT department's budget to hire the required extra personnel. As a result of identifying common interests or changing the interests of stakeholders, these stakeholders move to the right on the map.

3. *Reduce vulnerability to powerful conflicting stakeholders*: We may reduce our dependency on the critical resources that are owned or controlled by powerful conflicting stakeholders. These resources may include information, data, and people. We may find alternative sources of supply. Then we can switch suppliers or use the alternative suppliers to strengthen our bargaining position *vis-à-vis* the conflicting stakeholders: "If you do not collaborate with us, you will force us to use another supplier or partner."

4. *Strengthen weak aligned stakeholders*: We may strengthen weak aligned stakeholders in various ways. A principal may promote weak aligned internal stakeholders to higher positions in the company hierarchy. A principal may give these stakeholders more resources, such as budget, people, and information.

5. *Align weak conflicting stakeholders*: Tactics for aligning weak conflicting stakeholders are the same as those for their powerful counterparts: identifying common interests or changing the interests of the conflicting stakeholders.

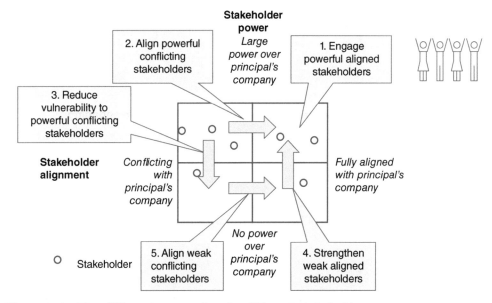

Figure 6.13 Five different approaches for different stakeholders

Mini Exercise

Think of a recent problem of a well-known company and use Internet research to identify the strongest opposing stakeholder for this case. Consider alternative approaches to handle this stakeholder.

PART 2: STAKEHOLDER COLLABORATION AND CONFLICT

Ensure stakeholder collaboration

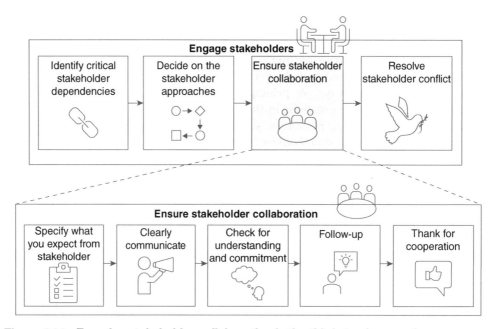

Figure 6.14   Ensuring stakeholder collaboration is the third step in engaging stakeholders

Specify what you expect from a stakeholder

We seek collaboration with stakeholders because we need something for our problem-solving. Figure 6.15 distinguishes between five categories of such needs.

Clearly communicate

We must be aware of what may go wrong when we work with stakeholders, even when their interests and values are aligned with ours. Stakeholders may be willing to collaborate, but they may misunderstand our data requests, workplans, and interview questions. Therefore, it is critical to clearly communicate what we want from stakeholders.

What you need	How to get it	A key trap	Tip
Data	Data request	Misunderstanding by the data owner	Write down everything in detail and check for understanding
Work (such as problem analyses and solution implementation)	Workplan with assignments	Misunderstanding by the assigned person	Same
Knowledge (such as experience, ideas, other insights, and judgment	Interview or workshop	Cognitive biases of participants	Ask critical questions to uncover any biases
Understanding and acceptance			
Approval and decisions			

Figure 6.15   Some traps when you seek resources from stakeholders

Check for understanding and commitment

We should not assume that stakeholders understand our requests for information and other forms of support. Stakeholders may have *cognitive biases* that hinder the understanding of our request. Therefore, we need to identify such biases. We should also not assume that stakeholders will be committed to fulfilling our requests for information and other forms of support. Stakeholders may have *social and interest biases* that come at the expense of commitment. We also need to identify these biases.

Identify cognitive biases

Stakeholders' cognitive biases may contribute to business problems. We must be aware that we also have cognitive biases. Cognitive biases are systematic thinking errors when people process and interpret information. They influence our judgment and decision-making. There are many types of cognitive biases. For clarification and simplicity, we only show some examples in Figure 6.16.

Identify social biases

We distinguish between individual and collective or social biases. Social biases are the result of interactions between the members of a group. We provide three examples.

- *Imitation*:
  - *Bandwagon effect*: We do something because others do it.
  - *Herd behaviour*: We follow the crowd because it is better to be collectively wrong than individually right.

- *Desire for conformity and harmony*:
  - ○ *Group think*: Our desire for conformity and harmony leads to irrational and dysfunctional decisions and behaviour. We ignore alternative viewpoints, suppress dissenting views, and isolate the group from outside influences.
  - ○ *Courtesy bias*: We give an opinion that is more socially correct than our true opinion.
- *Discrimination and prejudice*:
  - ○ *In-group bias*: We treat people differently based on whether they are part of our ingroup or from an outgroup, that is, insiders and outsiders, respectively.
  - ○ *Not-invented-here syndrome*: We have an aversion to ideas developed by outsiders – people who are not part of the group.

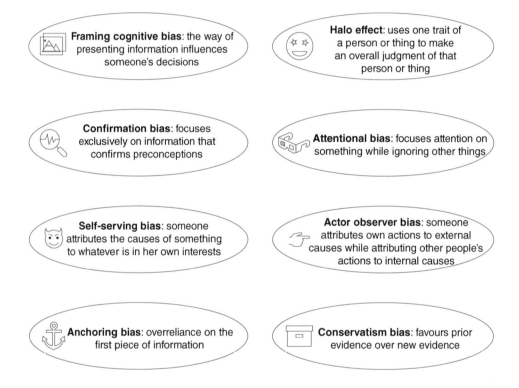

Figure 6.16   Some examples of cognitive biases

Identify interest biases

In addition to cognitive biases, people may have interest biases. Interest biases are not flawed judgments because of a failure to process information. They are a conscious distortion of reality to promote one's own interests at the expense of others. People may have an interest in not seeing a problem or misinterpreting a problem, for example, falsely blaming other people or external factors for causing a problem. People can also advocate a particular solution to a problem. This solution is not the best option for the company, but it is for them as individuals. For example, a finance director advocates the closure of a factory to reduce costs. Closure is not the best solution to the company's profit problem, but it does ensure that the finance director can stay within the budget.

Deal with biases

We need to be aware that we and the stakeholders have biases. Do you think you have no bias? That is a bias. We should not believe at face value everything people tell us. Biases cause people to knowingly or unknowingly give us wrong information. Therefore, we are critical and try to verify whether people's statements are true. Are there any signs of biases? We ask ourselves: Are these statements based on logic and demonstrable evidence? We are critical if stakeholders do not give reasons or evidence for their opinions. Critical thinking helps us to challenge any biases. We ask:

- Why do you think this is true? For example: Why do you think that the decline of sales is due to the account managers' lack of motivation?
- What evidence supports this view? For example: What proof do you have that account managers lack motivation?
- Where can we find evidence to support this opinion? For example: What sources can prove the account managers' lack of motivation?

 Pause and Reflect

Use your own experience of a recent project from your study or work. Do you recall any biases of the stakeholders and yourself? If so, what role did these biases play in the project?

Follow-up

We have submitted an information request to a stakeholder. In addition, we have explicitly indicated the period in which we would like to receive the requested information. The deadline has passed, and that stakeholder has not sent us anything. What may have happened?

- The stakeholder may have forgotten about our request.
- Alternatively, the stakeholder may have other priorities.
- Another possibility is that the stakeholder has encountered difficulties during processing our request and that the stakeholder for whatever reason does not want to inform us about these difficulties.

In all these scenarios, we must take follow-up action on our request. We can send the defaulting stakeholder a friendly reminder. We may also contact that stakeholder to ask why we have not yet received the information and offer our help if applicable. As a preventive action, we can also contact the stakeholder before the expiry of the term to inquire about the status of our request.

Thank for collaboration

After you have received information or other support from a stakeholder, thank that stakeholder for the collaboration. A small gesture like a thank-you note is enough. Problem-solving remains human work, and people are sensitive to a thank you or a compliment. We create goodwill with it. It is therefore in our own self-interest to thank others. Never forget to thank stakeholders for their collaboration.

 Pause and Reflect

Use your own experience of a recent project from your study or work. Did you receive information from a stakeholder who had a conflicting agenda? If so, how did you handle this situation? Did you ask yourself: Can this be true? What, if any, evidence supports this stakeholder's statement?

Running Case RobotCo

Tara talks with an engineer who skips the problem analysis and jumps straight to a solution.

- Engineer states: "I want more inventory at the warehouse."
- Tara thinks: What problem is this a solution for? Tara asks: "*Why* do you want a larger inventory?"
- Engineer answers: "The warehouse does not have the parts that I order."
- Tara thinks: I cannot ask *why* the warehouse does not have the order because then he will answer that the inventory is low. Instead, she probes into the problem by asking: "Is that always so?"
- Engineer answers: "No, in most cases, the warehouse has the parts in the inventory."
- Tara asks: "In what cases does the warehouse not have what you order?"
- Engineer answers: "Let me think about that. Sometimes the problem with the robot is so complex that I cannot diagnose the specific cause upfront. There is no time to take the robot fully apart. Then I must diagnose the problem with limited information. If the robot problem can be due to various causes, I order various parts for the various possible causes. I do this just to make sure that I always have the right parts for

the repair. After the arrival of the parts, I open the robot and partially disassemble the machine. Next, I do trial-and-error problem-solving. I replace parts to see whether a replacement solves the problem."

 Pause and Reflect

Use your own experience of a recent project from your study or work. Did you get stuck in a situation with a stakeholder? How did you handle the situation? Did you ask yourself: *Why* does this stakeholder act like this? What drives this behaviour?

Running Case RobotCo

Tara talks with a software developer who blames another stakeholder.

- Developer: "The engineers are the problem."
- Tara: "Why is that so?"
- Developer: "The engineers order too many parts or the wrong parts."
- Tara: "Why do they do that?
- Developer: "They misdiagnose the problem with the robots."
- Tara: "What evidence do you have for this explanation of the problem?"
- Developer: "We look at the unused parts. If engineers order too many parts or the wrong parts, then they will not need these parts for the repair jobs."

Resolve a stakeholder conflict

Identify the conflict with the stakeholder

Conflicts are about something:

- *Objectives* (what should we achieve?): we and the stakeholder have conflicting objectives
- *Actions* (how should we achieve it?): we and the stakeholder disagree about the actions needed to analyse or solve a problem
- *Resources* (such as, money, people, knowledge, data): we and the stakeholder disagree about the allocation of resources to a problem-solving project

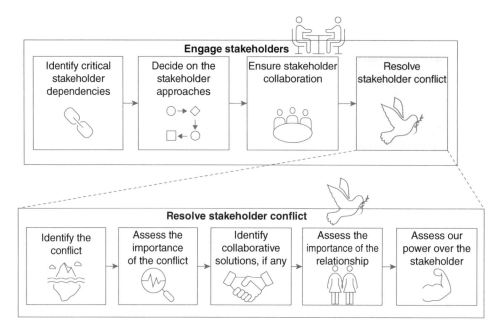

Figure 6.17   Resolving stakeholder conflict is the fourth step in engaging stakeholders

Causes of conflict include:

* opposition of *interests or values*: we and the stakeholder have conflicting interests or values
* opposition of *perceptions*: we and the stakeholder have opposite perceptions of the problem or solutions. Differences in perceptions may be due to information and communication problems.

Stakeholders who have a conflict with the principal can ask you to determine who is right. Do not be tempted to comply with this request because it is a pitfall. You are *not* a neutral referee. You work for the principal. Your job is not to referee but to help the principal solve the business problem.

Assess the importance of the conflict with the stakeholder

The conflict's importance to us (relative to its importance to the conflicting stakeholder) is a criterion for choosing a suitable approach to conflict resolution. For example, we need financial data from the business controller to run an analysis, but the data are not readily available. The business controller must raise a query in the database to retrieve the data from the system. The controller has other priorities and cannot make the query for another two weeks. But we want the data for analysis now. The questions are: How important are these analyses to our project and how important is it to do the analyses now instead of two weeks from now? The importance of the conflict will drive our assertiveness in conflict resolution. The more important the conflict is to us, the more assertive we should be.

Identify collaborative solutions, if any

The Kilmann and Thomas Conflict Model may help in finding a suitable approach to conflict resolution (Kilmann & Thomas, 1975). This model maps five approaches based on our attempts to satisfy our own concern and the concern of the conflicting stakeholder (see Figure 6.18).

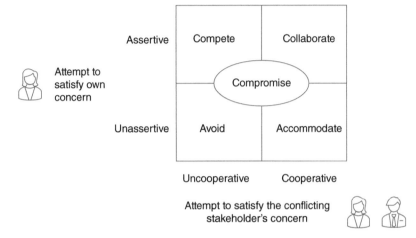

Figure 6.18   The Kilmann and Thomas Conflict Model
Source: Kilmann & Thomas (1975)

- *Avoid*: People can avoid a conflict with an opposing stakeholder. They may avoid the topic, downplay the conflict, or even deny the problem. People can make jokes about it to downplay it. Conflict avoidance can be a wait-and-see approach: the avoiders wait for better times.
- *Accommodate*: People in a conflict may also give in, yield to the other party, oblige the opponent, or try to smooth things out.
- *Compromise*: People may try to conciliate the other party. They may bargain or negotiate to find a solution that is acceptable to each party.
- *Compete*: People may also force the opposing stakeholder to act in their interest. This is about coercion. The powerful party may dominate the opponent.
- *Collaborate*: Finally, parties in a conflict may see their conflict as a creative opportunity and collaborate to seize it. They identify the concerns of each party. Then, they create a win–win solution that meets each party's concerns. A win–win outcome is superior to a compromise. A win–win outcome is satisfactory to each party whereas a compromise is acceptable but not necessarily satisfactory.

Assess the importance of the relationship

The importance of the relationship with the stakeholder is, besides the importance of the conflict, another criterion for choosing a conflict-resolution approach. The importance of the relationship depends on our dependence on this stakeholder. For example, do we need important information or support from this stakeholder? The length of the relationship is also important. Will we be dealing with this stakeholder for a long time or is this a one-off transaction? The importance of the relationship to us will drive our cooperativeness. The more important the relationship is to us, the more cooperative we will be.

Assess our power over the stakeholder

A third criterion is our power over the stakeholder. Dependence is also an important factor of power. Are we dependent on this stakeholder? For example, do we need her resources and approval? Is this stakeholder dependent on us? Is there a mutual dependency? Hierarchical relationships also determine power. In the case of *internal* stakeholders, are they below us, at the same level, or above us in the company hierarchy? Our power over the other party will allow for assertiveness. The more power we have over the stakeholder, the more assertive we will be.

Pause and Reflect

Use your own experience of a recent project from your study or work. Have you been in conflict with a powerful opposing stakeholder? If so, how did you approach the conflict and with what result?

Be wary of opportunism

Under some circumstances, it is tempting for good stakeholders to do bad things. By this, we mean the opportunity to do something bad with impunity. Opportunism is deliberately taking advantage of situations with little or no regard for the consequences for other people. We distinguish between five types of opportunism:

- *Distort information*: Cheat, lie, manipulate, and mislead others. For example, a stakeholder gives us manipulated cost data.
- *Withhold information*: Use private knowledge about the risks involved in a transaction to maximize our benefits at the expense of the other party (adverse selection). For example, a consultant does not tell the principal that he also advises a competitor.
- *Break promises*: Renege a contract, adopt free-rider behaviour, shirk on the job, and exploit the last period (i.e., self-conduct that goes unpunished because it occurs during the last interaction when the injured party no longer has a chance to respond). For example, in the last month of temporary employment, an employee cuts corners.
- *Take excessive risk if others bear the costs (moral hazard)*: For example, a distributor takes too great a risk because he knows that the manufacturer will come to the rescue in case of problems.

- *Spend too much money if it is someone else's money*: For example, a CEO pays too much for the acquisition because it is the shareholders' capital.

We distinguish between three conditions for opportunism:

- The situation allows for private benefits for the opportunist where others bear (most of) the costs. For example, an opportunistic employee secretly sells the employer's data as part of a personal side-job.
- Others cannot prevent the opportunistic behaviour, because:
  - either others have no or insufficient information to recognize the opportunistic behaviour. For example, an opportunist does not conduct an analysis thoroughly but gets away with it because others cannot check it.
  - or others have no external controls and sanctions, or they lack the power to enforce the controls. For example, an opportunist does not provide us with the requested data because she does not feel like it and we cannot force her to collaborate.
- The opportunist has no internal controls (they are immune to reason, have no empathy, and show no remorse, regret, guilt, or shame). Examples are the anti-social personality traits: narcissism, 'Machiavellinism,' and psychopathy (Muris, Merckelbach, Otgaar, & Meijer, 2017).

In a problem-solving project, we must be wary of stakeholder opportunism. We must try to ensure that no conditions arise that allow opportunistic behaviour to take place. We should prevent 'private benefits–public costs' situations from arising. Transparency is important to discourage the secretive behaviour of opportunists. Finally, we must have external controls and sanctions in place to discipline opportunists.

 Pause and Reflect

Use your own experience of a recent project from your study or work. Have you experienced the opportunistic behaviour of stakeholders? If so, how did you handle the situation and with what result?

Manage the relationship with the principal

Inform the principal

As we work for the principal, we must keep her in the loop and get her approval at project milestones. We set up a communication schedule to ensure regular meetings. It is vital to inform the principal about progress as well as any problems that emerge. We may also use her as a sounding board to receive feedback. Moreover, we can ask the principal questions, but we ask questions preferably in the first week because that is the only risk-free asking period. If we come up with questions later in the project, the principal may think: Do they only come up with that issue now? We can use casual settings such as coffee breaks and lunches for sensitive questions.

We should be ready anytime to inform the principal about the status of the project. We must be prepared if the principal asks us: "Can you update me on the project?" Then we should have an elevator pitch ready. We make sure that we have a 30-second answer ready for everything: the proposed approach, the analysis of the problem, and the current solution.

Manage the principal

If the principal asks difficult questions, we pause for three seconds before answering. There are several reasons to do so:

- A pause gives us time to think about the answer
- The principal sees that we are considering the question and taking it seriously
- The principal appreciates our answer more because of our silence
- A moment of rest prevents an overreaction or an emotional reaction

When communicating with the principal, we try to question more and talk less. We may use questions to turn 'no' into 'yes'. Rather than correcting the principal, we help her correct herself by using leading questions, for example "Do you think this analysis is feasible in one week?" Allowing the principal to discover that the right answer is better than stating the answer outright.

 Pause and Reflect

Use your own experience of a recent project from your study or work. How did you manage the relationship with the principal, whether it was your teacher (study project) or manager (work)?

Some principals may have all kinds of abstract ideas, which mean a lot of work. For example: "Find out for me how emerging technologies can strengthen our company's dynamic capabilities." If a principal wants to give us overwhelming tasks, we must push back. We do not ask ourselves: How can we get this done? Instead, we ask the principal questions.

1. Why do we need to do this task?
2. Is the task worth it?
3. How do the benefits of the task compare to the costs?
4. Are we the right people to do this task?
5. What is the timeline of this task?
6. How urgent is this task?

If the principal wants too much at once, ask for priorities: "What do you want me to pick up first?"

───── **Pause and Reflect** ──────────────────────

Consider how you may use these techniques for engaging stakeholders in your studies, work, and personal life.

SUMMARY

We briefly outline the main takeaways of this chapter.

- Develop a team contract
  - develop objectives for the team
  - identify values of the team
  - develop rules for the team
  - develop roles of the team members
- Identify the critical stakeholder dependencies
  - identify what we need from stakeholders for our problem-solving
  - explore how stakeholders can negatively affect our problem-solving
  - identify what stakeholders need from us
- Prioritise stakeholder approaches
  - assess the alignment of the stakeholder
  - assess the power of the stakeholder
  - identify options for approaches
    - engage powerful aligned stakeholders
    - align powerful conflicting stakeholders
    - reduce vulnerability to powerful conflicting stakeholders
    - align weak conflicting stakeholders
    - strengthen weak aligned stakeholders
  - evaluate options
  - decide on the approach
- Select a proper form of resolving a conflict with a particular stakeholder
  - identify the issue(s) with the stakeholder
  - assess the importance of the issue(s)
  - identify the conflict-resolution options, if any
    - assertive-cooperative: collaborate
    - unassertive-cooperative: accommodate
    - assertive-uncooperative: compete

     – unassertive-uncooperative: avoid
     – in-between assertiveness and cooperativeness: compromise

- ○ assess the importance of the relationship with the stakeholder
- ○ assess our power over the stakeholder
- ○ decide on the form of conflict resolution

Mini Exercise

Identify the key concepts and terms in this chapter, define them briefly and compile your own glossary.

REFERENCES AND FURTHER READING

Belbin, R. M. (1993). *Team Roles at Work*. Oxford: Butterworth-Heinemann.

Freeman, R. E. (1984). *Strategic Management: A Stakeholder Approach*. Boston, MA: Pitman.

Kilmann, R. H., & Thomas, K. W. (1975). Interpersonal conflict-handling behavior as reflections of Jungian personality dimensions. *Psychological Reports*, *37*(3), 971–980.

Mendelow, A. (1991). *Stakeholder mapping*. In Proceedings of the 2nd International Conference on Information Systems (pp. 10–24). Cambridge, MA.

Muris, P., Merckelbach, H., Otgaar, H., & Meijer, E. (2017). The malevolent side of human nature: A meta-analysis and critical review of the literature on the dark triad (narcissism, Machiavellianism, and psychopathy). *Perspectives on Psychological Science*, *12*(2), 183–204.

Develop Complete and Consistent Solutions

7

INTRODUCTION

In developing solutions for problems, we may fall into many pitfalls. For example, we may come up with solutions that do *not* address the principal's problem. When presenting our solution, the principal responds: "That is an interesting solution, but what does it have to do with my problem?" or "What problem is this a solution for?" Another pitfall is to create solutions that focus on the problem but do not build on the analysis of the problem. The principal then asks: "How does this solution deal with the causes of the problem?" This chapter outlines how to develop solutions that address the problem and build on the analysis of the problem.

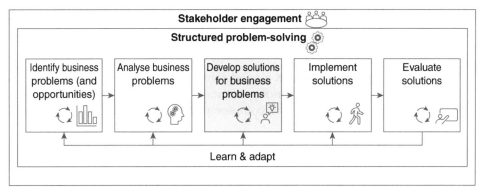

Iterative process of developing and testing hypotheses about problems, solutions, and implementation

Figure 7.1   Developing solutions is the third step of structured problem-solving

In some cases, we may know a possible solution. We may have solved the same or a similar problem before or we know analogical cases. Then we may use the Hypothesis Tree Method. Chapter 8 will outline how to develop and test a solution hypothesis. In this chapter we assume that we do not yet have a possible solution. We follow the Sequential Analysis Method (see Figure 7.2) and answer the fourth question: 'What *could* we do about the problem?' What are the *possible* solutions?

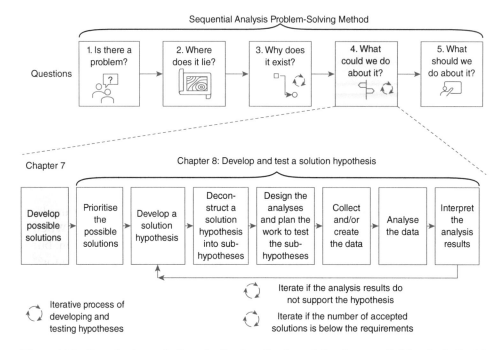

Figure 7.2   Developing solutions is the fourth step of the Sequential Analysis Problem-Solving Method

The chapter is structured as follows (see Figure 7.3):

1. We answer the question: What is a *good* solution?
2. We outline *how* to develop solutions and start with relatively simple problems.
3. We demonstrate our approach for complex problems.

MAIN LEARNING OBJECTIVES

After studying this chapter, you should be able to:

*   use analogical cases to develop solutions
*   use creative thinking to develop solutions

- use analytical frameworks to develop solutions
- understand that complex solutions are composed of choices
- use a morphological box to compose a complex solution

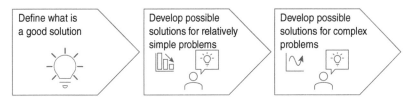

Figure 7.3 Chapter structure

DEFINE WHAT IS A GOOD SOLUTION

We may ask: What constitutes a *good* solution? Recall that we formulate a principal's problem as a key question: "How should the principal close the performance gap?" A good solution answers this question. Such an answer must be specific.

- A good solution is tailor-made to the principal's unique situation. The solution builds on the analysis of the problem:
  - ○ it focuses on the prioritised segment(s) of the problem
  - ○ and addresses the prioritised cause(s) of the problem
- A good solution meets the principal's evaluation criteria
- A good solution fits the principals' solution constraints

Distinguish between simple and complex solutions

We distinguish between simple and complex solutions (see Figure 7.4). Simple solutions consist of a single choice whereas complex solutions are composed of multiple choices. When do we need complex solutions? We need complex solutions when we need to solve complex problems. Complex problems *demand* complex solutions. Simple problems may *allow* for simple solutions.

For example, compare the two running cases:

- RobotCo has a (relatively) *simple* problem: the excessive waiting time for robot parts. How should RobotCo respond to the late delivery of parts problem? This waiting time is an *operational* problem. A solution for RobotCo's problem can be a single choice, such as: increase the parts inventory at the warehouse.
- In contrast, ConsultCo has a *complex* opportunity: How should ConsultCo seize the opportunity to internationalize? Where and how to expand internationally? The international expansion of a company is a *strategic* opportunity. Strategy is the highest level of complexity. An internationalisation strategy consists of multiple choices, such as:

- ○ country selection: what countries to enter?
- ○ entry mode selection: how to enter the selected countries?
- ○ competitive advantage: how to compete in the selected countries?

	Simple solution (single choice)	Complex solution (a set of choices)
Complex problem (multiple business functions) ConsultCo example: internationalization of the company	Not applicable	ConsultCo example: a set of choices, such as • foreign countries • entry mode • competitive advantage
Simple problem (single business function) RobotCo example: waiting time for parts	RobotCo example: Increase inventory	RobotCo example: a set of choices, such as • increase inventory • do preventative maintenance • create a support organization for inexperienced engineers

Figure 7.4   **Simple versus complex problems and solutions**

Composed solutions consist of multiple choices

We deconstruct complex problems into mutually exclusive and collectively exhaustive (MECE) structures of issues. Similarly, we *compose* complex solutions as MECE structures of choices. These choices are about the parts of the solution. Figure 7.5 provides an example a complex solution: a business strategy. We may view a business strategy, or a competitive strategy, as a structure of four interrelated high-level choices.

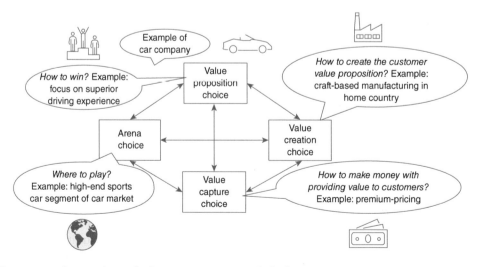

Figure 7.5   **A complex solution as a structure of choices**

DEVELOP POSSIBLE SOLUTIONS FOR RELATIVELY SIMPLE PROBLEMS

We revisit Coleman's bathtub model of problem-solving (Coleman, 1994; see Figure 7.6).

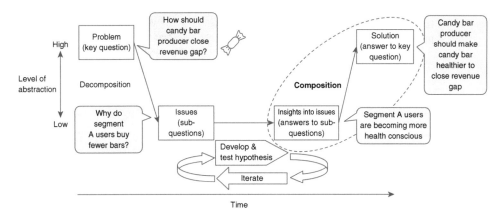

Figure 7.6   The composition of a solution is the final step in Coleman's bathtub of problem-solving (Coleman, 1994)

The solution must address the problem. Therefore, the solution development must build on the problem analysis (see Figure 7.7).

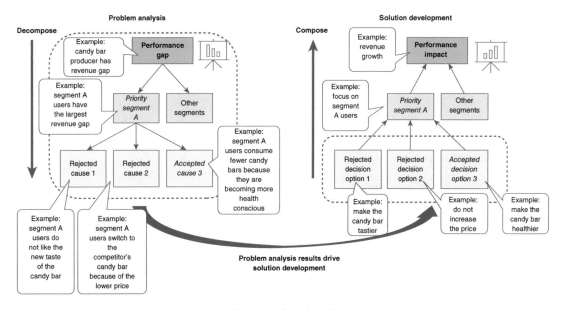

Figure 7.7   Problem analysis results drive solution development

Sequential Analysis Problem-Solving

We are now at the fourth question of the Sequential Analysis Problem-Solving Method (see Figure 7.8): What *could* we do about the problem?

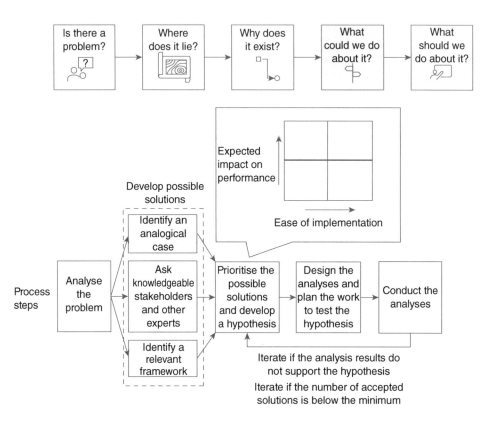

Figure 7.8   A Sequential Analysis process for developing and testing a solution

In Figure 7.8, we distinguish between three alternative approaches to develop possible solutions:

- Identify an analogical case
- Ask knowledgeable stakeholders and other experts
- Identify a relevant framework

In Chapter 4 we discussed these approaches for developing possible *explanations* for problems. In a similar way, we can use these techniques for developing possible *solutions*. Even if we think we already know the solution, we still engage stakeholders. They may have better ideas, and we may need their acceptance and support for the solution implementation.

Identify an analogical case

Analogical cases can inspire solution development as principals may learn from the best practices undertaken by other companies in the same industry or a similar one. But there may also be analogical cases inside the principal's company. We may be able to draw on a reservoir of experience about problems and solutions gained in the company's past. Then we need to identify the people in the company who have the relevant experience.

 Pause and Reflect

Use your own experience of a recent project from your study or work. Did you check first whether the principal's company had solved this kind of problem before?

Do not compare apples and oranges

We may already have an idea of the solution. We know that this solution works for other companies in the same industry or in similar industries. It is a proven successful solution that carries a low risk. Identifying analogical cases seems like an easy way to create solutions, but appearances can be deceiving. A big pitfall is to overlook critical differences between the principal's company and the analogical company. For example, the cultures of the two companies can differ or the economic conditions may differ. The analogical company may have implemented its solution during an economic boom whereas the principal company faces a recession. We should not compare apples with oranges.

 Pause and Reflect

Use your own experience of a recent project from your study or work. Did you use an analogical case? If so, did you take a critical look at whether that case was indeed analogical?

Do not copy, but customize

In practice, the current problem-solving project will not be a complete copy of previous projects. Every company and every problem have unique aspects. Principals will reject any standard, off-the-shelf solutions and argue that their problem is unique. That is why we will have to tailor the solutions of analogical cases to the principal's specific problem. Although the complete recycling of solutions rarely works, working with analogical solutions has excellent advantages for us. It makes a big difference whether we must develop new solutions from scratch or whether we can build on existing solutions.

Ask knowledgeable stakeholders and other experts

We may also ask knowledgeable stakeholders and other experts for possible solutions. These people know a lot about the problem and hopefully they have ideas for solutions. They may have experience in solving this problem or a similar one. But be critical of solutions put forward by knowledgeable stakeholders and other experts. Always ask follow-up questions. Why do you think this solution will work for this problem? What indications are there that this solution will be successful in this situation? Probing questions are important because stakeholders and experts can be wrong or have conflicting interests.

 Pause and Reflect

Use your own experience of a recent project from your study or work. How did you develop a solution?

Think creatively

Understanding problems is necessary for developing solutions. But solutions do not automatically flow from understanding. Answers to a principal's key question require creativity if there are no analogical cases or frameworks. Creating new and original ideas contributes to solution development.

Creativity benefits from a diversity of perspectives. Such diversity stimulates divergent thinking. Engaging knowledgeable stakeholders and other experts in the creative process contributes to the diversity of ideas. Therefore, we may want to engage a diverse range of stakeholders and experts in creative thinking sessions or workshops. For example, we can tap into the brains of a diverse group of managers and professionals in the principal's company. Certainly, in cases where different principals' employees do not or insufficiently communicate with each other, we can create value by talking to all these actors and combining their insights. The principal's employees may be locked in departmental silos and therefore have little or no knowledge of other relevant business functions, causing them to miss the crucial overview. For example, the R&D people rarely or never meet with the salespeople. We can collect the different perspectives through interviews with these stakeholders. But we can also bring the different people together through workshops to create a complete picture of what the solutions may look like.

Additionally, people outside the principal's organization may bring a fresh outsider perspective on solutions. Ideally, we engage independent people who are free to speak their own minds. We can use many techniques for stimulating creativity (see Figure 7.9 for some examples).

Technique | Examples

| Brainstorming & brainwriting (group discussion for coming up with ideas) | Identifying hidden presumptions (reversing your working assumptions, visioning if no limitations, etc.) | Associating (analogies, metaphors, random words, pictures, etc.) |

Changing perspectives (Six Thinking Hats, role play, brain shifter, etc.)

Visualising (mind mapping, storyboarding, brown paper method, etc.)

Force fitting (combining elements into one new idea)

Morphological analysis (analysing the total set of interrelationships in multidimensional problems)

Morphological matrix (table for presenting the total set of possible interrelationships)

TRIZ (Theory of Inventive Problem Solving: problem-solving based on patterns of invention)

Matrix of contradictions (map of all possible contradictions/problems and the suitable inventive principles)

Figure 7.9 Examples of creative problem-solving techniques

How To Do It?

Do not develop your solutions alone in your office behind your desk, but collaborate with knowledgeable stakeholders and other experts inside and outside the principal's organization.

Pause and Reflect

Use your own experience of a recent project from your study or work. How many alternative solutions did you develop? When and why did you decide to stop looking for more solutions?

Identify a relevant framework

We may use an off-the-shelf framework to develop solutions. A decision tree is a popular framework for identifying alternative solutions. For example, we can use a profit tree (see Figure 7.10). Alternatively, we can tailor an existing framework or even design a custom-made framework (see Figure 7.11).

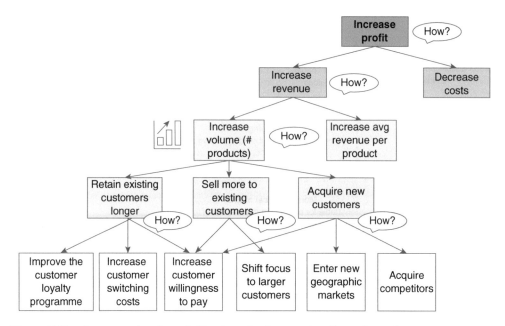

Figure 7.10   An example of a solution tree for increasing the sales volume

Notes: # means number; avg stands for average

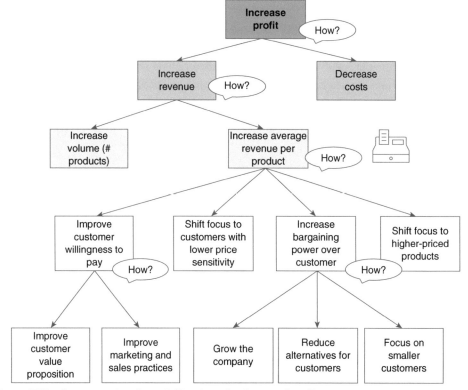

Figure 7.11   An example of a solution tree for increasing the average revenue per product

Note: # means number

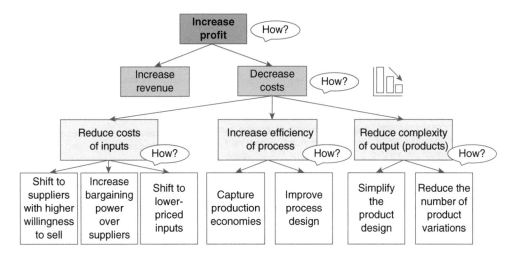

Figure 7.12   An example of a solution tree for decreasing the costs

Note: Examples of production economies are economies of scale and scope, experience effects, and capacity utilization

Tailor a profit tree

If we understand how the principal's company makes a profit, we can tailor a profit tree. An example is a company with large investments in a fixed production capacity, such as a hotel, a manufacturing plant, or an airline (see Figure 7.13). These types of companies make a profit if they use that capacity sufficiently. Their profit formula looks like this:

Profit = revenue – costs

Revenue = production capacity × utilization rate × revenue per utilized production unit

Costs = variable cost per production unit × number of utilized production units + fixed costs

Example for a hotel:

Hotel revenue per year = number of available 'room nights' per year × room occupancy rate × average room rate

Number of available 'room nights' per year = number of available rooms in hotel × nights per year that hotel is open

Hotel costs per year = (variable costs per occupied room night × number of occupied room nights per year) + fixed costs

Figure 7.14 visualizes the process for developing possible solutions for simple business problems.

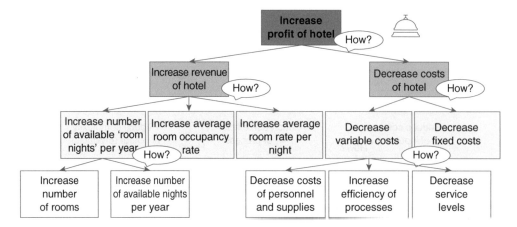

Figure 7.13   An example of a tailored solution tree for a hotel

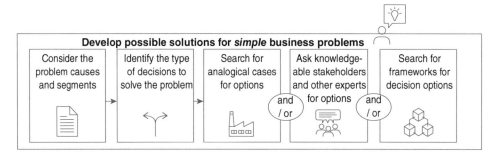

Figure 7.14   A process for developing solutions for simple business problems

―――――――――   Running Case RobotCo   ―――――――――

Recall the key question: "How should RobotCo respond to the late delivery of parts problem to increase its profit by 15 million euro in one year?" Tara considers the problem cause and the problem segment. Tara's problem analysis shows that the inexperience of engineers is the main explanation for the late deliveries problem. Inexperience causes wrong orders for parts that are not in the inventory of the warehouse.

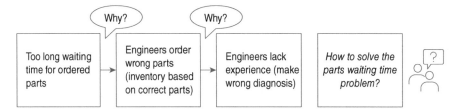

Figure 7.15   Insights from the problem analysis

Parts not being in the inventory leads to long waiting times. The warehouse needs to order these parts. Tara identifies the decisions that RobotCo can make (see Figure 7.16).

RobotCo may *increase the supply of parts* by stocking parts in the warehouse based on the (wrong) parts *ordering* instead of the parts *usage*. Then the company increases the inventory to anticipate wrong orders. But Tara concentrates on *reducing the wrong diagnosis* as this is the root cause. She asks herself: How should RobotCo correct the diagnoses? Increasing the experience of the engineer is an obvious answer but Tara does not stop after the first possible answer.

Tara looks for solutions from *analogical cases*. Some other companies provide their engineers with smart glasses (with a camera) that allow second-line support experts back at the company office to look over the engineer's shoulder to guide the problem diagnosis.

Please keep in mind that Tara does not have to come up with these solutions herself. Of course, it is fine if Tara has some ideas, but it is vital that she asks the knowledgeable stakeholders and other experts for their ideas. She must *engage stakeholders* who are close to the problem and therefore have the best chances of discovering solutions. Tara sets up workshops with knowledgeable stakeholders, such as engineers. Data show that even experienced engineers have 5 per cent unused parts (see Figure 5.31). Improving the engineers' experience will not take away the 5 per cent. Tara needs additional solutions for that. RobotCo may *prevent robot problems* through

- a better robot design
- better materials for the robots (inputs for the robot production process)
- a better robot production process

The company may also *predict up-coming problems with robots*: signalling a problem ahead of time leaves engineers more time for ordering parts. So, waiting time becomes less critical. But the main cause of the problem is engineers' lack of diagnosis experience. Therefore, RobotCo may reduce the challenge of diagnosing the problems of robots for engineers. The company may simplify robot design or create robots that can provide better information to engineers, for example more sensors in robots or a more extensive information display in robots. To address the experience problem, RobotCo may hire more experienced engineers. But the company may also train the inexperienced engineers better or provide them with support:

(Continued)

- a buddy system of more experienced engineers who can help
- a support organization (such as a helpdesk with experts on hand)
- an online AI-based knowledge system for complex diagnoses

Tara structures the possible solutions in a MECE-way (see Figure 7.16).

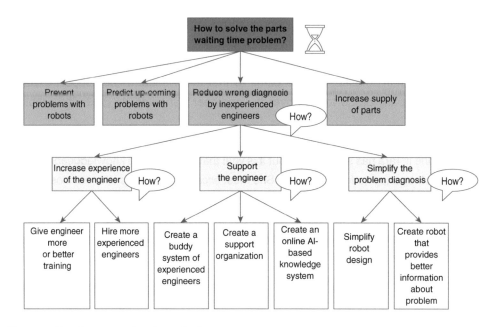

Figure 7.16   An example of a solution tree

 **Pause and Reflect**

Use your own experience of a recent project from your study or work. If stakeholders suggested a solution to you, did you ask yourself the following questions:

- Why does this stakeholder suggest this solution?
- Why would this be a good solution?
- What, if any, empirical proof is there for this solution?

DEVELOP POSSIBLE SOLUTIONS FOR COMPLEX SOLUTIONS

Solving complex problems differs from solving simple problems. Figure 7.17 shows a process for solving complex business problems:

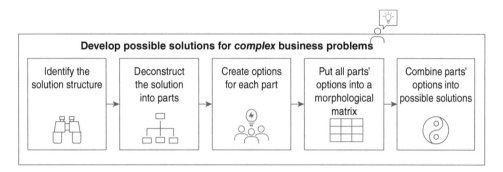

Figure 7.17   A process for developing solutions for complex business problems

Identify the solution structure

A solution for complex problems is a structure of choices. These choices are the parts of the solution. Frameworks can be structures of the solution parts. An example of a framework for a business function solution is the marketing mix. This framework presents the four parts of a marketing solution (see Figure 7.18).

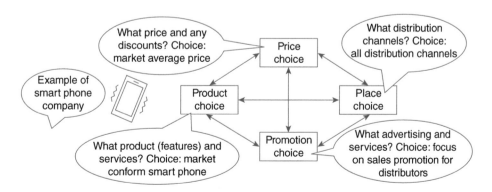

Figure 7.18   A marketing mix framework as a solution structure

Figure 7.19 provides an example of a framework for a solution for a business function problem, such as a manufacturing problem. Here we use the Nadler-Tushman Congruence Framework (Nadler & Tushman, 1980).

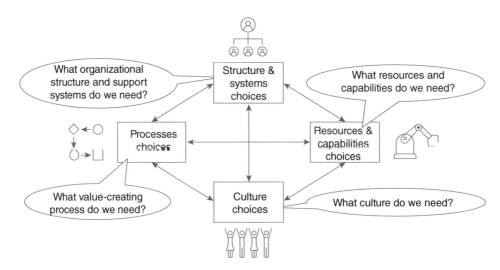

Figure 7.19   An example of a framework for a solution for a business function problem

Source: Author's interpretation of the Nadler-Tushman Congruence Framework (Nadler & Tushman, 1980)

Strategic problems are most complex as they encompass all business functions. For the solution, we need an integrated perspective on the principal's company. Strategies consist of structures or configurations of choices. There are many frameworks for strategy. Figure 7.20 provides some examples.

Topic	Framework (examples)
Competitive strategy	• Porter's generic competitive strategies (Porter, 1985) • Ansoff's growth strategies (Ansoff, 1957) • Blue Ocean Strategy (Kim & Mauborgne, 2004) • Strategy Diamond (Hambrick & Fredrickson, 2005) • Strategy Choice Cascade (Lafley & Martin, 2013) • Strategy Map (Kaplan & Norton, 2004) • D'Aveni's 7S for hyper-competition (D'Aveni, 1994) • Value Disciplines (Treacy & Wiersema, 1995) • Three Horizons framework (Baghai, Coley, & White, 1999)
International strategy	• Integration-responsiveness framework (Bartlett & Ghoshal, 1989)
Corporate strategy	• BCG Growth-Share matrix (BCG, 1968) • GE/McKinsey Nine-Box framework (McKinsey, 1970s) • Heartland matrix (Goold, Alexander, & Campbell, 1994)

Figure 7.20   Examples of strategy frameworks

Note: The GE-McKinsey Nine-Box Framework was developed in the early 1970s, but our source is Coyne (2008)

Deconstruct the solution into parts

What buttons can the principal push or what levers can she pull to solve the problem? We may have to ask the principal what types of decisions she can make to solve the problem.

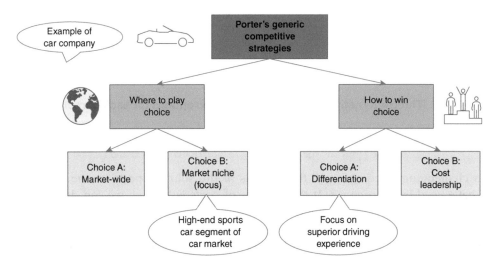

Figure 7.21   An example of the parts of a complex solution

Create options for each part

We create options, or alternative values, for the individual parts of a solution. We consider the options at the part level. We ask: What are the alternative values for each part of a solution from which we can choose? At this stage we do not look for complete solutions but for parts of a solution. What are the options for a single part? At this step we do not yet worry about the relationships between the parts.

To make the approach concrete, we use the metaphor of a dinner. We visit a restaurant and look at the menu to make a selection for a meal consisting of a starter, a main dish, and a dessert.

1. For the starter, we consider three alternative values or options: tomato soup, shrimp cocktail, and salad.
2. For the main dish, we also distinguish between three options: chicken, fish, and vegetarian.
3. For the dessert, we consider the following options: ice cream, fruit salad, and chocolate mousse.

We distinguish between three alternative approaches to create options for each part of a solution (see Figure 7.22). We already discussed these approaches in the context of problem segmentation and explanation (see respectively Figure 4.33 and Figure 4.43).

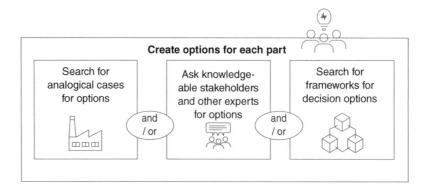

Figure 7.22   Three alternative approaches to develop options for each part of a solution

Put all parts' options in a morphological matrix

It is challenging to combine all the options of the solution parts in one go. So far, we have used tree structures. If the number of parts is limited, we can draw a decision tree. As the number of solution parts grows, the number of branches of the tree increases. If solutions consist of more than three parts, tree structures may become unmanageable. Then it is best to exchange the tree structure for another structuring technique. We can borrow an alternative modelling technique from *General Morphological Analysis* (hereafter GMA), which is the study of structural interrelationships between organisms (Ritchey, 2013). We use GMA to help us combine large numbers of solution parts. Morphological analysis is also used for creative problem-solving. This technique helps us to develop creative solutions by examining the possible combinations of solution parts. GMA can help to develop combined or composite solutions. In this chapter we focus on the process of combining parts of a solution. Simply put, morphological analysis is a sequential assessment of the combinations of solution parts that are consistent with each other. We will illustrate it later. Figure 7.23 presents a 'morphological matrix' to assess the options, or alternative values, for each part of a solution, so that each part can be compared to find the best fit. As an example, we use a marketing mix solution.

Morphological matrix		Alternative values for parts		
Solution parts	Product	Very basic product	Product conforms to the market	Highly differentiated product
	Price	Lowest price	Market average price	Premium price
	Place	Only via own stores and website	Network of exclusive distributors	All distribution channels
	Promotion	Focus on web advertisements	Focus on influencers	Focus on sales promotions for distributors

Figure 7.23   An example of a morphological matrix for structuring the options for each part of a solution

Figure 7.23 shows that for each part there are three alternative values from which to choose. The number of alternatives does not have to be three, but it should be at least two. We should not have more than seven alternatives to keep the overview clear and the combinatory process feasible. We only want to include the most effective and feasible values in the morphological matrix. We are not interested in theoretical values that will not have much effect or have low feasibility. The number of values may vary by solution part. Not all parts have to have the same number of values.

Combine parts' options into possible solutions

We use the main simplification principle in GMA, which is sequencing. Instead of the simultaneous assessment of all possible relationships between all choices, GMA sequentially compares pairs of decision options. We also use pairwise comparisons of partial solutions (or the options for a part of the solution). We create consistent and reinforcing combinations of the partial solutions. We ask ourselves: What choice for solution part B fits with and reinforces a particular option for part A?

For example, we combine the four components to create a complete and consistent marketing mix solution:

1. We begin with the product component.
2. Now we consider a price to go with the chosen product.
3. We choose a place to match with the product and the price.
4. Finally, we select a promotion to arrive at a complete solution.

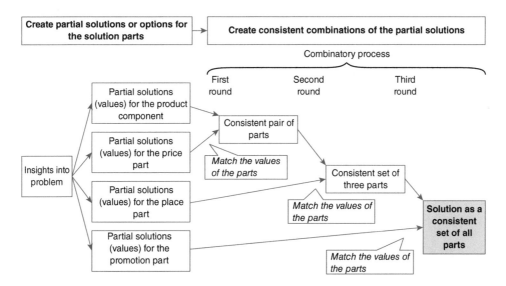

Figure 7.24   A combinatory process for creating a consistent solution

Create consistent combinations of the partial solutions

After creating the options per part, the next step is to combine these partial solutions into a complete solution, which is a consistent and reinforcing combination of all parts of a solution (see Figure 7.24). We begin the combinatory process with just two parts or a pair. Figure 7.25 visualizes the combinatory process in a morphological matrix. In the example, we select the product part and the price component. We form a pair of two matching values for these parts. Then we add to this pair a suitable value for a third part: the place. Next, we choose an appropriate value of the fourth part: the promotion. Now we have a combination of consistent values for the four parts of a solution: the four options in the circled cells.

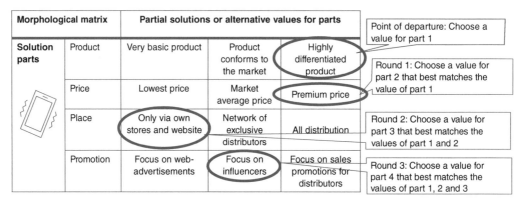

Figure 7.25 An example of a combinatory process in a morphological matrix

We may ask: In what order do we combine the partial solutions? The answer is: we select a logical sequence. If a principal's flexibility differs by part, we start with the most constrained and least flexible part. Subsequently, we add parts where the principal has more room for manoeuvre and flexibility. In the example, the product is the least flexible part.

We may also wonder: How to match the values of the parts of a solution? We provide three guidelines (see Figure 7.26).

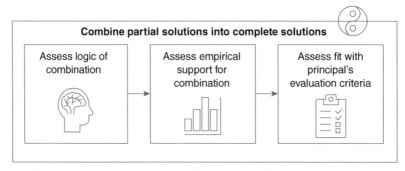

Figure 7.26 A process for combining partial solutions into complete solutions

1. *Assess the logic of the combination*. Is the combination of values logical? There should be no logical contradiction between the values. A framework may point to logical combinations. For example, take a strategy framework (see Figure 7.21). The first part is: Where to play? One value is to target price-sensitive customers. The second part is: How to win? Alternative values are differentiation and cost leadership. Cost is logical given our customer target. Differentiation typically demands a premium price. A high price logically contradicts targeting price-sensitive customers.

2. *Assess the empirical support for the combination*. Is there empirical evidence for this combination of values? Do we see this combination in practice? Is it common, rare, or have we never seen it in practice? For example, there is no company in this industry or similar industries that uses a network of exclusive distributors (see Figure 7.25). If there is no empirical evidence because we are the first, for example, then we can still choose this combination. But we do have to be extra critical when we test the solution.

3. *Assess the fit with the principal's evaluation criteria*. Does this combination meet the principal's evaluation criteria, including norms? For example, charging a high price for a basic product violates the principal's criterion that the company should offer customers value for money.

 Pause and Reflect

Use your own experience of a recent project from your study or work. Did you take a critical look at your solution?

Complex solutions meet three criteria

How to assess complex solutions? A complex solution is a composition of partial solutions. Such a solution must meet three criteria:

- *Complementarity*: The partial solutions are mutually exclusive. There must be no overlap.
- *Completeness*: The set of partial solutions is collectively exhaustive. There are no missing parts.
- *Consistency*: The partial solutions fit each other, and preferably, reinforce each other. Consistency is about the harmony of the parts with one another. All choices within a solution should perform similarly, namely contribute to solving the focal problem. Good choices are not only consistent but also reinforce each other. For example, the premium pricing reinforces the high level of product differentiation (see Figure 7.25).

Distinguish between five different forms of solution consistency

Besides the partial solutions being consistent, there are other forms of consistency that determine the quality of solutions (see Figure 7.27).

- A solution must be consistent with the problem analysis, that is, the performance gap, problem segments, and explanation.
- Furthermore, a solution must be consistent with the principal's internal organization because the solution must suit the principal.
- The solution must also fit the external environment of the principal. For example, the solution must anticipate the behaviour of competitors.
- Finally, the implementation of a good solution is feasible. The implementation must be consistent with the principal's resources and capabilities. Admittedly, there is some overlap between feasibility and these other forms of consistency, but with this classification certainly no aspect is left unexplained.

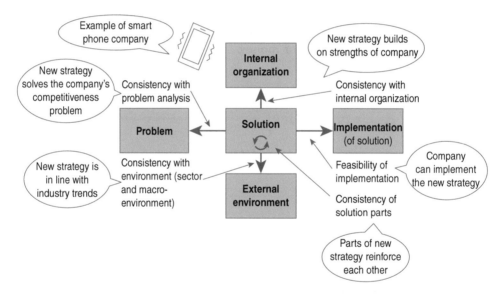

Figure 7.27 **The five different forms of consistency of a complex solution**

Running Case ConsultCo

Recall the key question: 'How should ConsultCo seize the internationalisation opportunity to increase its profit?' An internationalisation strategy in its simplest form consists of the answers to three sub-questions:

- 'Where to play?' Alternative values or options are countries A, B, or C.
- 'How to enter?' Options are

- o   to export to the foreign country
- o   to establish a wholly owned subsidiary in the foreign country
- o   to undertake a joint venture with a company in the foreign country
- • 'How to compete?' Options are
  - o   cost leadership (lowest consultancy fee)
  - o   thought leadership (most innovative advice)
  - o   client intimacy (best relationship of trust between client and consultant)

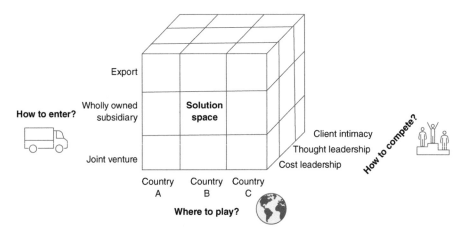

Figure 7.28   An internationalisation strategy as a combination of three choices

Figure 7.28 visualises the possible combinations of part values. It looks like a Rubik's cube.

Morphological matrix		Alternative value for parts		
Solution parts	Where to play?	Foreign country A	Foreign country B	Foreign country...
	How to enter?	Export	Wholly-owned foreign subsidiary	Joint venture
	How to complete?	Cost leadership	Thought leadership	Client intimacy

Figure 7.29   An example of a morphological matrix

Figure 7.29 presents a morphological matrix for the parts of an internationalisation strategy.

(Continued)

1.   Arpit starts with the question: "*Where* to play (abroad)?" It is a logical starting point. We cannot consider entry modes without choosing a country to enter. Arpit evaluates and prioritises the options with the MP and the other partners. They prefer country B.

2.   Arpit considers the second choice: "*How* to enter that country?" An international business framework distinguishes between three entry modes. Arpit engages the partners to assess the best entry mode. He uses the evaluation criteria from the framework. The attractiveness of exporting to country B diminishes because of the distance between the home country and the foreign country. Distance is not just geographic, but also includes other dimensions, such as cultural distance. The option of exporting is not an attractive option for country B. A joint venture with a foreign business partner suits if the foreign country's regulations demand local partners, or if the principal lacks relevant resources and capabilities for operating in the foreign country and therefore needs a local partner. Country B does not have such regulations and ConsultCo seems to have the relevant resources and capabilities. Therefore, a wholly-owned subsidiary in the form of a new office in country B seems to be the best entry mode.

3.   Arpit considers the third choice: "How to *compete* in that country?" For this choice he uses a strategy framework: value disciplines by Treacy and Wiersema (1995). The partners choose the thought leadership option.

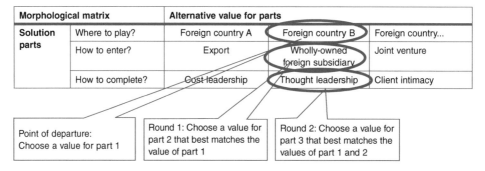

Figure 7.30   An example of a combinatory process in a morphological matrix

 **How To Do It?**

Keep your principal informed of the possible solutions. Avoid unpleasant surprises during the presentation of your recommendations.

Mini Exercise

Think of a recent market entry by a well-known company of your choice and use Internet research to create a morphological box for this case.

 Pause and Reflect

Consider how you may use these techniques for developing complete and consistent solutions in your studies, work, and personal life.

SUMMARY

We briefly outline the main takeaways of this chapter.

- Use analogical cases to develop solutions
  - do not compare apples and oranges but pay attention to differences between the principal's case and an analogical case
  - do not copy but customize the solution to the principal's specific situation
- Use creative thinking to develop solutions
  - brainstorming
  - morphological analysis
- Use analytical frameworks to develop solutions
  - use or customize an off-the-shelf framework, such as a profit tree
  - customize an off-the-shelf framework, such as a profit tree for an airline
  - create your own framework, for example a decision tree
- Understand that complex solutions are composed of partial solutions
  - criteria for complex solutions
    - choices for partial solutions are complementary: they are mutually exclusive
    - a set of partial solutions is complete: it is collectively exhaustive
    - a set of partial solutions is consistent
      - internally consistent: the partial solutions reinforce each other
      - consistent with the problem analysis: the complete solution solves the problem
      - consistent with the internal organization: the complete solution builds on strengths of company

- ☐ consistent with the external environment: the complete solution is in line with industry trends
- ☐ feasible implementation: the company can implement the complete solution
  - ○ process for developing complex solutions
    - identify the solution structure
    - deconstruct a solution into parts
    - create options for each part of a solution
    - put all parts' options into a morphological box
    - combine parts' options into complete solutions
      - ☐ assess the logic of a combination of parts' options
      - ☐ assess the empirical support for a combination
      - ☐ assess the fit of a combination with the principal's evaluation criteria

 Mini Exercise

Identify the key concepts and terms in this chapter, define them briefly and compile your own glossary.

REFERENCES AND FURTHER READING

Ansoff, H. I. (1957). Strategies for diversification. *Harvard Business Review*, *35*(5), 113–124.

Baghai, M., Coley, S., & White, D. (1999). *The Alchemy of Growth: Practical Insights for Building the Enduring Enterprise*. Reading, MA: Perseus Books.

Bartlett, C. A., & Ghoshal, S. (1989). *Managing Across Borders: The Transnational Solution*. Boston, MA: Harvard Business School Press.

Boston Consulting Group (1968). *Perspectives on Experience*. Boston, MA: The Boston Consulting Group.

Brandenburger, A. M., & Stuart Jr, H. W. (1996). Value-based business strategy. *Journal of Economics & Management Strategy*, *5*(1), 5–24.

Coleman, J. S. (1994). *Foundations of Social Theory*. Cambridge, MA: Harvard University Press.

Coyne, K. (2008). Enduring ideas: The GE-McKinsey nine-box matrix. *McKinsey Quarterly*, *4*(9), 142.

D'Aveni, R.A. (1994). *Hypercompetition: Managing the Dynamics of Strategic Maneuvering*. New York: Free Press.

Goold, M., Alexander, M., & Campbell, A. (1994). *Corporate-level Strategy: Creating Value in The Multibusiness Company*. New York: Wiley.

Hambrick, D. C., & Fredrickson, J. W. (2005). Are you sure you have a strategy? *Academy of Management Perspectives*, *19*(4), 51–62.

Kaplan, R. S., Kaplan, R. E., & Norton, D. P. (2004). *Strategy Maps: Converting Intangible Assets into Tangible Outcomes*. Boston, MA: Harvard Business Press.

Kim, W. C., Mauborgne, R. (2004). *Blue Ocean Strategy: How to Create Uncontested Market Space and Make the Competition Irrelevant*. Boston, MA: Harvard Business School Press.

Lafley, A. G., & Martin, R. (2013). *Playing to Win: How Strategy Really Works*. Boston, MA: Harvard Business Press.

Liedtka, J., & Ogilvie, T. (2011). *Designing for Growth: A Design Thinking Tool Kit for Managers*. New York: Columbia University Press.

Minto, B. (1987). *The Pyramid Principle: Logic in Writing and Thinking*. London: Pearson.

Nadler, D. A., & Tushman, M. L. (1980). A model for diagnosing organizational behavior. *Organizational Dynamics, 9*(2), 35–51.

Porter, M. E. (1985). *Competitive Advantage: Creating and Sustaining Superior Performance*. New York: Free Press.

Ritchey, T. (2013). *General morphological analysis. A general method for non-quantified modelling*. Revised paper. Swedish Morphological Society. Retrieved on April 14, 2021, from www.swemorph.com/ma.html

Treacy, M., & Wiersema, F. (1995). *The Discipline of Market Leaders: Choose Your Customers, Narrow Your Focus, Dominate Your Market*. Reading, MA: Addison-Wesley.

Evaluate Solutions and Make Decisions under Uncertainty

INTRODUCTION

Here we identify a couple of pitfalls regarding solution development.

- Some people recommend untested solutions. To serve the principal as quickly as possible, these people skip the test.
- Some people advise solutions that are unacceptable to some influential stakeholders. These people are so focused on the principal's needs that they overlook the interests of other key stakeholders.
- Some people offer solutions that are not feasible. Their recommendations look good on the PowerPoint slides but when the principal tries to implement the recommendations, she discovers implementation is not feasible.

This chapter outlines how structured problem-solving (see Figure 8.1) avoids such pitfalls.

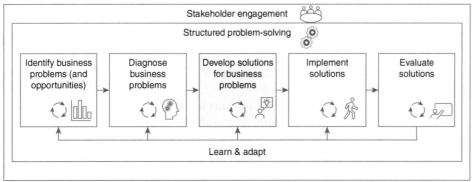

Figure 8.1 Developing solutions is the third step of structured problem-solving

Developing and testing a solution hypothesis is part of the fourth step of the Sequential Analysis Method (see Figure 8.2).

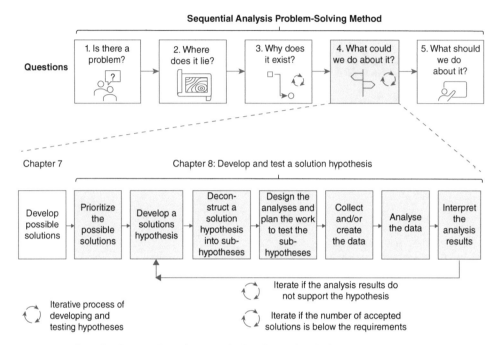

Figure 8.2   **Developing and testing a solution hypothesis is part of the fourth step of the Sequential Analysis Method**

We deconstruct the hypothesis development and testing process into a sequence of steps. This iterative process provides us with opportunities for learning and improvement (see the loop in Figure 8.2). We iterate hypothesis development and testing for two reasons:

- We reject a solution hypothesis. The analysis results do not support the hypothesis. Therefore, we need to develop and test an alternative hypothesis. We continue until we can accept a hypothesis.
- We accept a solution hypothesis, but we need other solutions as well. We do not want to stop after the first solution.
  - Our first solution meets the requirements, but we want to see if there are better solutions available.
  - Principals may demand multiple options to choose from (the minimum number to be determined in consultation with the principal).
  - Principals may ask: "What alternative options have you considered?"
  - Principals may criticize us: "Why did not you consider alternative option X?"

This chapter will also address the *final* question of the Sequential Analysis Method: What *should* we do about the problem? (See Figure 8.3.)

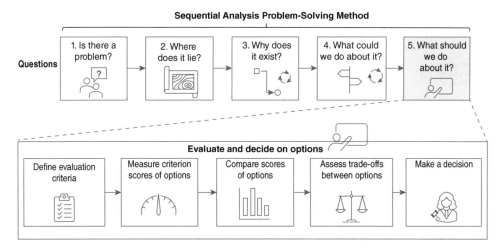

Figure 8.3   Evaluating and deciding on options are the fifth step of the Sequential Analysis Method

The chapter is structured as follows (see Figure 8.4). The first four items do not consider uncertainty about the future. In the final two items, we account for uncertainty.

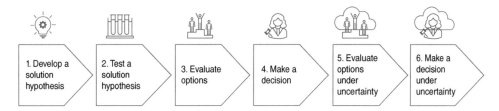

Figure 8.4   Chapter structure

MAIN LEARNING OBJECTIVES

After studying this chapter, you should be able to:

- evaluate and prioritise the possible solutions
- develop a solution hypothesis
- test a solution hypothesis
- assess the level of uncertainty about the future
- make a business case for a solution
- decide under uncertainty

DEVELOP A SOLUTION HYPOTHESIS

Prioritise a set of possible solutions

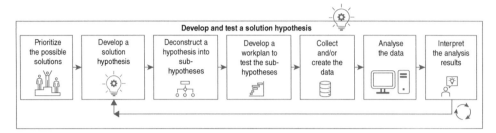

Figure 8.5   A process for developing and testing a solution hypothesis

We may develop *several* possible solutions to the principal's problems (see Chapter 7). We always continue after the first solution and look for alternatives. The first solution does not have to be the best. When we only present a single solution, critical principals will ask which alternative options we have considered. If we must then admit that we did not look beyond our first solution, we are not making a good impression on the principal.

Moreover, some principals have the urge to choose from a range of options. Options give these principals a feeling that they are in charge. Then we must develop several solutions to meet the principal's choice needs.

Create confidence in a solution

The *possible* solutions we have developed are just *ideas*, and these solutions have yet to be proven successful. The saying is: The real proof of the pudding is in the eating. Therefore, solution implementation is the real test of solutions. But before the principal decides to implement a solution, he wants to have confidence in the effectiveness and feasibility of the solution. Therefore, we test the possible solutions before we present our recommendation to the principal.

Distinguish between complementary and alternative solutions

We distinguish between complementary and alternative solutions.

- *Complementary* solutions A and B allow for a combination of A and B. Complementary solutions can be combined. In the RobotCo case, we may solve the waiting time problem by improving the robot design *and* hiring experienced engineers to replace inexperienced ones.
- *Alternative* solutions are substitutes, and we must choose between them: A or C. We cannot combine alternative solutions. To address RobotCo's problem, we may train inexperienced engineers in our workforce *or* hire experienced engineers to replace inexperienced ones.

───────── **Running Case ConsultCo** ─────────

ConsultCo may see opportunities in both countries A and B. The company can enter both countries simultaneously. A and B are so-called *complementary* solutions. But if any resource constraints prevent ConsultCo from entering both countries simultaneously, ConsultCo must decide on the order: Which country comes first?

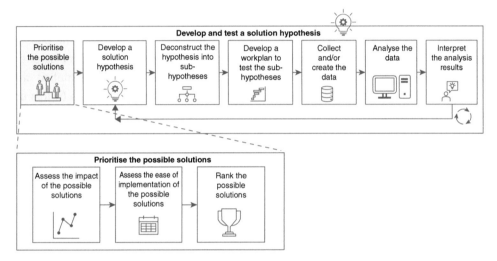

Figure 8.6　A process for prioritizing the possible solutions

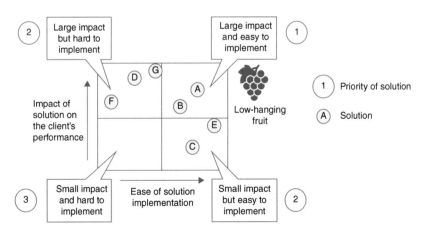

Figure 8.7　An example of a solution evaluation

Testing all possible solutions generally takes too much time and effort. Therefore, we will most times be unable to test all solutions. Then we assess and rank all possible solutions and prioritise the top-ranked solutions. To evaluate, we will use the principal's evaluation criteria. Figure 8.7 shows an example of a simple assessment using two criteria: the performance impact of a possible solution and the ease of implementation.

Running Case RobotCo

Recall the key question: "How should RobotCo respond to the problem of the late delivery of parts to increase its profit by 15 million euro in one year?" Tara evaluates the possible answers with two criteria: the solution's impact on the profit and the ease of implementing this solution (see Figure 8.8). RobotCo sets a solution constraint: an implementation must occur in one year. Therefore, Tara distinguishes between short-term solutions (within one year) and longer-term solutions.

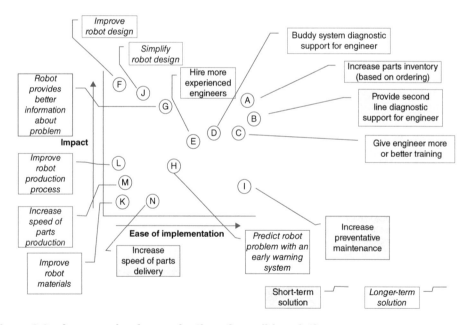

Figure 8.8   An example of an evaluation of possible solutions

Tara prioritises the following possible solution: Increase the inventory (based on parts ordering) as the engineers order more parts than they use. Therefore, RobotCo should no longer base the stock on parts usage (for robot maintenance and repair) but on parts ordering by engineers. The inventory should account for wrong ordering. The solution hypothesis is: *An increase in parts inventory based on ordering (instead of usage) enables RobotCo to reduce the waiting time for parts by X per cent in one year to achieve the 15 million euro profit objective. X is a to be specified number.*

Pause and Reflect

Use your own experience of a recent project from your study or work. After you had developed a solution, did you ask yourself: Why may this solution *not* work? Did you also ask this question to knowledgeable stakeholders and other experts who oppose this solution?

Develop a solution hypothesis

We select the prioritised solution as a solution hypothesis (see Figure 8.9).

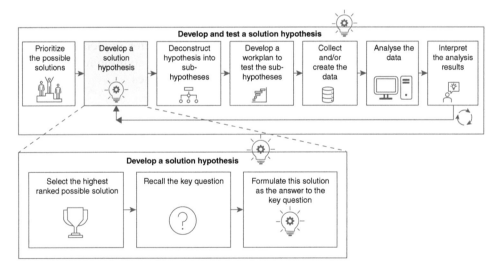

Figure 8.9   A process for developing a solution hypothesis

The principal will typically use multiple criteria. If one possible solution wins on all criteria, we call it a 'natural winner'. This winner is the candidate for the (initial) solution hypothesis. The assessment may produce a mixed picture. For example, option A wins on the criterion 'impact', but option B wins on the criterion 'ease of implementation'. How do we address such a trade-off between criterion outcomes? We may ask the principal for the weights of the criteria. We must identify these weights before an assessment to avoid the appearance of manipulation. The criteria and their weights should be in the problem statement. We prioritise the option with the highest sum of the weighted scores for all criteria.

> The weighted sum of option = weight of 'impact' × impact score + weight of 'ease' × ease score
>
> Example: weighted sum of option A = 0.4 × 5 + 0.6 × 2 = 3.2

The chosen solution is the subject of our initial solution hypothesis. A generic solution hypothesis looks like this:

> *Hypothesis: This solution will close the principal's performance gap.*

TEST A SOLUTION HYPOTHESIS

Deconstruct a solution hypothesis into sub-hypotheses

The solution hypothesis differs from the problem hypothesis. A problem hypothesis *explains* a problem. Recall that our problem hypothesis is a possible answer to the question: Why does the problem exist? In contrast, the solution hypothesis *prescribes* a solution and predicts that this recommendation will close the principal's performance gap. Solutions and their predicted performance improvements are not facts that we can verify before solution implementation. Only after implementation can we measure any performance impact. Therefore, prescriptive solution hypotheses are more challenging to test than explanatory problem hypotheses.

Think critically

You may wonder: *How* do we test prescriptive solution hypotheses? Perhaps the principal is putting pressure on us to find proof for his desired solution. Focusing only on data that confirms a hypothesis while ignoring data that does not support the hypothesis is a *confirmation bias*.

For an objective test, we deconstruct a solution hypothesis into *sub-hypotheses or assumptions* (see Figure 8.10). We ask: *What do we need to know or believe in to accept this solution?* Or, formulated differently: What are the premises of the hypothesized solution? Instead of testing the hypothesis, we test the underlying assumptions. Identifying the underlying assumptions is sometimes tricky. There may be hidden beliefs, so people are unaware of them. For example, in a company, there is an unspoken assumption that all customers are price sensitive. Identifying assumptions requires critical thinking.

We may identify the sub-hypotheses or assumptions by asking the people who suggested the solution and those who are in favour of this solution. We ask specifically what the conditions are for the success of the solution. For example, we ask: What should we assume about customers, competitors, the principal's company, and

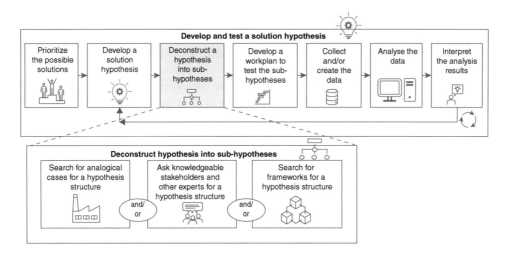

Figure 8.10 A process for deconstructing a solution hypothesis into sub-hypotheses

other stakeholders? But we must also invite opponents or critics of a solution. They can tell us why the solution will *not* work. Their assumptions are also relevant.

Moreover, we may also conduct a 'pre-mortem analysis,' which is a thought experiment. We imagine that the solution has failed. Subsequently, we work backwards to determine what potentially could cause the failure. We can then investigate the factors that could lead to possible failure.

Develop a workplan to test the sub-hypotheses

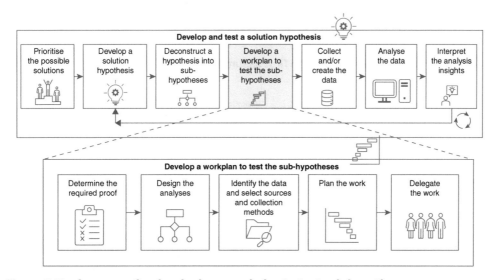

Figure 8.11 A process for developing a workplan to test sub-hypotheses

As we test the sub-hypotheses or assumptions, we ask for each premise: What is the required proof for the principal and other essential stakeholders to accept this assumption? Then we design for each assumption the analysis that *can* provide the desired proof. The analysis design points to the required data. We ask: What data should we analyse? Subsequently, we identify the data sources. Finally, we select the most appropriate way to collect the data. Just as with a problem hypothesis, we put everything for a test together in a workplan.

Running Case RobotCo

Tara identifies the assumptions and sub-assumptions of the solution hypothesis by discussing the solution with the principal and other knowledgeable stakeholders. Then she draws a logical structure (see Figure 8.12). In practice, the profit objective belongs in the hypothesis, but to keep the example manageable, we do not include the profit objective. We use a simplified hypothesis: *An increase of parts inventory based on ordering (instead of usage) enables RobotCo to reduce the waiting time for parts by X per cent in one year.*

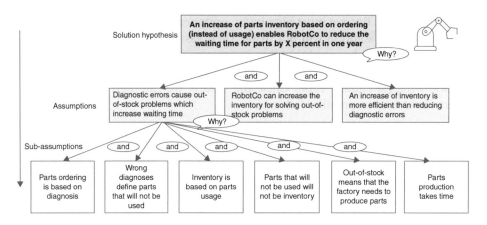

Figure 8.12   A deconstruction of the first assumption

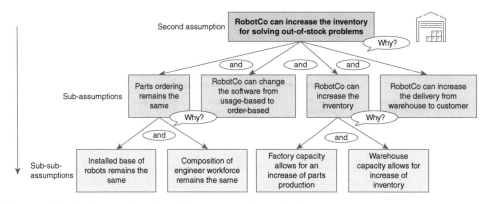

Figure 8.13   A deconstruction of the second assumption

After deconstructing the hypothesis into assumptions, Tara creates a workplan for testing these assumptions. Figure 8.14 shows the workplan for testing the second assumption.

Sub-assumption	Analysis design	Data	Data source	Data collection method
Installed base of robots remains the same	Deconstruction analysis of installed base: predict the components of the base: • New customers • Loss of customers • Loyal customer	Robot investment and divestiture plans of customers	• Customers • RobotCo sales people	• Data requests • Interviews
Composition of engineer workforce remains the same	Deconstruction analysis of workforce: • New hires • Leavers	• Hiring plans • Prediction of leavers	RobotCo HR Department	• Data requests • Interviews
RobotCo can change the software from usage-based to order-based	Comparison analysis of analogical software changes	Analogical software changes at: • RobotCo • Other companies	RobotCo IT department	Data requests
Factory capacity allows for an increase of parts production	Comparison analysis of factory spare capacity and required production increase	• Factory spare capacity • Production increase	RobotCo factory	Data requests
Warehouse capacity allows for increase of inventory	Comparison analysis of warehouse spare capacity and required inventory increase	• Warehouse spare capacity • Inventory increase	RobotCo warehouse	Data requests
RobotCo can increase the delivery from warehouse to customer	Comparison analysis of delivery spare capacity and required delivery increase	• Delivery spare capacity • Delivery increase	RobotCo delivery department	Data requests

Figure 8.14 A workplan for testing the second assumption

 Mini Exercise

Think of a recent product introduction by a well-known company of your choice and treat it as a solution hypothesis. Use Internet research to deconstruct that hypothesis into sub-hypotheses (use a maximum of two levels of sub-hypotheses).

Pause and Reflect

Use your own experience of a recent project from your study or work. Did the principal know what you were doing? Did you always keep the principal in the loop?

Collect and create data for testing solution hypotheses

It is time to implement the workplan. We must collect and create the data for the hypothesis test (see Figure 8.15). The process is the same as for the problem hypothesis (see Figure 5.21), so we refer to the previous description.

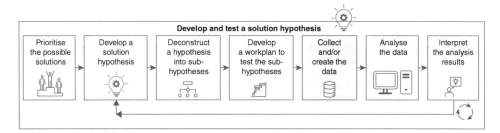

Figure 8.15   Collecting and creating the data is the fifth step in the process of developing and testing a solution hypothesis

The workplan specifies what data to collect (and how) and what data to create (and how). Figure 8.16 presents a process for deciding on (forms of) data collection and data creation. This process is also like that for the problem hypothesis (see Figure 5.23).

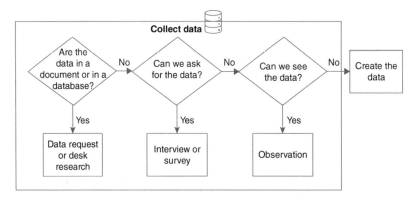

Figure 8.16   A process for deciding on data collection and data creation

Figure 8.17 presents three different approaches to creating data. We already discussed this process for the problem hypothesis (see Figure 5.27).

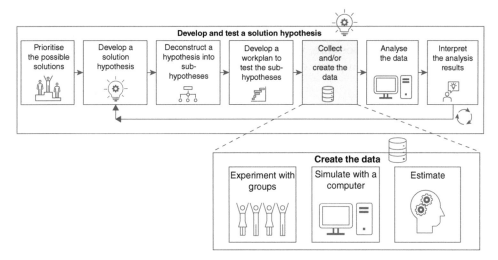

Figure 8.17 Three different approaches for creating data

Create the data

In contrast to *problem* hypotheses, much of the data for testing *solution* hypotheses may not be available for collection. Solutions are promises for performance improvement in the future. If we base the solution on an analogical case, we may use proof from that case to test the hypothesis. In other situations (not based on analogical solutions), we must wait until solution implementation before collecting proof about any performance improvement. After implementation, we expect solutions to improve the principal's performance. But there are no facts about the future available. We cannot collect all the data we need to test the assumptions of our solution hypothesis. Therefore, we must resort to *creating* data.

Experiment

We may use experimentation, computer simulation, and estimation to create the necessary data (see Chapter 5). With our help, principals can implement several solutions simultaneously as field experiments or pilots on a small scale. In this way, principals try these solutions in practice. Then we monitor the results of each small-scale solution implementation. If the experiments with specific solutions are successful, principals will gain confidence and increase the scale of implementation. But in the case of failures, principals end the experiments with these solutions.

Make assumptions

When testing solution hypotheses, we may make estimates about unknown future developments. To make these estimates we need to make assumptions about these future developments. It may seem weird that we make assumption-based estimates to test the sub-hypotheses, which are assumptions of a solution hypothesis. If estimates are inevitable, we must ensure that the assumptions underlying an estimate are logical, realistic, and as concrete as possible. It is valuable to involve knowledgeable stakeholders and other experts in making estimates. Ideally, we let them create the estimates. If that is not possible, we ask them to review the estimates that we made. We use any criticism to improve our estimates.

Analyse the data

Once we have collected and created the data, we can analyse the data. We use the workplan analysis design to test the sub-hypotheses. After the analysis, we check the results (see Figure 8.18). This process is also like that for the problem hypothesis (see Figure 5.28).

Check the output

We can do a so-called 'sanity check'. We ask: Can this analysis result be true? For example, we analysed the mobile phone market in country X, and the result was 50 million mobile phones. We ask ourselves: Can this be true? As a check, we calculate this country's average number of phones per habitant. A population of 5 million inhabitants implies that each habitant would own on average 10 telephones!

Interpret the analysis results

The project managers interpret the data, the analysis, and the analysis results created by the team members (see Figure 8.19). We already discussed this process for the problem hypothesis (see Figure 5.29).

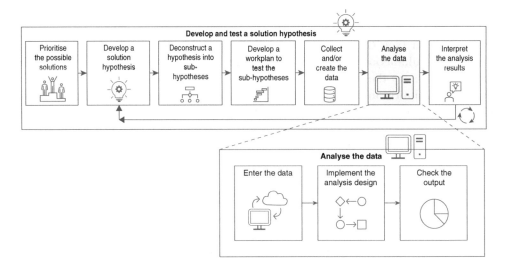

Figure 8.18   A process for analysing the data

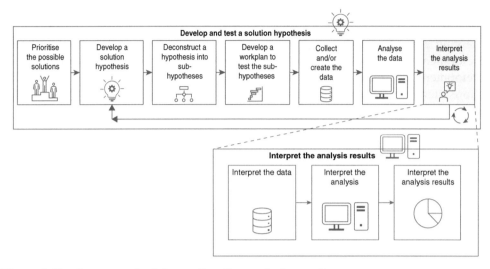

Figure 8.19   A process for interpreting the analysis results

Before the hypothesis test, managers have defined the proofs that the principals require in order to accept the sub-hypotheses. After the test, managers compare the analysis results to the required proofs. Do the analysis results meet or exceed the needed proof?

- If the analysis results meet or exceed the needed proof, the managers accept the sub-hypothesis or assumption. Because the results meet or exceed the principal's requirements, the principal will also accept the assumption. Accepting *all* assumptions of a solution hypothesis means accepting that hypothesis, and this hypothesis becomes an accepted solution option for the principal.
- If the analysis results do not match the required proof, managers reject the sub-hypothesis. *One* single rejected sub-hypothesis or assumption is enough to reject a solution hypothesis. The managers do not take a rejection as a personal failure, because, as a result of the rejection, the managers know that this hypothesized solution is not correct. This is a valuable insight if the principal or stakeholders thought that the hypothesized solution was correct.
  - In the case of a hypothesis rejection, we need to iterate the process of hypothesis development and testing.
  - In some cases, we can improve the rejected solution hypotheses. We may learn from rejections how to enhance these solutions. These improved solutions can pass the hypothesis test.

Since solutions are about the future and data about the future do not exist, the proofs of solution hypotheses will often rely partly or wholly on *created* data. As a result, these proofs are uncertain compared to the empirical evidence of collected data. The decision to accept or reject a solution hypothesis is therefore not entirely suitable for rational decision-making based on empirical evidence. In addition, we will have to use our intuition to make that decision.

Develop multiple options

Accepting a single solution hypothesis does not mean we are done with solution development. We always strive for multiple solutions and continue with hypothesis development and testing until we have accepted a minimum number of solution options. Iterations of hypothesis development and testing not only result from rejections of hypotheses, but also arise from the requirement of multiple solutions.

Pause and Reflect

Use your own experience of a recent project from your study or work. Would you have chosen the recommended solution if you were the principal?

EVALUATE AND DECIDE ON THE OPTIONS

We have developed and accepted several alternative solution options. These are our answers to the fourth step of the Sequential Analysis Problem-Solving process: What *could* we do about the problem? Now we are ready for the fifth process step: What *should* we do about the problem? We develop multiple solutions, but the principal can implement only *one* solution. Therefore, we evaluate all solution options (recall that these are all accepted solution hypotheses) with the principal's evaluation criteria and select the best option as our recommendation or advice (see Figure 8.20).

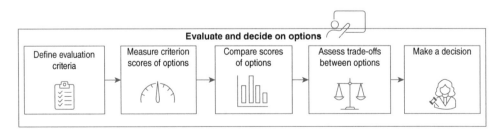

Figure 8.20   A process for evaluating and deciding on options

Define the evaluation criteria

At the beginning of the project, we define the evaluation criteria (see Figure 8.21). We include the principal's criteria, but we also consider the criteria of other powerful stakeholders. These criteria will be in the problem statement (Chapter 2). We should keep these criteria after we have developed solutions. If we were to change the criteria, then some stakeholders may accuse us of manipulation and opportunism.

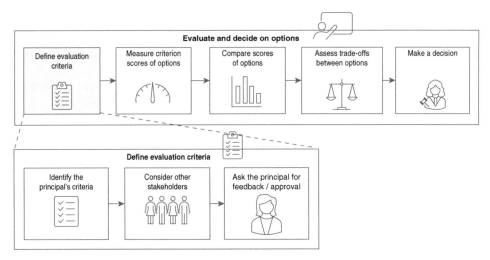

Figure 8.21 A process for defining evaluation criteria

Benefits and costs

An essential evaluation criterion is a solution's contribution to the principal's performance. Closing the principal's performance gap in time is a requirement. But some options may perform better than others. Therefore, we must assess our solutions' expected business impact or performance improvement. We use the criteria to predict the benefits and costs of the solutions (see Figure 8.22).

Criteria	Solution benefits	Solution costs
Profit	Revenue growth	Revenue decline
	Cost reduction	Cost increase
Society	Safety of customers and employees	Safety incidents
	Health of customers and employees	Health issues
	Job satisfaction of employees	Job dissatisfaction
	Fair wages for employees	Unfair wages
	Job creation and employment	Job loss and unemployment
	Tax revenue for the government	Costs for the government
The planet	Pollution reduction or elimination	Pollution increase
	Resource usage reduction	Resource usage increase

Figure 8.22 Examples of benefits and costs of a solution

Measure the criterion scores of the options

We collect data to measure how each option scores on each criterion. If we cannot collect data, then we create data (see Figure 8.23).

There are various analyses for the profit impact of an option. We provide three examples:

- The *return on investment* equals the extra profit due to the solution divided by the capital investment required for the solution.
- The *earn back period* equals the time to earn back the investment required for the solution. Time equals investment divided by annual earnings.
- A *break-even analysis* is about the minimum production volume to cover the solution's fixed costs. To calculate the break-even volume, we divide the fixed costs by the contribution margin per unit, which is the unit selling price minus the unit variable cost.

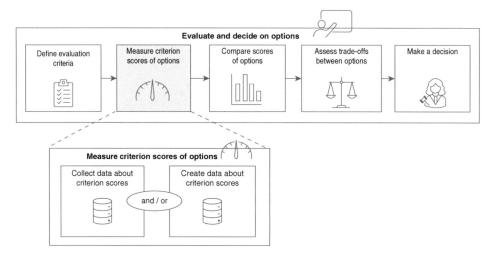

Figure 8.23   A process for measuring criterion scores of options

 **How To Do It?**

Always calculate the business impact of your solution *yourself*. Do not leave the calculation to the principal because you lose control. The principal may be unable to calculate the impact or may want to avoid doing it (for example, it is not a priority for them).

We may use a simple method, the so-called 'calculation on a napkin' or the 'calculation on the back of an envelope'. It is a quick and informal calculation with rounded numbers to develop a rough estimate or a ballpark figure.

Compare the scores of the options

We compare the options' scores on the evaluation criteria (see Figure 8.24). We have a natural winner if one option wins on all criteria. This winner is undeniably the best solution, and our recommendation is clear.

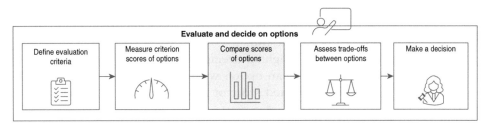

Figure 8.24 Comparing scores of options is the third step in the process of evaluating and deciding on options

Assess the trade-offs between the options

The selection of the best option gets trickier when there is no natural winner among the options. One option has the highest score on one criterion, and the other option has the highest score on another measure. In such cases, we need to assess the trade-offs between the options (see Figure 8.25).

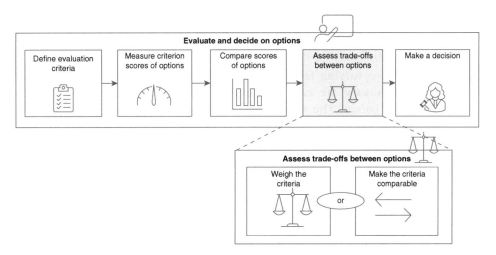

Figure 8.25 Assessing trade-offs between options is the fourth step in the process of evaluating and deciding on options

We can assess trade-offs between options in two ways:

- *Weigh the criteria*. We do not look at the absolute scores per criterion but calculate a weighted average for all criteria. If the principal does not give an explicit weighting to the criteria, we can propose a weighting.

  - The weights enable us to make conditional recommendations. 'If profit improvement is most important to you, then option X is best. However, if you think the implementation efforts are the most important criterion, then option Y would be better for you.'
  - We can also calculate a weighted average for the options. We multiply for each criterion the score of an option with that criterion's weight and then calculate the average weighted score of this option for all criteria.

- *Make the criteria comparable*.

  - The principal will have financial and non-financial criteria. To make the criteria comparable, we *determine the financial equivalents of non-financial criteria*. For example, one option ranks higher on profit, while another ranks higher on carbon emission reduction. We determine the financial equivalent of emission reduction. We may use a carbon credit price for carbon emission reduction as there is a market for credits. Another example of a non-financial criterion is waste. We may calculate the cost of the waste, such as the cost of the wasted material and the cost of cleaning up the trash. We may also ask knowledgeable stakeholders and experts to assess the financial equivalent of non-financial criteria. If we have expressed all the criteria in financial terms, then we can compare them. But we admit that in some cases, it is difficult or unethical to express impact in financial terms.

    An example is the reduction of the safety of employees because of an option. We can calculate the cost of medical treatment, and we may ask knowledgeable stakeholders what proper financial compensation for victims of an option's health impact would be. Still, it is unethical to sacrifice stakeholder health for company profit.

  - We may have varying feasibility per option, and the odds or likelihood of success may vary. We can make these options comparable by *calculating expectancy values*. The expectancy value is the impact of an option multiplied by the likelihood of that impact. For example, an option has an 80 per cent chance of a profit of 10 million euros and a 20 per cent chance of a profit of 5 million. The expected value of this option is 9 million ($0.8 \times 10 + 0.2 \times 5 = 9$).

Running Case RobotCo

Tara must assess how the options rank per evaluation criterion. She uses her judgment and involves the principal and relevant stakeholders. Then Tara selects the option to increase the parts inventory by basing it on parts ordering (instead of parts usage). She makes a 'back-of-the-envelope calculation' to assess the performance improvement (see Figure 8.26).

Decrease of annual revenue due to late parts = % late parts × % customer loss due to late parts × total number of customers × average annual revenue per customer

Because customers remain customers for five years on average (customer lifetime), RobotCo misses out on annual profits five times. Avoiding this loss is the yield of the option to increase the inventory.

Late parts	40%
Customer loss due to late parts	25%
Total number of customers	75
Average annual revenue per customer (€ m)	4
Annual revenue decrease due to late parts (€ m)	30
Profit margin	50%
Annual profit decrease due to late parts (€ m)	15
Average customer lifetime (years)	5
Lifetime profit decrease due to late parts (€ m)	75

Figure 8.26   An example of a back-of-the-envelope calculation of the revenue impact of an option

Tara also considers the costs of increasing the inventory (see Figure 8.27). Forty per cent of the parts are not in the warehouse inventory. The stock is therefore 60 per cent of the orders. The stock must increase by 67 per cent to have 100 per cent of the orders in the warehouse. For this quick analysis, Tara makes the simplifying assumption that warehouse costs increase proportionally with the inventory. In 40 per cent of the orders where parts are not in stock, RobotCo must deliver the missing parts in a second shipment. If all orders are in the inventory, the 40 per cent additional shipments are no longer necessary. The number of shipments can decrease by 29 per cent (from 140 to 100). For this quick analysis, Tara makes the simplifying assumption that shipping costs decrease proportionally with the number of shipments. The decrease in shipment costs is a benefit of the option to increase the inventory.

Inventory increase	67%	formula $0.4/(1-0.4)$
Warehouse costs (€ m)	8	formula 0.67×8
Increase of warehouse costs (€ m)	5.33	
Shipping decrease	29%	formula $0.4/(1+0.4)$
Order shipping costs (€ m)	7	
Decrease of shipping costs (€ m)	2	formula 0.29×7

Figure 8.27   An example of a back-of-the-envelope calculation of the cost impact of an option

Figure 8.28 shows an example of an options evaluation. Tara makes a high-level analysis of the implementation of options to assess the ease of implementation. What will it take to implement a solution? How much time and effort does the implementation require? The evaluation criterion 'risk' is about what may go wrong during implementation and the likelihood that things go wrong. 'Employee buy-in' points to whether involved employees will accept and commit to a specific option. Buy-in assumes that this option aligns with the employees' interests and values.

		Evaluaton criteria					
		Financial performance improvement	Environmental performance	Ease of implementation	Risk	Employee buy-in	**Overall**
	Weight of criterion	0.4	0.2	0.2	0.1	0.1	1
Solution options	A: increase inventory	9	7	8	8	8	6.8
	B: second line support	8	9	9	7	7	6.4
	C: increase or improve training	7	9	7	7	6	5.5

Figure 8.28   An example of an options evaluation

Pause and Reflect

Use your own experience of a recent project from your study or work. After you had developed a solution, did you ask yourself: What will relevant stakeholders think of it?

Running Case RobotCo

Tara makes a prognosis of the benefits and costs of increasing the inventory. The benefits of avoiding customer loss increase during the first five years and remain the same afterwards. The benefits stabilise after five years because customers stay with RobotCo for an average of five years. After five years, customers switch suppliers even if RobotCo does not have late parts. Figure 8.29 shows Tara's spreadsheet model.

	Year 1	Year 2	Year 3	Year 4	Year 5
Avoidance of annual profit decrease due to late parts[1]	15	30	45	60	75
Decrease of shipping costs	2	2	2	2	2
Increase of warehouse costs	5.33	5.33	5.33	5.33	5.33
Net benefits[2]	11.67	26.67	41.67	56.67	71.67

Figure 8.29   An example of a spreadsheet model

Notes: Numbers are in millions of euros. 1: accumulation of annual customer loss avoidance; 2: net benefits = profit decrease avoidance + shipping costs decrease - warehouse costs increase

Make a decision

We try to convince the principal that she should accept the recommendation. The next chapter will elaborate on how to convince the principal and other relevant stakeholders. Please note that *we* do not decide on a solution. It is the principal who decides on the solution. We *support* principals in their decision-making by providing the principal with information about the options. Figure 8.30 shows the decision-making process for a principal.

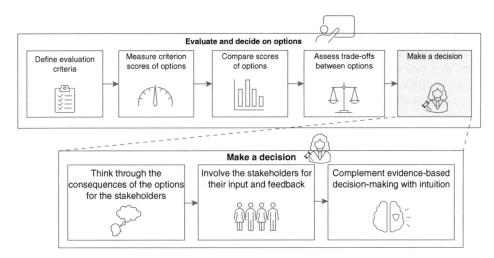

Figure 8.30   A process for decision-making

Think through the consequences for the stakeholders

The principal must think through any consequences of the options for relevant stakeholders. This is not the first time that we think about stakeholders. The entire problem-solving process is embedded in stakeholder engagement. We engage stakeholders in the problem analysis. When determining the criteria and constraints for the solution, we take stakeholders into account. We also involve stakeholders in the development of solutions. Finally, we consider the stakeholders when choosing between alternative solutions.

It is ethical to think through the consequences for stakeholders because we do not want to choose solutions that negatively affect specific stakeholders, society, or the planet. Considering the stakeholders is also in our self-interest. On the one hand, we need some stakeholders to accept, approve, and support our solution. On the other hand, we want to avoid negative responses by stakeholders who disapprove of our solution.

Involve the stakeholders

In many cases, the decision about a solution depends on more than just the principal. The principal may need the approval of specific stakeholders. For example, a general manager may need permission from the supervisory board. Even if the principal does not require the consent of other stakeholders, she may still be interested in the stakeholders' acceptance of the solution. The principal may involve stakeholders who have the right of consent in the evaluation and decision-making. There are also stakeholders without the right of consent who are critical for solution implementation. Taking these stakeholders into account is a critical success factor for a successful implementation.

Complement evidence-based decision-making with intuition

We previously discussed the need to combine evidence-based decision-making with intuitive decision-making in the case of uncertainty about a proof that is based wholly or partly on created data. Both the trade-offs between the options and the principal's dependence on some stakeholders with different objectives, values, and views increase the complexity of decision-making about the options. Since there are limits to the complexity that rational, evidence-based decision-making can handle, we should certainly *also* use intuitive decision-making when deciding between the options if we face: (a) trade-offs between options; or (b) dependencies on stakeholders. Then, the decision about the solution requires a judgment call. The principal cannot be certain about the chosen option before the implementation, but she must have enough confidence in this solution to implement it. This confidence in its turn can create a self-fulfilling prophecy. If the principal has faith in a specific solution, she will do her best to make the implementation of that solution a success. But if she has doubts, she will bet less on this solution, and she will give up sooner in the face of adversity. The same applies to all stakeholders whose support is required for the implementation. They also need confidence in the solution.

 Pause and Reflect

Use your own experience of a recent project from your study or work. After developing the solution, did you ask yourself whether all relevant stakeholders would accept this solution?

EVALUATE AND DECIDE ON OPTIONS UNDER UNCERTAINTY ABOUT THE FUTURE

We have yet to assess the uncertainty *about the future*. What do we do if the future is uncertain? Here we discuss a process for evaluating and deciding on options *under uncertainty* (see Figure 8.31).

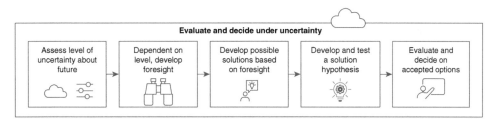

Figure 8.31   A process for evaluating and deciding on options under uncertainty

Assess the level of uncertainty about the future

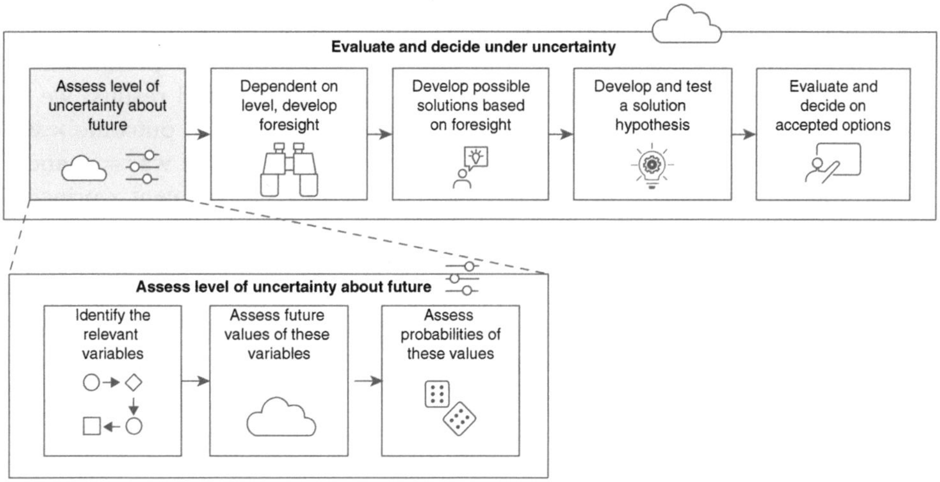

Figure 8.32   Assessing the level of uncertainty about the future is the first step in the process of evaluating and deciding under uncertainty

Four levels of uncertainty about the future

A solution always relates to the future. At present, a solution is just a proposal. The principal must accept the solution first. Then the principal must implement the solution. Implementation is in the future. Therefore, we must have a vision of the future, but we do not have a crystal ball. The difficulty of predicting the future is associated with uncertainty that may vary by time and place. We distinguish between four levels of uncertainty about the future (see Figure 8.33).

Level of uncertainty about the future	1	2	3	4
Characteristics of the future	Future is like the past	A set of alternative futures with known probabilities	Range of plausible futures (known unknowns)	Unknown unknowns
Example of tools to deal with uncertainty	Extrapolation	Game theory	Scenario planning	Scanning and experimenting

Figure 8.33   Four levels of uncertainty about the future

Source: Author's interpretation of Courtney, Kirkland, & Viguerie (1997)

1. *Level 1*: We can extrapolate past *trends* of relevant variables because the future will be like the present or the past. These variables can influence our solution's performance. An example is market growth. We can extend a range of values of relevant variables by inferring unknown future values from trends in the known values of the past. For example, we may extrapolate demographic trends.

2. *Level 2*: We cannot extrapolate trends because the future value of a variable will differ from the present or the past. For example, the behaviour of the principal's main competitor is unknown. We do not know what the future outcome will be, but we can predict alternative future developments. For example, we may predict whether the principal's competitor starts a price war or not (which provides two alternative future outcomes). We can also assess the odds or probabilities of alternative outcomes. Therefore, we can quantify the expected results. We may assess *expectancy values*. Expectancy value = probability of an outcome × value of that outcome. For example, the expectancy value of a price war = chance of price war × outcome of a price war. Expectancy value = 20 per cent × principal's loss of 5 million euro = 1 million euro loss.

3. *Level 3*: The number of unknowns (variables with unknown future values) is too large for a small set of alternative futures. Moreover, we cannot assess the odds or probabilities of alternatives. But we can imagine a couple of plausible futures or so-called *scenarios*. For example, we may create four scenarios about the future energy price.

4. *Level 4*: We cannot even identify all the unknowns, and we may only know some variables (unknown future values) that will be relevant to the principal's future. Therefore, we cannot develop scenarios. For example, we cannot create scenarios of the principal's industry in 50 years' time.

 How To Do It?

We assess the level of uncertainty about the future in three steps (see Figure 8.32).

1. Identify the relevant variables. Ask yourself: What variables can influence the performance of our solution? You face level 4 uncertainty if you cannot identify the relevant variables.

2. Assess the future value of these variables.

    a. If you can extrapolate past values, you are at the first level of uncertainty.

    b. You are at level 2 or 3 if you can distinguish different future values.

3. Assess the probabilities of future values.

    a. If you can assess probabilities, then you are at the second level.

    b. If you cannot, then you face level 3.

Dependent on the level, develop foresight

Figure 8.34 presents a process for developing foresight for the third level of uncertainty.

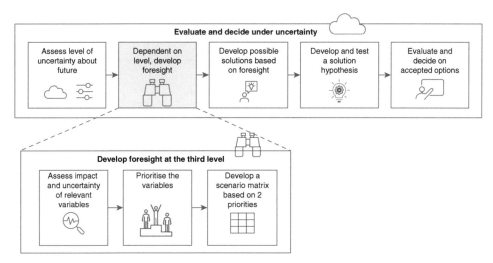

Figure 8.34   Developing foresight is the second step in the process of evaluating and deciding under uncertainty

In Chapter 1, we discussed the concept of VUCA. To refresh your memory, it is an acronym that stands for the Volatility, Uncertainty, Complexity, and Ambiguity of the environment. VUCA point to the third and fourth levels of uncertainty. We cannot develop foresight at the fourth level, but foresight development is feasible at the lower levels. Here we present a process for developing foresight at the *third* level of uncertainty.

1. *Assess the impact and uncertainty* of the relevant variables, which are the variables that can influence the performance of our solution.

2. *Prioritise* variables based on their impact and uncertainty. Variables of high impact and medium uncertainty drive the alternative scenarios. Rare phenomena (high uncertainty) are not a basis for scenarios whereas certain phenomena are part of all scenarios.

3. *Develop a scenario matrix* based on two prioritised variables. For each variable, we create a spectrum with two opposed values at the ends. Then we map the two ranges on each other to create a matrix of four scenarios. For each combination of driver values, we develop a scenario. We provide a brief sketch of each future and create an appealing title for each scenario.

Running Case ConsultCo

ConsultCo offers an example of the third level of uncertainty. Together with the principal and knowledgeable stakeholders, Arpit develops four scenarios (see Figure 8.35). The two biggest unknowns *at the time of the case* (2021) were international politics and the status of viruses (COVID-19). At that time, there were various domestic and international political tensions. In addition, the world was struggling with the COVID-19 pandemic. At that time, it was unknown how this virus would develop and whether other viruses would emerge.

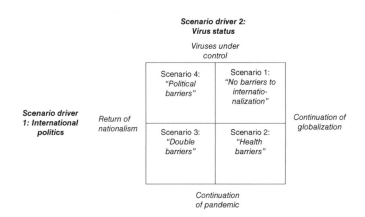

Figure 8.35   An example of a scenario matrix
Disclaimer: figure is an illustrative example that is not based on research

 Mini Exercise

Think of a well-known company of your choice that needs to make large and long-term investment for its future. Use Internet research to create a scenario matrix for this case.

Pause and Reflect ────────────

Use your own experience of a recent project from your study or work. To what extent did you consider the level of uncertainty?

Develop possible solutions based on foresight

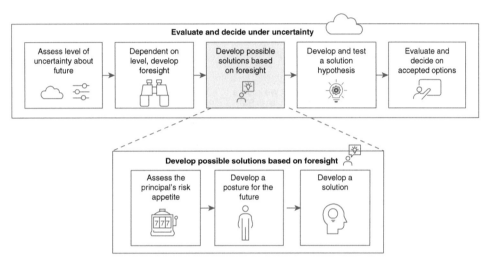

Figure 8.36   Developing possible solutions is the third step in the process of evaluating and deciding under uncertainty

Assess the principal's risk appetite

We assess the principal's risk appetite. Uncertainty about the future entails risk for the principal. Therefore, the principal's appetite for risk, or their risk attitude, is relevant. We focus on three factors that influence risk appetite.

- The principal's *personality*: Some personalities take risks more easily than others. Ask the principal about her risk appetite.
- The *resilience* of the principal's company: To what extent can the company afford the risk? Does the company have the financial buffers and other capabilities to recover from setbacks?
- The *power* of the principal's company to reduce risk: Macroeconomic risks, such as inflation and recessions, are beyond the reach of even the world's largest corporations. But large companies may influence risk factors at the industry level. For example, major industry players may influence the choice of technology as the industry standard.

Develop a posture for the future

We have estimated the level of uncertainty about the future. Now we are faced with the question: How to approach an uncertain future? Here we discuss six ways to deal with uncertainty or six different postures to an uncertain future (see Figure 8.37).

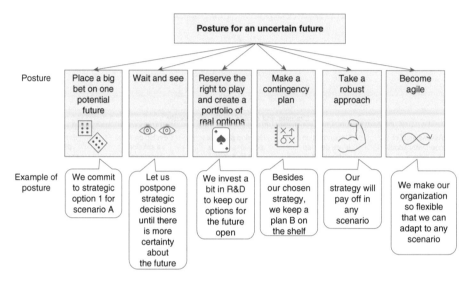

Figure 8.37   Six postures for an uncertain future

Source: Author's interpretation of Courtney et al. (1997)

- *Big bet*: We place a big bet (our solution) on one (1) alternative future (level 2 uncertainty) or plausible future (level 3). We tailor our solution fully to this future rather than other plausible futures. We can make a big bet if we can shape the future or are confident that the specific future we bet on will emerge. We should be able to afford the loss if we are wrong. We do not bet on the company.
- *Wait and see*: We postpone our decision-making about a solution until the future becomes clearer. This posture assumes that we have time and can afford to wait. Sometimes it is good to wait. We can learn from the beginner mistakes the pioneers make.
- *Reserve the right to play*: This is a solution between total investment and waiting. We invest just enough to be able to participate fully later. It is an option to participate later when the future is clearer. This posture is proper if we cannot afford to wait and see what will happen. For example, our competitors are already investing and will have an unstoppable lead. If we do not know which solution will win, we can invest a little bit in several alternatives simultaneously. We create a portfolio of real options, which is like betting on multiple horses in a race.
- *Contingency plan*: We create a 'plan B' in addition to our preferred solution A. Plan B prepares us for a different future. If the future turns out differently from our expectation, we will swap our original solution for plan B. We may have even more plans, such as plan C and plan D.

- *Robust approach*: We choose a solution that will work in *any* future. Such a solution is typically a compromise and provides a satisfactory performance in any future instead of an optimum performance for a specific future.
- *Become an agile organization*: We make our organization agile or flexible. Our organization knows how to adapt to whatever the future will bring.

We also acknowledge so-called '*no regret moves*'. These are actions that will always work in the future. Since these solutions are always good, we will never regret them. An example is combatting inefficiencies and waste in a production process.

Develop a solution

The process is like solution development under certainty, but it includes foresighted problems and opportunities. We distinguish between three alternative approaches to developing possible solutions:

- Identify an *analogical case*: In the case of foresighted problems, we need insights into companies and industries that are ahead of the principal. They are further along in their development and have already solved the principal's foresighted problems.
- Ask *knowledgeable stakeholders and other experts* about the industry's future: There may be people who have a sound vision of the future of the principal's industry.
- Identify a relevant *framework*: There are frameworks that can structure the dynamics of products, markets, companies, and strategies. Examples are product life cycle, market life cycle, and company life cycle frameworks.

─────────────── **Running Case ConsultCo** ───────────────

ConsultCo can illustrate the six postures for an uncertain future.

- *Big bet*: ConsultCo commits to the "health barriers" scenario (see Figure 8.35). The consultancy invests in an IT infrastructure for virtual internationalisation.
- *Wait and see*: ConsultCo postpones its decision to internationalize until there is more clarity about the future.
- *Reserve the right to play*: ConsultCo develops relationships with several foreign consultancies as candidates for international collaboration. The consultancy starts several small international collaboration projects as experiments.
- *Contingency plan*: ConsultCo chooses a solution for one scenario (virtual internationalisation for the "health barriers" scenario) but also creates a backup plan for an alternative scenario (setting up a foreign office for the "no barriers to internationalisation" scenario).

(Continued)

- *Robust approach*: ConsultCo's solution works in every scenario. The consultancy sets up local partnerships with foreign consultancies as partners (beyond the single project of the 'reserve the right to play' posture).
- *Agility*: ConsultCo chooses an export model. It serves foreign clients from the home country (consultants travel back and forth to foreign clients) and collaborates with local freelance consultants in foreign countries.

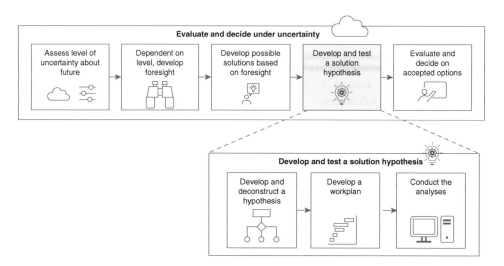

Figure 8.38   Developing and testing a solution hypothesis form the fourth step in the process of evaluating and deciding under uncertainty

Develop and test a solution hypothesis

We must develop and test a solution *hypothesis* (see Figure 8.38). Therefore, we prioritise the possible solutions. The prioritised solution is our *initial* hypothesis, and we deconstruct that hypothesis.

The process for testing a hypothesis varies with the level of uncertainty.

1. Level 1 is certainty about the future. We can measure the values of relevant variables, and the proofs of the hypothesis assumptions consist of measured values.
2. Level 2 is about the probabilities of alternative futures. We can assess the probabilities of the alternative values of relevant variables. Therefore, we can determine expectancy values of these variables. The proofs of the hypothesis assumptions use expectancy values.
3. Level 3 precludes assessment of the probabilities of alternative futures. We can only identify plausible alternative futures. Therefore, the proofs use the plausibility of values.

4. Level 4 means that we have no idea about the future. The relevant variables for the future performance are unknown. As there is no proof of the hypothesis, we must revert to experimenting.

Evaluate and decide on accepted options

Hypothesis testing becomes more challenging as the uncertainty increases. The assumption proofs become weaker if the level of uncertainty increases. But even under higher levels of uncertainty, the principal needs to evaluate options and make a decision (see Figure 8.39).

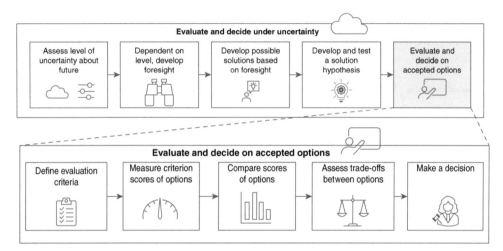

Figure 8.39   Evaluating and deciding on accepted options form the fifth step in the process of evaluating and deciding under uncertainty

We have already outlined the process for evaluating and deciding on options (see Figure 8.30). The uncertainty about the future reduces the applicability of evidence-based decision-making and forces us to rely more on intuitive decision-making. We may support the principal's decision-making under uncertainty by modelling how the various options perform under varying conditions. Examples of decision-support techniques are sensitivity analysis and regret analysis.

Conduct a sensitivity analysis

We develop a financial model of our solution to test how robust the solution is under uncertainty. Sensitivity refers to the extent to which a model's output variable is sensitive to changes in a model's input variable. Examples of output variables are a principal's revenues and costs. An example of input variables at *company* level is the success rate of a principal's R&D projects. An *industry*-level example of input variables is changes in competitors' prices in response to the principal's solution. Interest rates are an example of *macro-environmental* level input variables. We may also develop scenarios to assess how sensitive solutions are to alternative futures or how much the principal's performance varies with alternative futures. Figure 8.40 provides an example.

Conduct a regret analysis

Regretting a decision is the difference between the value of that decision and the value of the optimal decision.

1. For each decision in each scenario, we estimate the value or outcome (see Figure 8.40).
2. We then determine the regret per scenario (see Figure 8.41).
3. Finally, we compare the maximum or worst regret per decision (see Figure 8.41).

Running Case ConsultCo

Arpit conducts a sensitivity analysis. He assesses the business impact of solutions of a scenario. Arpit measures the impact by the return on investment. He makes a back-of-the-envelope calculation by tapping the brains of the principal and other knowledgeable stakeholders. Figure 8.40 shows the outcome of the sensitivity analysis. Variation is the difference between the highest and the lowest return for a particular solution in the various scenarios. The 'wholly owned foreign subsidiary' solution has the largest variation. Therefore, it is the most sensitive solution: variation is 6 as the highest return is 7 ("no barriers") and the lowest return is 1 ("double barriers").

Return		Scenarios				
		No barriers	Health barriers	Double barriers	Political barriers	Variation
Solutions	Export	4	2	0	1	4
	Wholly owned foreign subsidary	7	3	1	2	6
	Joint venture	5	3	2	5	3
	Best return	7	3	2	5	

Figure 8.40   **An example of a sensitivity analysis**

Arpit uses the best returns to calculate the regrets (see Figure 8.41). The regret of a specific solution is the difference between the best return in a scenario and the return of that solution. The regret for "export" in the "no barriers" scenario equals 3, namely 7 (best return for "no barriers") minus 4 (export's return). A joint venture has the slightest worst regret: 2.

Regret		Scenarios				
		No barriers	Health barriers	Double barriers	Political barriers	Worst regret
Solutions	Export	3	1	2	4	4
	Wholly-owned foreign subsidary	0	0	1	3	3
	Joint venture	2	0	0	0	2

Figure 8.41 An example of a regret analysis

 ━━ **Pause and Reflect** ━━━━━━━━━━━━━━━━━━━

Consider how you may use these techniques for testing and evaluating solutions and making decisions under uncertainty in your studies, work, and personal life.

SUMMARY

We briefly outline the main takeaways of this chapter.

- Develop a solution hypothesis
    - prioritise the possible solutions
    - develop a hypothesis based on the prioritised solution
    - a solution hypothesis is a possible answer to the key question

- Test a solution hypothesis
    - deconstruct a hypothesis into sub-hypotheses or assumptions
    - identify the required proof of an assumption
    - design the analyses
    - identify data sources
    - identify data collection techniques
    - create a workplan
- Evaluate and prioritise alternative solutions
    - accepted hypotheses are alternative solutions or options
    - evaluate the options using the evaluation criteria from the problem statement
    - select the best-evaluated option as the recommendation
- Deal with trade-offs between alternatives
    - weigh the criteria
    - make the criteria comparable

- determine financial equivalents of non-financial criteria
- calculate expectancy values

- Assess the level of uncertainty about the future
  - distinguish between four levels of uncertainty
  - choose a posture for dealing with uncertainty
- Make a business case for a solution
  - assess the impact of a solution on the principal's performance objective
- Decide under uncertainty
  - hypothesis proofs weaken if the level of uncertainty increases
  - higher levels of uncertainty demand a judgment call
  - do a sensitivity analysis and regret analysis to support decision-making

 Mini Exercise

Identify the key concepts and terms in this chapter, define them briefly and compile your own glossary.

REFERENCES AND FURTHER READING

Courtney, H. (2001). *20/20 Foresight: Crafting Strategy in an Uncertain World*. Cambridge, MA: Harvard Business School Press.

Courtney, H., Kirkland, J., & Viguerie, P. (1997). Strategy under uncertainty. *Harvard Business Review*, 75(6), 67–79.

Schoemaker, P. (2012). *Profiting from Uncertainty: Strategies for Succeeding No Matter What the Future Brings*. New York: The Free Press.

Schwenker, B., & Wulf, T. (Eds.). (2013). *Scenario-based Strategic Planning*. Roland Berger School of Strategy and Economics. Wiesbaden: Springer Fachmedien Wiesbaden.

Spetzler, C., Winter, H., & Meyer, J. (2016). *Decision Quality: Value Creation from Better Business Decisions*. Hoboken, NJ: John Wiley & Sons.

Communicate the Recommended Solution

9

INTRODUCTION

Communicating a recommended solution to a principal may look easy. We point to some pitfalls.

- We may assume that the audience is as interested in the subject as we are, which is one reason why we tend to dwell on our presentation for too long. But people in the audience often have very different problems on their minds. Therefore, we should keep our presentations short and straightforward.
- Another trap is to show how much work we have done. We must prove our worth during presentations. Some people may want to show their smartness and make their presentations far too complicated. Such presentations will exhaust the audience and people will lose interest and give up listening.
- We may also talk too long. People can listen to another person speaking for only so long. After that time, people become distracted, and their focus on the speaker's story drops off fast.

The purpose of a presentation of a recommended solution is to convince the audience to *say yes* to the recommendation. To succeed, we benefit from a communication method. This chapter will outline a proven successful method for communicating recommendations (see Figure 9.1).

The chapter is structured as follows (see Figure 9.2).

MAIN LEARNING OBJECTIVES

After studying this chapter, you should be able to:

- choose a proper presentation structure for a specific audience of stakeholders
- develop an overall presentation structure
- develop a storyline
- structure a slide
- visualise the information
- deliver a presentation to an audience
- interact with the audience

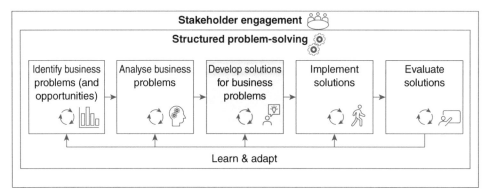

Figure 9.1   **After developing solutions, we communicate our recommendation**

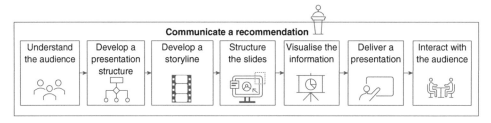

Figure 9.2   **Chapter structure**

UNDERSTAND THE AUDIENCE

We make sure that we know to whom we will present. Not only do we need to know *who* will attend the presentation, but we also need to understand *how* these people relate to the project. Their relation to the project brings us back to the stakeholder analysis. When we are going to present, we need to know what kind of stakeholders are in the room, and we must map the stakeholders in the audience (see Figure 9.3).

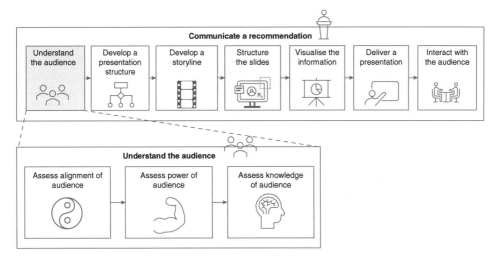

Figure 9.3   Understanding the audience is the first step in the process of communicating a recommendation

1. *Assess the alignment of the audience with the principal.* We must learn whether their interests are the same as or conflict with the principal. Will these people find the recommendation controversial or embrace it?
2. *Assess the power of the audience over the principal.* We need to know whether stakeholders have significant power over the principal.
3. *Assess the audience's knowledge about the problem and the recommended solution.* It is not only about the alignment and the power of the audience. Also essential is the audience's understanding of the problem and the solution. The less prior knowledge the audience has, the more we should explain.

 Pause and Reflect

Use your own experience of a recent project from your study or work. Did you ask yourself before the presentation of the recommendation:

- Who is in the audience?
- What are their interests?
- Why would they care about your recommendation?

DEVELOP A PRESENTATION STRUCTURE

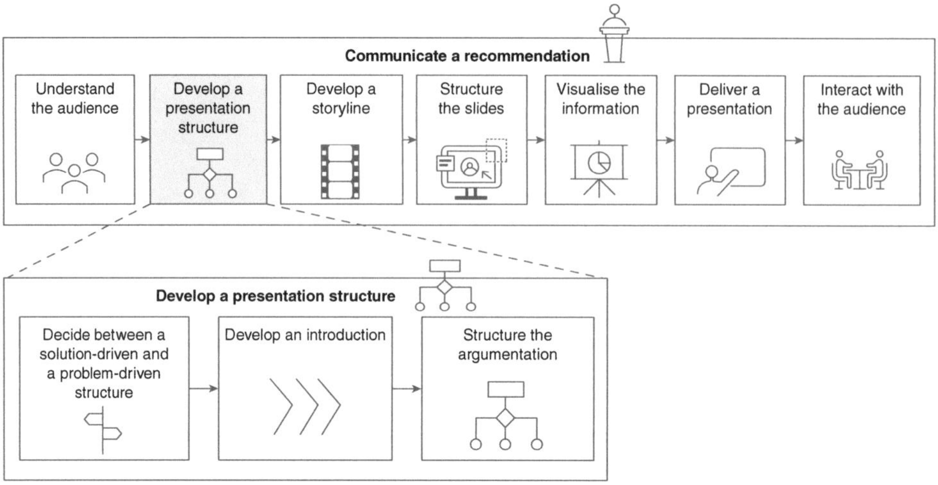

Figure 9.4   Developing a presentation structure is the second step in the process of communicating a recommendation

Decide between a solution-driven and a problem-driven structure

When presenting the recommendation to an audience, we distinguish between two starting positions of the audience.

- *The principal and all stakeholders in the audience know the problem.* We informed the principal and the stakeholders in advance about the results of the problem analysis. This audience knows the problem, where it lies, and why it exists. These people have a shared understanding of the problem. But they need to learn how to solve the problem. The relevant question for them is: *How should we solve the problem?* Therefore, we decide on a *solution-driven* presentation structure.
- *Some members of the audience need to learn the problem.*
  - ○ We inform the relevant stakeholders during the problem-solving on a need-to-know basis. These stakeholders may only receive the necessary information to contribute to that process. Therefore, they lack the big picture of the problem-solving process.
  - ○ Some audience members were not involved in the problem-solving. They may have a flawed understanding of the problem, or their interpretations may differ. Stakeholders may blame each other for causing the problem. People may deny the problem's existence, whereas others may even be unaware of the problem.
  - ○ For such an audience, the relevant question is: *Is there a problem?* Therefore, we decide on a *problem-driven* presentation structure.

Pause and Reflect ─────────────────────────────

Use your own experience of a recent project from your study or work. Did you consider how much prior knowledge the audience had about the problem or solution?

Develop an introduction

Distinguish between two different introductions

Each starting position demands a specific introduction consisting of four parts: situation, problem or complication, key question, and purpose. This structure is based on the author's interpretation of Barbara Minto's Pyramid Principle (Minto, 2003).

- The first part is the '*situation*', which is a brief description or profile of the principal's company. It must be recognizable to the audience because we want to avoid any controversy over the opening lines of our presentation. We want the audience to agree with the first thing we say. We want to show that we understand the principal's company.
- The second topic is the '*complication*'. Recall that the complication is the aspect that complicates the problem-solving (see chapter 2). From this point on, the structures for the two different starting points of audiences diverge. For *a knowledgeable audience*, the complication is: There is a problem and we do not know how to solve it.
- Then we present the third part: the '*key question*'. This question is the most critical one in the mind of this audience. We repeat the key question: How should the principal respond to the problem to achieve her performance objective in time?
- The fourth part is the '*purpose*' of the presentation. We inform a knowledgeable audience that we will present our recommended solution to the problem.

Figure 9.5 displays the suitable introduction for a knowledgeable audience. For clarity, this figure is about a problem, but the technique is also applicable to opportunities.

- We use a different introduction for *an audience that lacks knowledge about the problem*.
  ○ The situation is the same.
  ○ For these people, the complication is that they do not know whether there is a problem or not.
  ○ Then we must make explicit the *key question* that lives in the minds of this audience. This question is: Is there a problem, and if so, how should we solve it? Subsequently, we clarify the purpose of our presentation. For this audience, we present our analysis of the problem and recommend a solution in the case of a verified problem. Figure 9.6 displays a suitable introduction for this starting position.

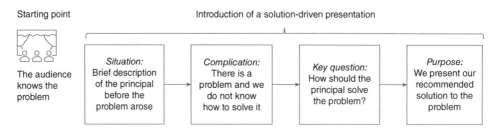

Figure 9.5   An introduction to a solution-driven presentation for a knowledgeable audience

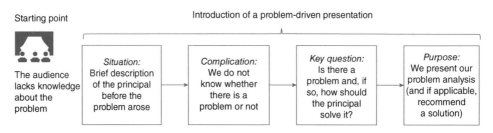

Figure 9.6   An introduction of a problem-driven presentation for an audience that lacks knowledge

Structure the argumentation

We can use the 'Minto Pyramid Principle' (Minto, 2003; see Chapter 4) for presenting our recommendation in a structured way. This principle deconstructs the presentation's main message into a hierarchy of sub-messages that resembles a (two-dimensional) pyramid. The main message is the recommendation.

There is a problem. The principal wonders: "What should I do about the problem?" Our answer is the main message or the *governing thought* of the presentation. Depending on the principal's needs, we may deconstruct our messages into arguments (an explanation of our recommendation) and proposed actions (the suggested implementation of our recommendation).

1. First, principals want to know *why* this is the best solution to their problem. They want arguments or explanations. Arguments answer the why-questions. We need to develop an argument structure.
2. When a principal accepts the recommendation, she wants to know *how* to implement this solution. The principal wants to learn about the implementation actions as the actions answer the how questions. We develop an action structure.

Develop argumentation structures to answer why-questions

We need to convince the principal of the value of our recommendation. We provide a set of arguments to answer the principal's why-questions: "Why is this the best solution for my problem?" The collection of arguments should be MECE. Figure 9.7 presents only a single level of arguments. Still, we can deconstruct these arguments into sub-arguments, thereby creating additional explanations.

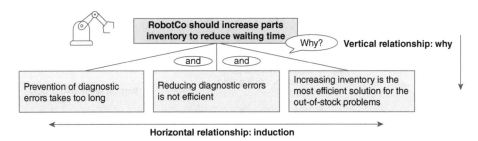

Figure 9.7   An example of an argumentation structure for an inductive answer to a why-question

Note: 'and' (in the ovals) means that the lower-level elements *together* answer the why-question

- The *vertical* relationship between the two levels in the structure in Figure 9.7 is the why-question. The lower-level elements provide arguments for the higher-level statement or recommendation.
- The organization of elements at the same level is about the *horizontal* relationship. We can structure our arguments in an inductive format (see Figure 9.7) or by using *deduction* (see Figure 9.8):
  - An induction means no order or sequence of arguments
  - A deduction goes from general to specific statements

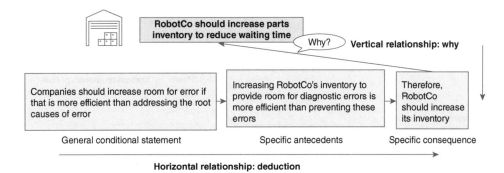

Figure 9.8   An example of an argumentation structure for a *deductive* answer to a why-question

The example uses the same arguments for the parallel and the deductive structures (Figure 9.8). In practice, the arguments may differ.

Develop action structures to answer how-questions

The principal who accepts the recommendation will ask: "How should we implement the recommendation?" We will provide a set of actions for implementation. We may group the actions by business function, such as IT, manufacturing, and logistics. Figure 9.9 presents an action structure for a *functional grouping* to answer the how-question.

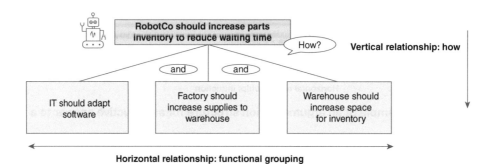

Figure 9.9   An example of an action structure for a functional grouping of answers to a how-question

The *vertical* relationship between the two levels in the structure in Figure 9.9 is the how-question: the lower-level elements indicate how to implement the higher-level recommendation. The set of implementation actions should be MECE. We can present our activities in *functional groups* (see Figure 9.9) or in *chronological order* (see Figure 9.10). Functional and chronological order are examples of *horizontal* relationships. Figures 9.9 and 9.10 show only a single level of actions, but we can deconstruct these actions into sub-actions (see Chapter 10).

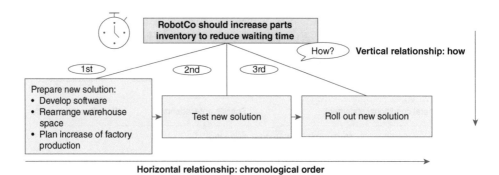

Figure 9.10   An example of an action structure for a *chronological order* of answers to a how-question

How To Do It?

Always ask the principal in advance how much time you have for the presentation.

Pause and Reflect

Use your own experience of a recent project from your study or work. Did this presentation have a specific structure? If so, what kind of structure was it and why did you choose it?

Develop a solution-driven presentation structure

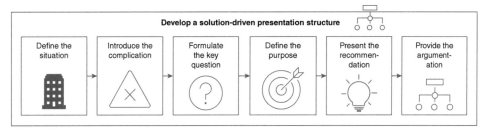

Figure 9.11   A process for developing a solution-driven presentation structure

A knowledgeable audience

Here we discuss the presentation of a recommendation to a *knowledgeable* audience. The purpose is to convince the audience to accept the recommendation. We face the first starting position (see Figure 9.5): the audience knows the problem.

Arouse the audience's interest first

How do we convey the message to the audience? Some presenters believe that the audience is on the edge of their seats to listen to the presentation. Unfortunately, in practice it is often very different. The audience members already have plenty of other things on their minds. Their heads are full of other problems and concerns. We will encounter resistance if we want to impose our message. The audience will not be open and will pay little or no attention to our presentation. The members of the audience are only interested in information that answers their struggling questions.

Therefore, we must first make them aware of the question that our recommenda-tion answers. Questions make the audience interested in our presentation because we answer their questions. For knowledgeable audiences, we use the project's key question. After all, the key question was the reason for the project. The principal and other stakeholders in the audience want an answer to this question.

Figure 9.12 shows a solution-driven structure for a knowledgeable audience. We have kept the structure very simple to make the picture clear and understandable. However, we can expand the structure.

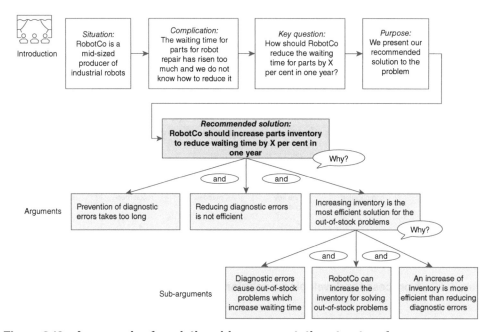

Figure 9.12   An example of a solution-driven presentation structure for a knowledgeable audience

Figure 9.12 is elementary. A more detailed presentation looks like this.

1. After the introduction and presenting the purpose of our presentation, we offer *the principal's evaluation criteria and solution constraints* as a starting point for solution development (not shown in Figure 9.12).
2. We present *a methodological justification*: how did we develop solutions? We explain our method and data for developing solutions (not shown in Figure 9.12).
3. We discuss *the different possible solutions*. We provide an overview of the alter-native accepted solution hypotheses (not shown in Figure 9.12).
4. We *evaluate these options* based on the principal's criteria and constraints. The recommended solution emerges from this evaluation as the best option (not shown in Figure 9.12).
5. We present the details of *the recommended solution* (not shown in Figure 9.12).

How To Do It?

Do not push your recommendation but pull in the audience with the question to which your recommendation is the answer.

Mini Exercise

Think of a recent product introduction by a well-known company and use Internet research to develop a solution-driven presentation structure for this product.

Introduce the recommendation

Figure 9.12 visualizes the whole structure of the presentation, which runs from the top to the bottom. We start with an introduction structure suitable for a knowledgeable audience. Because these people already know the problem, we can spend less time on it and move on to the recommended solution quickly. The focus of a presentation for a knowledgeable audience is the solution. Therefore, we call it a *solution-driven presentation*. We ask ourselves: What will the audience think when we present our recommendation?

Convince the audience

They will wonder *why* this advice is a solution to their problem. Why would this solution solve the problem? This question pops up in their minds when we present our recommendation. Therefore, we need to answer that why-question. We must argue why our advice will provide the best solution to the problem. The recommendation is an accepted solution hypothesis. We tested the hypothesis by assessing its assumptions. These assumptions are what people need to know or believe in to accept the solution. We have analysed the assumptions and shared the analysis results with the principal and relevant stakeholders. These people have bought into these findings and have thus accepted the assumptions. Now we can use the accepted results of the analyses as arguments to support our recommended solution. The supported assumptions of the solution hypothesis become the arguments for the recommendation. In this way, we convince the audience of the value of the recommended solution. Here it comes down to our persuasiveness. How convincing are our arguments? How compelling are we as presenters?

Structure the argumentation

The argumentation structure of Figure 9.12 equals the hypothesis assumptions in Figure 8.12. To keep the picture clear, Figure 9.12 only shows the arguments and sub-arguments. But we also have sub-sub-arguments. If the available time is limited, we present only the first level of arguments. If there is sufficient time and the audience asks for it, we offer a second or even a third level of argument. Even if the presentation time is limited, we should be prepared to answer questions about lower-level arguments.

Present the next steps

After the audience accepts our recommendation, they wonder *how* to implement it. We should anticipate that question and prepare suggestions for the implementation.

Develop a problem-driven presentation structure

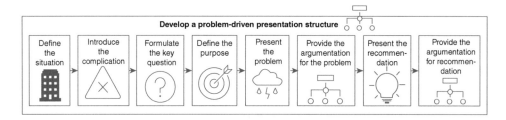

Figure 9.13   **A process for developing a problem-driven presentation structure**

Addressing an audience that does not know the problem

The principal knows the key question, but some people in the audience may need to be more familiar with it or have varying interpretations of the problem. Then we start our presentation with an introduction that everybody recognizes. If we start immediately with something unknown to some people, these people will not comprehend it and then we are likely to lose their attention. Therefore, we develop introductions that will be familiar to all people in the audience.

Start with the problem

Figure 9.14 visualizes the presentation's whole structure, which runs from the top to the bottom. We start with an introduction structure that is suitable to an audience that needs to learn the problem (see Figure 9.6). Because (some) people in the audience need to understand the problem, we must spend a significant amount of time on the problem. We must move on to our recommendation slowly. If we introduce the solution too soon, (some) people in the audience will wonder about the problem that our solution must solve. The focus of presentations for such audiences is the problem. Therefore, we call it a problem-driven presentation.

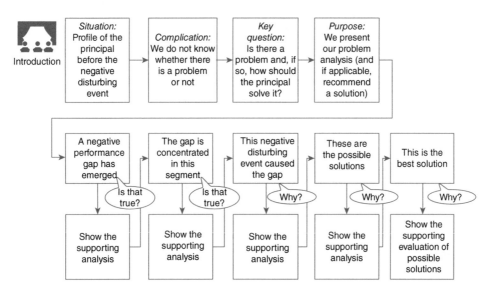

Figure 9.14   A problem-driven presentation structure for an audience that lacks knowledge

Use the Sequential Analysis Method

The problem-driven presentation structure mirrors the Sequential Analysis Method (see Figure 9.15). These questions come into the audience's mind in succession.

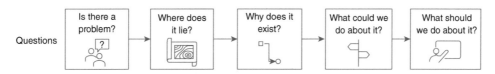

Figure 9.15   The Sequential Analysis Method for a problem

Convince the audience to accept the problem

We start with the first question: "Is there a problem?" This question is vital for people who are unaware of the problem or deny it. An adequate answer to this question presents the negative performance gap. This gap is a factual and objective answer to the first question.

Convince the audience to accept the location of the problem

After this convincing proof of the problem's existence, the audience will wonder *where* the problem is. The location of the problem is a potentially sensitive topic. The question "Where is the problem?" relates to the question "Who is to blame?" Therefore, we must again provide factual answers. We present the quantitative distribution of the performance gap across the segments to show where the gap is most extensive. Our analysis shows what products, customers, plants, or other segments have the most significant gap. The presentation of the facts prevents endless discussions in which everyone defends their truth.

Convince the audience to accept the explanation of the problem

After the audience accepts the location of the problem, we answer the following question in the audience's mind. The audience now wants to know what caused the problem. Our answer is the accepted *problem* hypothesis or hypotheses in case of multiple causes. We use the results of our analyses of the hypothesis-assumptions as the arguments of the problem cause(s).

Present the alternative solutions

After the audience accepts the explanation of the problem, they have sufficient knowledge of the problem. We answer the question of the fourth step of the Sequential Analysis method: "What are the possible solutions?" We present an overview of the possible solutions. These are the accepted solution hypotheses. By offering alternative solutions, we show that we have oriented ourselves broadly. Subsequently, we use the principal's evaluation criteria to evaluate and rank the possible solutions. Based on this evaluation, we present our recommended solution.

Support the principal's decision-making

The *decision* about the solution is the principal's mandate. We recommend and the principal decides. To make deciding easier for the principal, we substantiate our recommendation as much as possible. We base arguments as much as possible on factual analyses. Here we can use our analyses of the assumptions of the solution hypothesis. Entirely fact-based substantiations of recommendations are not feasible. Solutions are about the future, and there are no facts about the future. The principal's decision, therefore, is ultimately a matter of judgment. In any case, we must provide logical arguments and realistic assumptions for our recommendation to facilitate the principal's judgment and support the decision-making.

We cannot please everyone

We hope that the audience is happy with our recommendation. But our advice may also encounter resistance from (some) stakeholders in the audience. As indicated earlier, the interests and values of stakeholders can differ. For example, for environmental movements, the sustainability aspects of solutions are critical. For works councils, employment and the well-being of the workforce are decisive. There will probably be stakeholders in the audience who prefer different solutions because every possible solution can have advantages and disadvantages for specific stakeholders. Some stakeholders favour one specific solution, and others want another option. The choice of a solution is therefore also a *political* choice.

Let the principal present

A political situation brings us to the question: "*Who* should present the solution?" So far, we have assumed that we present the solution, but that is not always the case. If some stakeholders find messages hard to accept, presentations may evoke resistance from these people. The principal can leave such difficult messages for us. In such cases, we are the bogeymen, and the principal watches how we answer the stakeholders' critiques. Then we become the bad guys while the principal can play the good guy.

Although we can provide good arguments for the solution, it is often better for the principal to present it herself. In this way, the principal shows that she is committed to the solution and takes responsibility for its implementation. A presentation by the principal indicates that it is the principal's solution rather than our solution. In this way, the principal can prevent the 'not-invented-here syndrome'.

 How To Do It?

Do not try to please everyone in the audience at all costs. Focus on the principal because it is the principal who has hired you.

Running case RobotCo

Tara has created a problem-driven presentation structure because the audience lacks knowledge (see Figure 9.16).

(Continued)

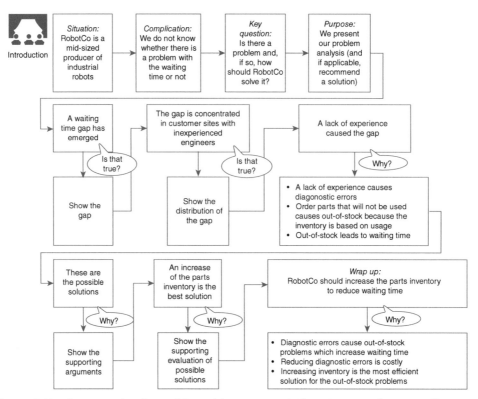

Figure 9.16   An example of a problem-driven presentation structure for an audience that lacks knowledge

DEVELOP A STORYLINE

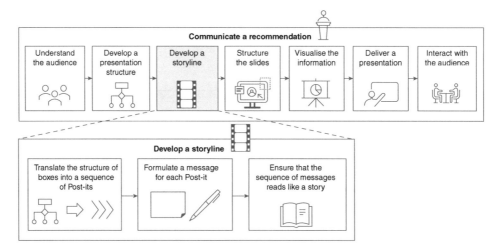

Figure 9.17   Developing a storyline is the third step in the process of communicating a recommendation

Translate the structure of boxes into a sequence of Post-its

After designing the presentation structure, we develop a storyline. We can use the Post-it notes on a storyboard because this flexible approach allows us to make changes to the storyline if new insights emerge (see Figure 9.18).

Formulate a message for each Post-it

Each Post-it note gets a line with a message, which always contains a noun and a verb. We distinguish between different types of messages.

- Conclusion:
  - Explanation: We explain a problem (or an opportunity). For example, "Diagnostic errors cause out-of-stock problems".
  - Recommendation: We make a recommendation. For example, "RobotCo should increase the inventory".
- Argument: We present an argument that may refer to explanations and recommendations. Here we provide an example of an argument for an explanation: "Inexperience contributes to diagnostic errors".
- Action: We present an action for implementing our recommendation. For example, "RobotCo must increase the warehouse space".

Ensure that the sequence of messages reads like a story

The lines or messages of a series of Post-it notes should read as a story (see Figure 9.18). The sequence of messages is the storyline. We call it the '*horizontal flow*' of the presentation to distinguish it from the 'vertical flow', which we will introduce later. The horizontal flow must be clear and convincing. The storyline is the basis for the PowerPoint presentation, but we can also turn a storyline into a text report. We structure both a PowerPoint presentation and a text report as a storyline, or a sequence of messages, on slides and pages, respectively.

We also need to consider the audience's need for additional explanation or details. Depending on the audience's needs, we create backup slides with detailed descriptions of methods and data or a more detailed analysis of the problem. For a text report, we provide appendices. Finally, we may add an executive summary to our presentation or report.

 Pause and Reflect

Use your own experience of a recent project from your study or work. Look at the slide titles. To what extent can you identify a horizontal flow in the slide titles?

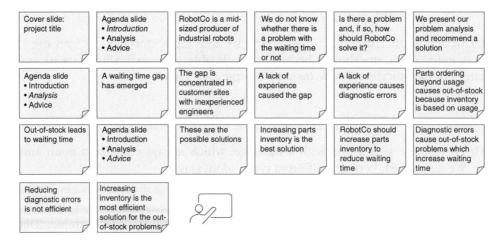

Figure 9.18   An example of a presentation structure in Post-it notes on a storyboard

Present an opportunity

So far, we have discussed *problem* cases. But we also analyse the principal's *opportunities*. We can use a solution-driven presentation structure if the audience is knowledgeable about the opportunity. But (some people in) the audience may need to learn or believe that the company has an opportunity. There may also be people who deny or question the opportunity. Then we use an opportunity-driven presentation structure.

Follow the order of the Sequential Analysis Method

An opportunity-driven structure differs from a problem-driven structure. Like the sequential analyses of opportunities differ from problems, so do the presentations vary. Unlike a problem, the beginning of an opportunity-driven structure is not a performance gap. We distinguish three steps for the sequential analysis of an opportunity (see Figure 9.19).

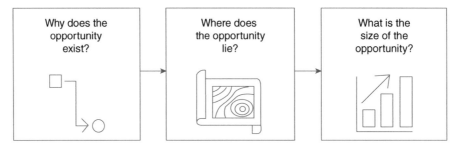

Figure 9.19   The first three questions of the Sequential Analysis Method for an opportunity

We structure our opportunity-driven presentation as follows:

1. We explain *why* the principal has an opportunity.
2. We present *where* the opportunity is.
3. We show *what* the estimated size of the opportunity is. We present how much performance can improve if the principal seizes the opportunity.

Running Case ConsultCo

Arpit creates an opportunity-driven structure for a presentation to an audience that does not know about the opportunity (see Figure 9.20). There will likely be a few people in the audience who have no knowledge of or deny ConsultCo's opportunity.

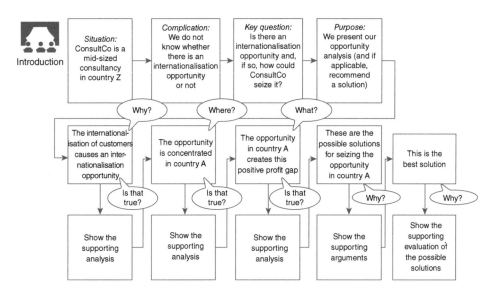

Figure 9.20   An opportunity-driven presentation structure for an audience that lacks knowledge

STRUCTURE THE SLIDES

Put the message at the top of the slide

We distinguish between three components of a slide:

*   a slide title at the top
*   a slide body in the middle
*   a slide justification at the bottom

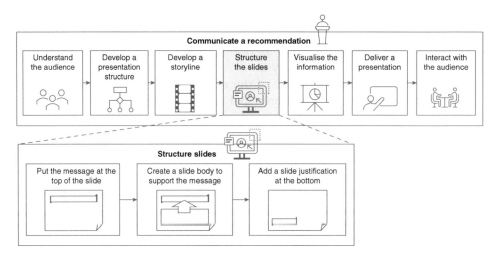

Figure 9.21   Structuring slides is the fourth step in the process of communicating a recommendation

We take the message from a Post-it note in the storyboard and make it the title of a slide. Figure 9.18 shows a storyboard of messages on Post-it notes. Each Post-it note message becomes the title of *a slide*. Every slide must have one (1) message. No more, no less. One message makes the slide relatively simple and easy to understand for the audience.

Create a slide body to support the message

We design a slide body that supports the message. The principle is as follows: *No conclusion in the slide title without supporting facts in the slide body*. We strive to support every message with facts. We minimize conceptual slides, that is, slides without facts. The slide body must be consistent with the slide title. We call the relation between the slide title and the slide body the '*vertical flow*' of the slide (see Figure 9.22). We keep the slide body as simple as possible. The principle is as follows: *No facts in the slide body that are not necessary for the conclusion in the slide title*.

Add a slide justification at the bottom

The justification of the slide body concerns the source reference. The audience may ask: From where do the facts come? Therefore, we need to present the sources of the slide body facts.

Suppose the underlying analytical method and techniques are complex. In that case, we may place an explanatory note at the bottom of the slide. If we need an elaborate explanation that does not fit a footnote, then we create a backup slide to provide this explanation.

─────────────── **Running Case ConsultCo** ───────────────

Arpit translates one of the messages in the storyline into a slide (see Figure 9.22). He uses the message to develop the slide body.

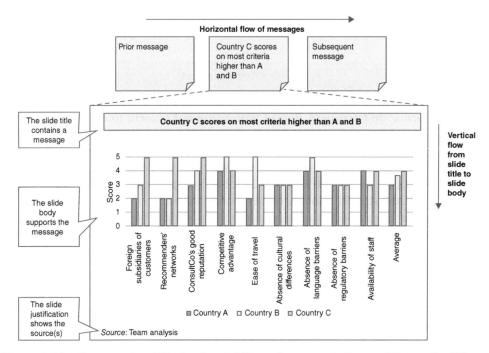

Figure 9.22   An example of the horizontal flow of a presentation and the vertical flow of a slide

Keep it simple

There is a tendency to put too much information on a slide. Information overload primarily occurs if there is a limit to the number of PowerPoints the principal allows for the presentation. Then people want to put too many messages on a slide. But we must stick to only one single message per slide. Besides, people may place more information in the slide body than is necessary to support the message. But the slide body should only support the title: no more and no less. We refrain from unnecessary information in the slide body because unnecessary data makes it more challenging for the audience to understand the slides.

 Pause and Reflect

Use your own experience of a recent project from your study or work. Look at the slides. To what extent do you recognize a vertical flow in the slides?

Avoid wordy slides

PowerPoint presentations are not text reports. The report pages should provide *complete* information to readers. Report writers are not present to explain their writing. Reports are different from PowerPoint presentations. Unlike pages, slides do not have to do communication work independently. The presenter and the slides *together* communicate the message to the audience. Therefore, we do not create PowerPoints that look like report pages. See Figure 9.23 for an (exaggerated) example of a wordy slide. Slide bodies should contain the essence but not too much detail. There is not enough space on a slide for large numbers of words. We do not want to use a font size smaller than 16. We should not treat a slide presentation as a substitute for a report.

RECOMMENDATIONS

- You have to do this, and this and this
- You also have to do these three things: (a) this, (b) this, and (c) this
- Furthermore, it is necessary that you do this and this
- In addition, you have to consider this and that
- We also recommend that you do this and this
- You need to do that also
- For the implementation phase, you have to do this, this and this
- In case of this, you need to do these things: a, b and c
- You have to do this, and this and this
- You also have to do these three things: (a) this, (b) this, and (c) this
- Furthermore, it is necessary that you do this and this
- In addition, you have to consider this and that
- We also recommend that you do this and this
- You need to do that also
- For the implementation phase, you have to do this, this and this
- In case of this, you need to do these things: a, b and c

Figure 9.23   A slide should not be like a text page

 **How To Do It?**

Do not try to make PowerPoints that do not require an oral explanation. Slides should convey the messages together with a verbal explanation.

VISUALISE THE INFORMATION

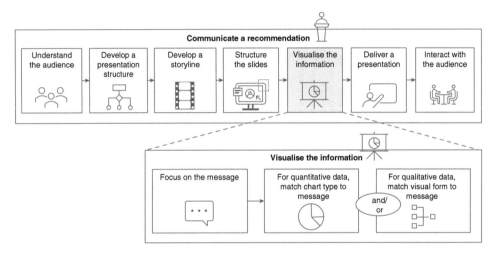

Figure 9.24 **Visualizing information is the fifth step in the process of communicating a recommendation**

Focus on the message

The purpose of a slide is to convey a message. Therefore, we focus on the message. We must resist the temptation to create fancy-looking charts. PowerPoint and other computer programs can produce so many graphs. One push of a button is enough to make the most fancy-looking charts. It is tempting to be creative, but the form may then take precedence over the content. The audience will be less charmed by the graphic art pieces we can get from software. Remember that the audience should understand our presentation with little effort. We should not exhaust our audience with visual art that unnecessarily complicates slides.

We make clever use of the software to make presentations easier to digest instead of more complex. The software can interpret our data, but we need to frame it to meet the message we want to convey.

—— **Running Case ConsultCo** ——

Arpit prepares two bar charts using the same data (see Figure 9.25). The left-hand bar chart of Figure 9.25 organizes data by country evaluation criteria. But, as the right-hand bar chart shows, we can also rank the data by country. What graph should Arpit use? It depends on the message that he wants to convey. For example, assume that the message is: "Country C wins on subsidiaries, networks, and reputation." Then the left-hand chart is the best choice. But Arpit's message may also be: "Subsidiaries, networks, and reputation are the strengths of country C." Then the right-hand chart is better, but without countries A and B because the message is only about C.

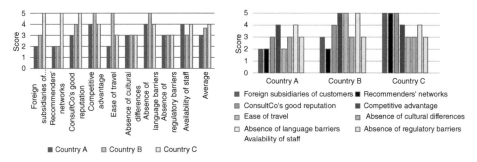

Figure 9.25   Same data but different types of bar chart

For quantitative data, match the chart type to the message

We visualize our data as much as possible because most people understand visuals more easily than texts and tables. Audience members want to avoid reading slides packed full of text and tables. These people should not think about having to understand tables consisting of 15 rows and 10 columns full of numbers in an 8-point font size. Digesting such slides takes too much energy from an audience. After a few slides, the audience gets tired, and their attention weakens. Therefore, we visualize the information whenever possible. If we have quantitative data, we do not show tables but charts. Figure 9.26 provides some suggestions for matching chart types to messages.

For qualitative data, match the visual form to the message

Visualizing *quantitative* data with charts is a well-known practice, but how do we display *qualitative* data? We want to make as many subjects as possible measurable, and we measure as much as possible. But we cannot quantify everything, and there are limits to what we can quantify without appearing artificial. Some parts of the problem analysis and solution may lend themselves to something other than quantification. These parts of the presentation are qualitative.

Message is about:	Comment	Recommended chart type
Comparisons	Comparisons in general	Bar chart
	Comparisons of components	• Stacked bar chart • Funnel chart
Components	Components in general	• Pie chart • Radar chart • Sunburst chart • Tree map
	Decomposition of a performance gap	Bar waterfall chart
Relations	Relations in general	• Scatter plot (2 variables) • Bubble chart (3 variables) • Surface chart (3 variables)
	Portfolio of products, projects or businesses	2 by 2 matrix (or variants, such as 3 by 3)
Time series	Time series in general	• Column chart • Line chart • Combo chart (column and line)
	Time series in combination with comparison	• Stacked column chart • Area chart
	Contribution of solution to performance	Column waterfall chart

Figure 9.26   Different chart types for different messages

Besides numbers, we can use text. However, we want something other than PowerPoints designed as text pages (see Figure 9.23). We present keywords instead of sentences, and we visualize relationships between keywords using boxes, arrows, chevrons, and other graphic forms. Computer programs offer many ready-to-use forms to visualize textual information. Think, for example, of PowerPoint's SmartArt. Some software may have digital libraries of icons and other visual formats. Figure 9.27 presents some examples of visual forms to show process flows, categories, and other structures of qualitative data.

 How To Do It?

If you distribute the design of slides across team members, ensure that the slide designs are consistent.

- Do all slides have the same layout, font types, and use the same jargon? Do not use different words on different slides if you want to indicate the same thing. For example, do not alternate between 'customers' and 'clients'.
- Check for any typos and miscalculations on slides.
- Make sure that all slides are correctly numbered and referenced.

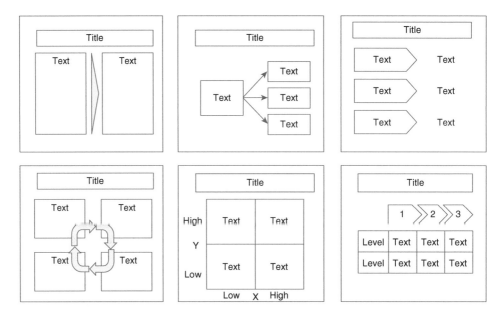

Figure 9.27   Some visual forms to present qualitative information

Visualise a presentation structure

We need to pay attention to the structure of our presentation. The audience must have the structure well in their mind. Otherwise, the following questions may arise:

- Where are we now in the presentation?
- How does this slide fit into the bigger picture?
- How far along are we with the presentation?

By emphasizing the presentation structure, we can manage the audience's expectations. We distinguish between two techniques: show an agenda and use a tracer.

- *Show an agenda*: A well-known technique for structuring presentations is the agenda. We present an agenda slide at the beginning of our presentation. We repeat the agenda slide every time we arrive at a new item. We indicate the current topic by placing a box around it. The left-hand side of Figure 9.28 shows an agenda slide.
- *Use a tracer*: Another technique for structuring presentations is the 'tracer'. Tracers are small visualisations or texts in each slide's top-right or top-left corner. The right-hand side of Figure 9.28 shows a slide with a tracer in the top-right corner. Tracers inform the audience where slides fit in the bigger picture of presentations. Tracers may point to agenda items. More sophisticated tracers, as in Figure 9.28, have multiple components. Each component may point to an agenda item. We highlight the focal component of the tracer. For example, in Figure 9.28, the

tracer consists of three chevrons. We highlight the first chevron, which points to the presentation's first section. But we can also use the chevrons to indicate the various process steps, such as the principal's value-adding processes or a process for implementing our recommendation.

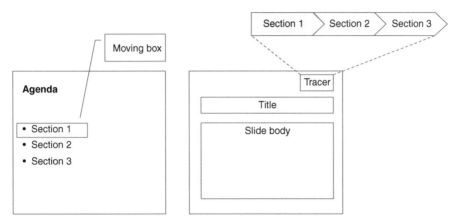

Figure 9.28   Visual techniques to emphasize the presentation structure

Mini Exercise

Use the solution-driven presentation structure for the recent product introduction by a well-known company that you developed for the previous mini exercise. Design one critically important slide from this presentation.

Pause and Reflect

Use your own experience of a recent project from your study or work. Did you consider the ability of the audience to understand your presentation?

DELIVER A PRESENTATION

Practise, practise, practise

This chapter's focus is on the screen content of presentations, but personal delivery of presentations is a crucial factor to their success. A comprehensive discussion of all aspects of effective presentation is beyond the scope of this book, but Figure 9.30 provides some practical advice.

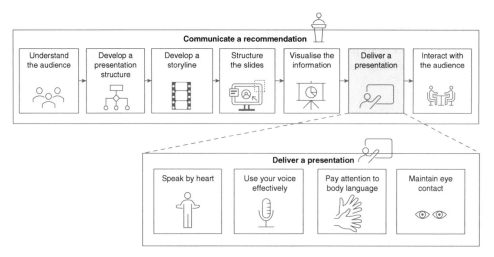

Figure 9.29 **Delivering a presentation is the sixth step in the process of communicating a recommendation**

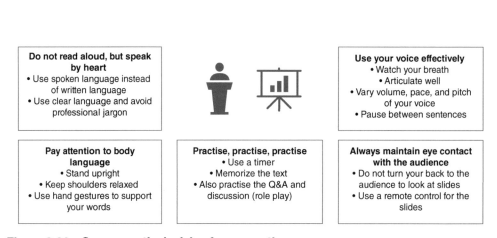

Figure 9.30 **Some practical advice for presenting**

Pause and Reflect

Use your own experience of a recent project from your study or work. Did you ask yourself in advance: How will the audience look upon me and my presentation? Will they have preconceived thoughts, opinions, prejudices, and biases?

INTERACT WITH THE AUDIENCE

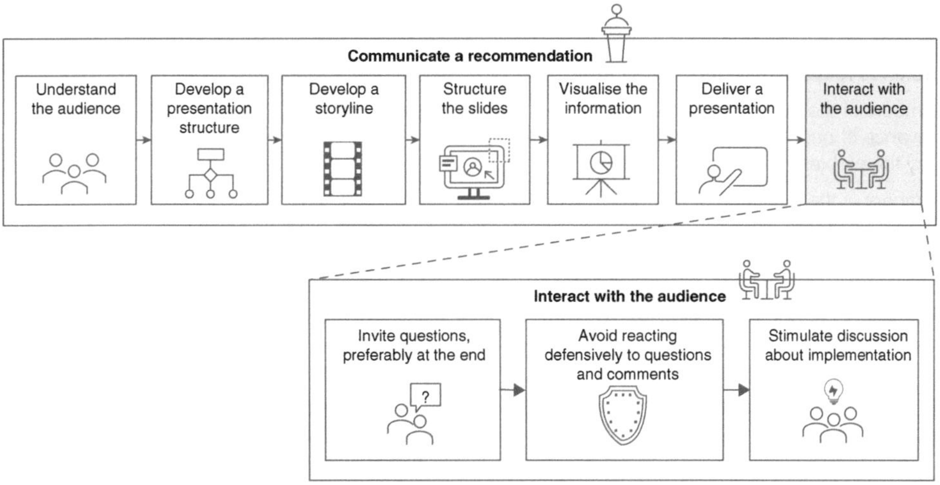

Figure 9.31 Interacting with the audience is the seventh step in the process of communicating a recommendation

Invite questions

We prefer to take questions at the end. But during a presentation, we may have to handle questions and comments. Presenting is not lecturing but convincing the principal to say yes to our recommendation.

After our presentation, we launch the conversation. We distinguish between three scenarios.

- The audience is thoroughly convinced and therefore accepts our recommendation. These people want to discuss the implementation, and then we share our implementation plan. We have prepared slides about the implementation.
- The audience has questions about our analysis of the problem or our recommendation and requests a clarification or explanation. We should be happy with these questions because they allow us to better explain our problem analysis and recommendation. We make sure we are prepared to answer questions and explain our work. For these reasons, we create extra (backup) slides.
- The audience has a critique of our analysis of the problem and recommendation. We discuss this scenario in Figure 9.32.

Avoid reacting defensively to questions and comments

It is tempting to become defensive when the audience has critical questions and comments. We must resist that temptation because a defensive position is often unproductive. Figure 9.32 provides recommendations for responding to critical questions and comments.

Audience response to our presentation	Recommended actions
Members of the audience do not see the relevance of our recommendation because they deny the problem	Show the empirical evidence of the problem gap
Members of the audience do not understand our problem analysis	• Take more time to explain the analysis • Use simpler language • Take smaller steps and ask control-questions: Is this answer clear?
Members of the audience reject our problem analysis	• Better explain the problem analysis • Elaborate on the analytical method and show the empirical evidence
Members of the audience do not understand our recommendation	• Take more time to explain the recommendation • Use simpler language • Take smaller steps and ask control questions: Is this answer clear?
Members of the audience reject our recommendation Members of the audience prefer another solution	• Better explain the solution development process • Elaborate on the method and show the empirical evidence • Show the relationship between the recommendation and problem • Show the option evaluation for a comparison of the recommendation and the other options
Members of the audience think they cannot implement our recommendation	Show a feasibility assessment of the high-level implementation actions

Figure 9.32   **Recommended actions for audience responses**

Stimulate a discussion about the implementation

After the principal and other relevant stakeholders have accepted our recommendation, we should stimulate a discussion about implementing that solution. It is essential to talk about implementation: only through implementation can we demonstrate the value of our recommendation.

 **Pause and Reflect**

Use your own experience of a recent project from your study or work. Did you want everybody to like your presentation, and agree with you?

Add a disclaimer to a presentation slide deck

We may give the principal a digital copy of the slide deck. The principal may distribute the slide deck to stakeholders who did not attend our verbal presentations. The people who were absent during these meetings will not have the same understanding as those who were present. The absentees miss the presenters' verbal explanations. Therefore, we may put a disclaimer on slide decks, such as: "This presentation is not complete without a verbal description."

Do not share the PowerPoints with the audience but turn the slide deck into a PDF. You want to prevent people from using individual slides in a different context or, worse, make changes to your slides and then share them with others.

 Pause and Reflect

Consider how you may use these techniques for communication in your studies, work, and personal life.

SUMMARY

We briefly outline the main takeaways of this chapter.

- Choose a proper presentation structure for a specific audience of stakeholders
  - if the audience knows the problem, we choose a solution-driven structure
  - if (some people in) the audience lack knowledge about the problem, we need a problem-driven structure
- Develop an overall presentation structure
- Develop an introduction
  - introduce a solution-driven presentation structure
    - key question: how should the principal respond to the problem (opportunity)?
    - purpose of presentation: we present our recommended solution
  - introduce a problem-driven presentation structure
    - key question: is there a problem, and if so, how should the principal solve it?
    - purpose of presentation: we present our problem analysis and if applicable, our recommended solution
- Structure of the arguments for the recommendation
  - Why is this a solution: inductive or deductive structure of the arguments
- Structure of the actions for the implementation
  - How to implement: functional grouping or chronological order of the actions

- Create a storyline
  - ○ translate the structure of boxes into a sequence of Post-it notes
  - ○ formulate a message for each Post-it
  - ○ ensure that the sequence of messages reads like a story: the *horizontal* flow of messages
- Structure a slide
  - ○ put the message at the top of the slide in the title
  - ○ create a slide body to support the message: the *vertical* flow from the message to supporting facts
  - ○ add a slide justification at the bottom
- Deliver a presentation to an audience
  - ○ speak by heart
  - ○ use your voice effectively
  - ○ pay attention to body language
  - ○ maintain eye contact
- Interact with an audience
  - ○ invite questions, preferably at the end
  - ○ avoid reacting defensively to questions and comments
  - ○ stimulate discussion about implementation

 Mini Exercise

Identify the key concepts and terms in this chapter, define them briefly and compile your own glossary.

 REFERENCES AND FURTHER READING

Minto, B. (2003). *The Minto Pyramid Principle: Logic in Writing, Thinking and Problem Solving*. London: Minto International.

Zelazny, G. (2007). *They Say it with Charts Complete Toolkit*. New York: McGraw-Hill.

Prepare for Solution Implementation

INTRODUCTION

Solution implementation *looks* simple compared to problem analysis and solution development. Therefore, we tend to underestimate implementation. We may think: "Now that we have come up with the solution, others can implement it." Implementation often fails because it is complex and challenging; therefore, we must systematically prepare an implementation. This chapter will outline a method for preparing an implementation.

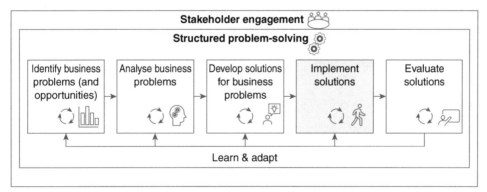

Figure 10.1   Implementing solutions is the fourth step of structured problem-solving

The chapter is structured as follows (see Figure 10.2).

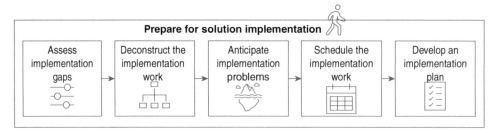

Figure 10.2   Chapter structure

MAIN LEARNING OBJECTIVES

After studying this chapter, you should be able to:

- assess implementation gaps
- develop implementation actions
- schedule implementation actions
- conduct a pre-mortem analysis of an implementation
- assess the implementation readiness of stakeholders required for implementation
- develop an implementation plan

ASSESS THE IMPLEMENTATION GAPS

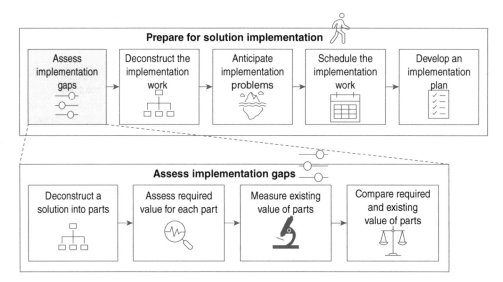

Figure 10.3   A process for assessing implementation gaps

Deconstruct a solution into parts

A complex solution is a structure of parts.

Running Case RobotCo

The solution is to increase the inventory. Tara uses an operations framework consisting of the following four parts:

- processes
- resources and capabilities
- structure and systems
- culture

Solutions to operational problems mean changes to the framework parts (see Figure 10.4).

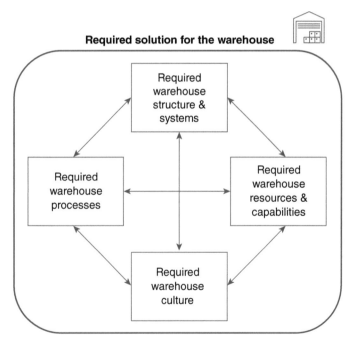

Figure 10.4   An example of a deconstruction of an operational solution into parts

Assess the required value for each part

We assess the *required* value for each part of the solution.

Running Case RobotCo

Tara asks herself: What consequences will the solution have for the warehouse? Figure 10.5 shows that RobotCo needs a new value for each of the four parts of the warehouse solution. For example, warehouse space is an aspect of warehouse resources. The solution requires a warehouse space of 2 million cubic feet.

Measure the existing value of solution parts

We also measure the *existing* values of these parts if we do not already know them. For example, Tara understands that the existing warehouse space is 1.5 million cubic feet. Measuring, observing, estimating, and asking knowledgeable stakeholders and other experts are examples of approaches to obtaining the existing values.

Compare the required and existing value of solution parts

We compare the required and the existing values of the solution parts. For example, the gap between the required and existing warehouse space amounts to 0.5 million cubic feet.

Running Case RobotCo

Since the four parts (see Figure 10.5) must complement and reinforce each other, Tara probably also needs to do something about the other parts when changing one part. Therefore, solutions to operational problems usually mean changes to all four parts. Implementation of the solution is an integrative change of that business function.

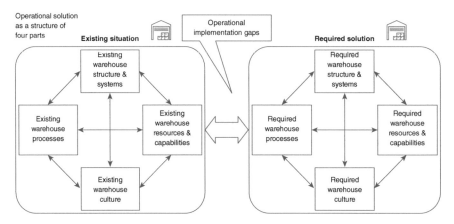

Figure 10.5   Gaps between the existing and required values of an operational solution for a warehouse

Figure 10.6 compares the existing and required values for the parts of an operational solution for the warehouse.

Solution parts	Existing values	Required values
Warehouse processes	• Ordering and stocking parts based on actual use • Frequent extra ordering of parts because they are out-of-stock	• Ordering and stocking parts based on engineers' orders • No or infrequent extra ordering needed
Warehouse structure & systems	Software plans inventory based on real use	Software plans inventory based on engineers' orders
Warehouse resources & capabilities	• Inventory based on real use • Warehouse capacity 1.5m cubic feet	• Larger inventory based on orders • Warehouse capacity 2m cubic feet
Warehouse culture	Expect all engineers' orders to be correct	Acceptance that some engineers' orders are incorrect

Figure 10.6   An example of the required and existing values of the parts of an operational solution

Note: m means million

══════ Running Case ConsultCo ══════

For a *strategic* solution, we may use a different framework. Arpit uses a strategic framework consisting of the following parts:

• arena
• value proposition
• value creation model
• value capture model

Solutions to strategic problems mean a change of the four parts of the principal's strategy. Since these four parts must reinforce each other, Arpit must do something about the other parts when changing one part. Therefore, solutions to strategic problems mean changes to all four parts – an integrative change of strategies. For example, Arpit recommends ConsultCo to change its arena: ConsultCo should operate in two countries instead of one. With a pen stroke, the principal can change the value of ConsultCo's arena. To implement this ambitious change meaningfully, the principal must tailor the consultancy's value proposition to the new arena. Adapting this proposition means adapting models for value creation and value capture. As a result, ConsultCo faces strategic gaps in its arena, value propositions, and models for value creation and capture (see Figure 10.7).

(Continued)

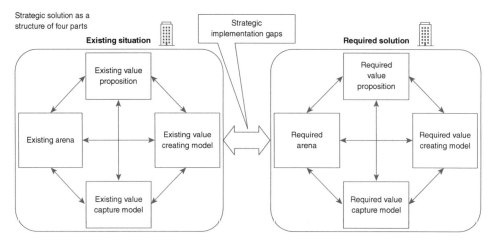

Figure 10.7   Gaps between the existing and required new values of a strategic solution for a company

Figure 10.8 compares ConsultCo's existing situation and the required solution for the new strategy. Between the existing and the required value of each part, Arpit finds implementation gaps.

Solution parts	Existing values	Required values
Arena	Operate in the home country only	Operate both in the home country and the foreign country
Value proposition	Value proposition is tailored to the home country	• Keep existing value proposition for the home country • Adapt value proposition for the foreign country to that country's culture
Value creation model	• One office in the home country only • Value creation model is tailored to the home country	• Keep the office in the home country • Keep the existing value creation model for the home country • Add an office in the foreign country with local staff • Adapt the value creation model to the foreign country's culture and collaborate with the home office
Value capture model	Value capture model is tailored to the home country	• Keep the existing value capture model for home country • Adapt the value capture model for the foreign country to that country's economy

Figure 10.8   An example of a comparison of the required and existing values of the parts of a strategic solution

Understand the relationship between strategic and operational solutions

A *strategic* solution guides most, if not all, company business functions. Figure 10.9 shows the relationship between a strategic solution and the *derived* operational solutions for the relevant business functions. For clarity, the figure provides only two examples of marketing and sales. We may have to consider many more business functions in a real-world project.

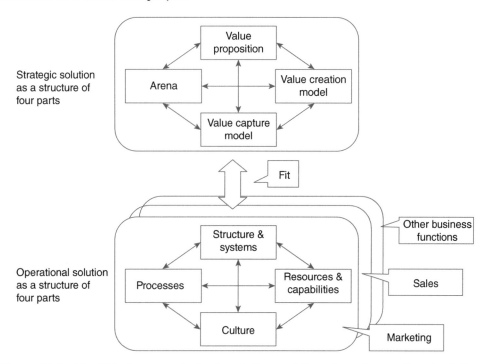

Figure 10.9   The fit between a strategic solution and the relevant operational solutions

Implement a strategic solution

The parts of a strategic solution are more abstract than the parts of an operational solution. For example, a value creation model is more abstract than a business process. The gaps between the existing and required values of the parts of a company strategy are more abstract than the gaps between the existing and required values of the parts of a *business function*. Operational gaps are easier to translate into concrete actions for implementation than strategic gaps. As discussed, strategy and business functions are related (see Figure 10.9). A new strategy calls for new values of the relevant business functions. To bridge *strategic* implementation gaps between the existing and required values of the strategic parts we need to bridge *operational* implementation gaps between the existing and required values of the parts of the relevant business functions. Figure 10.10 shows the links between strategic and operational gaps.

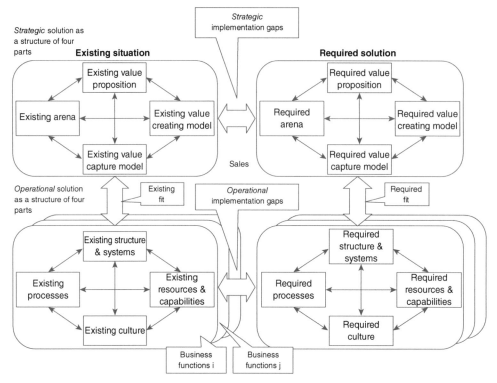

Figure 10.10   Links between strategic implementation gaps and derived operational implementation gaps

— **Mini Exercise** —

Think of a recent strategic product introduction by a well-known company and use Internet research to identify the strategic implementation gaps for this case.

— **Pause and Reflect** —

Use your own experience of a recent project from your study or work. Did you think about implementation gaps?

DECONSTRUCT THE IMPLEMENTATION WORK

We know the implementation gaps between the existing and required values of the parts of a solution. The next question is: *How* will we close the implementation gaps? We determine the implementation work to close these gaps.

We deconstruct the implementation work to close a high-level, abstract implementation gap into a hierarchy of increasingly concrete actions. We implement these actions at the business function level, and this hierarchy of actions is a '*work breakdown structure*'. This deconstruction of the implementation work follows the same principles of logical structuring that we use for structuring problems, solutions, and presentations. A structure of implementation actions should be MECE. Figure 10.11 presents three alternative approaches for deconstructing the implementation work. We already discussed these approaches in the context of problem analysis and solution development (see Figure 4.33, 4.43, and 7.22).

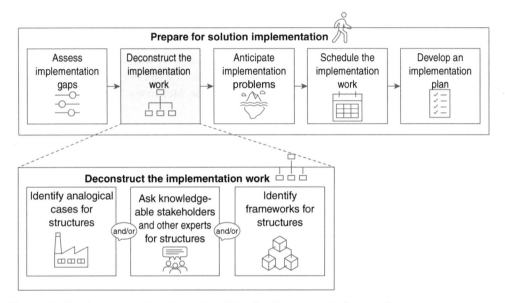

Figure 10.11   A process for deconstructing the implementation work

Identify analogical cases for structures

We may use analogical cases for structuring implementation work. For example, the principal's company may have done the same or a similar implementation before. But there may also be other companies with relevant implementation cases.

Ask knowledgeable stakeholders and other experts for structures

The deconstruction of implementation work requires in-depth knowledge of the principal's company. Lower levels of deconstruction are increasingly concrete and detailed. To obtain knowledge about these lower levels, we must have access to the principal's lower-level managers and frontline professionals. We look for employees who work on the factory floor or shopfloor and have direct contact with customers, suppliers, and other business partners. During the deconstruction process, we follow a cascade down the principal's organizational hierarchy from the top management to the middle management, to the lower management, and finally to the frontline professionals.

We not only benefit from the stakeholders' *knowledge*. We also create stakeholder *commitment* to the implementation work. Engaging with stakeholders leads to an inclusive approach to implementation. The engaged stakeholders may develop a feeling of ownership of the implementation. Such ownership is the opposite of the 'not-invented-here' syndrome, in which people resist implementation because they are not part of the implementation preparation process. Because of their engagement in the deconstruction process, the engaged stakeholders buy into the implementation. They become committed to making the implementation successful.

Identify frameworks for structures

We may also use frameworks to structure the implementation work. In particular, the literature on organizational change may be a source of frameworks. Well-known examples are the change models of Kotter (1996) and Lewin (1947). But we may also benefit from organizational frameworks, such as the McKinsey 7S-model (Peters & Waterman, 1982).

——— Running Case RobotCo ———

Tara deconstructs the work to close the implementation gaps of an operational solution (see Figure 10.12).

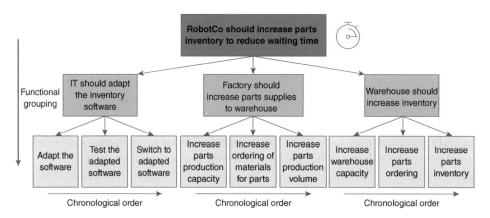

Figure 10.12   An example of a deconstruction of an implementation of an operational solution

The first deconstruction in Figure 10.12 is a *grouping*, and Tara deconstructs by business function: IT, manufacturing (factory), and logistics (warehouse). The second deconstruction in Figure 10.12 follows a *chronological order*. The order is a sequence of implementation steps for changing the values of the solution parts. Grouping and chronological ordering are the two logics for deconstructing implementation work into concrete actions.

Running Case ConsultCo

ConsultCo intends to enter a second country, which is a strategic decision. This case illustrates the deconstruction of implementation to close the implementation gaps of a strategic solution. Arpit wants to implement a new value for 'the arena' part of the strategy. He asks himself: "What actions are relevant for setting up a new office in a foreign country?" Figure 10.13 shows a deconstruction of the implementation work for a new office. The logic is grouping.

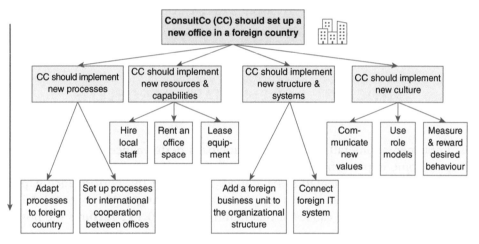

Figure 10.13   An example of a deconstruction of an implementation of a strategic solution

How To Do It?

It is hard to deconstruct an abstract solution into concrete actions for the shopfloor. Refrain from deconstructing abstract implementation gaps in concrete actions on your own. It would help if you had input from the stakeholders on the shopfloor who must perform these actions. Using the ideas and know-how of the stakeholders required for the implementation enables you to concretise the actions *and* gives you the support of these people to implement these actions.

Mini Exercise

Think of a recent strategic product introduction by a well-known company and use Internet research to deconstruct the implementation work for this product (to a maximum of two levels of actions).

Pause and Reflect

Use your own experience of a recent project from your study or work. Did you ask yourself: What should stakeholder X do tomorrow to contribute to the implementation?

ANTICIPATE IMPLEMENTATION PROBLEMS

Conduct a pre-mortem analysis

Most implementations fail to close the principal's performance gap. Therefore, we anticipate some implementation problems. Before we plan an implementation, we *imagine* that the implementation has failed. Recall that the performance gap was the problem, and the solution was supposed to close that gap. We try to think backwards about the possible causes of that failure. Figure 10.14 structures the possible causes.

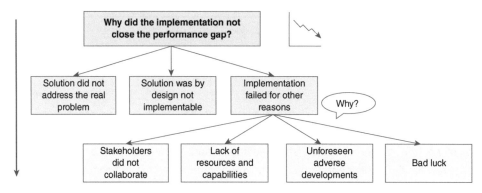

Figure 10.14 **Possible causes of the failure to close a performance gap**

Stakeholders are critical for implementation success. They must be *'ready'* for the implementation:

- they must be aware of the problem, the solution, and the intended implementation
- they must be aligned with the solution and the intended implementation
- they must be able to contribute to the intended implementation

If they are not ready for the implementation, they can cause implementation problems. In Figure 10.15, we outline a process for anticipating implementation problems because stakeholders still need to be ready.

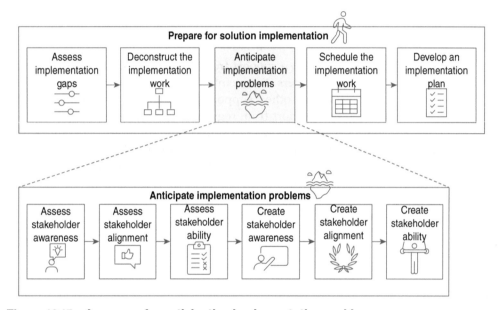

Figure 10.15   A process for anticipating implementation problems

Map the stakeholders in the implementation

The principal must close the solution's implementation gaps for success. The company's top managers must delegate most implementation actions to their lower *managers and professionals*. But the principal may also depend on the approval, collaboration, and passive support of various *external* stakeholders, such as customers, labour unions, and the government. Will these stakeholders do what the principal needs them to do for implementation? We should not take the contributions of these stakeholders for granted.

At the start of a project, we map the stakeholders. But during the project, we deepen our understanding of the problem, which may affect the power-interest map (see Figure 10.16). The development of a solution may also have implications for this map. Power and alignment may vary with the nature of the solutions.

Assess what the principal needs from stakeholders

We identify the stakeholders we need in order to close the implementation gaps. We distinguish between their different needs.

- There is a need for stakeholders' *passive support* of a solution implementation.
  - The principal may need external stakeholders, such as the government, regulators, shareholders, and lenders, to *approve* the chosen solution.
  - The company's managers and professionals must accept the solution. Besides, external stakeholders, such as, labour unions, non-governmental organizations (NGOs), the public, and the media, must *accept* the solution. The acceptance of the solution by these internal and external stakeholders legitimizes the solution. The legitimization gives the principal a 'social licence to operate', that is, to implement and use the solution.
- There is also the need for *active support* from stakeholders. The principal may need resources from stakeholders. For example, governments may provide subsidies, tax arrangements, and other support to the principal's company. The principal may also require support from regulators. The principal may lobby for changes in regulations to accommodate or support the solution. For example, the company wants an import duty to protect itself against foreign competition. Moreover, shareholders and lenders may help the principal by providing financial funding for the solution implementation. Other stakeholders, such as customers, suppliers, and other business partners, may commit their time and knowledge to support the implementation.

Identify natural opponents

Besides stakeholders who must support the implementation of the solution, we also identify any powerful stakeholders with conflicting interests who may *undermine* the implementation. They may try to make the implementation fail by, for example, hijacking the necessary resources, spreading misleading information, or manipulating key stakeholders. The principal's competitors are the most obvious example of powerful conflicting stakeholders or natural opponents.

─── Running Case RobotCo ───

Tara analyses the stakeholders in the chosen solution.

- First, she looks at the power of stakeholders. Who has power over the implementation?
- Second, Tara focuses on the alignment of the powerful stakeholders. Who is aligned with the implementation, and who is not?

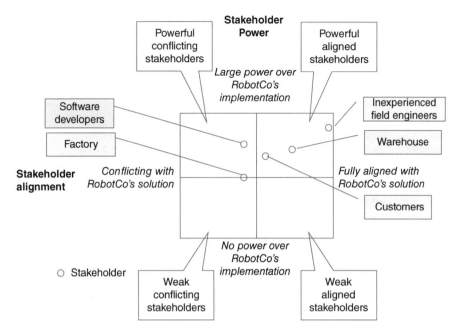

Figure 10.16 **An updated map of some important stakeholders in the chosen solution**

 Pause and Reflect

Use your own experience of a recent project from your study or work. Did you ask yourself: Are the powerful stakeholders with conflicting interests going to sit on their hands to wait until the principal has implemented the chosen solution?

Assess the readiness of stakeholders

Here we discuss stakeholders whose support the principal needs for the implementation. These are the *required* stakeholders. Will these stakeholders be ready to help the principal to close the implementation gaps? We distinguish between three necessary conditions for stakeholder readiness: awareness, alignment, and ability.

Figure 10.17 shows these conditions. We can assess stakeholder readiness through, among other things, interviews, surveys, and the observation of stakeholder behaviour. The readiness assessments allow us to identify gaps between the existing and the required levels of stakeholder awareness, alignment, and the ability for implementation.

	Awareness	Alignment	Ability
Problem (opportunity)	Awareness of the principal's problem (opportunity)		
Objective	Awareness of the principal's objective	Alignment with the principal's objective	
Solution and intended implementation	Awareness of the principal's solution and intended implementation	Alignment with the principal's solution and intended implementation	Ability to implement the principal's solution

Figure 10.17   The readiness of stakeholders to implement solutions: awareness, alignment, and ability

Assess the awareness of the required stakeholders

To implement a solution, the required stakeholders must be aware. What do we mean by 'aware'? Awareness is about knowledge.

- The required stakeholders must know the problem or the opportunity. It is not self-evident that all stakeholders are aware of the problem or opportunity.
- The required stakeholders must also know the performance objective of the principal's company. They need to know what this company wants to achieve. As discussed earlier, objectives do not have to be limited to profit. Companies can also focus on objectives regarding people and the planet. In contrast, opportunities allow new, higher performance objectives. The required stakeholders should know the new objective.
- The required stakeholders must know the solution that the principal's company has chosen. They need to know what the solution is and why the company chose this specific solution.
- To implement the solution, the required stakeholders must know what to do. They must know their role and responsibility in the intended implementation.

Assess the alignment of the required stakeholders

The required stakeholders should align with the principal's company. We distinguish between three areas of alignment: objectives, solutions, and implementation.

- The required stakeholders must be aligned with the principal's performance objective(s). We should not take the alignment of internal stakeholders for granted. For example, in cases of opportunities, the internal stakeholders may be inclined to oppose a new, higher objective. The higher the objective, the greater the challenge for these stakeholders to achieve the desired performance.
- The required stakeholders should also be aligned with the chosen solution and the intended implementation. They must agree with how the principal's company

wants to solve the problem or seize the opportunity. The stakeholders' opinions on the chosen solution's perceived correctness or ethics may vary. For example, the principal has a plan to reduce costs. The labour unions are against the plan because they expect the cuts in the number of employees will lead to an irresponsibly high workload for the remaining staff.

Assess the ability of the required stakeholders

The required stakeholders must be able to implement the solutions. For example, the managers and professionals of the principal's company should have the knowledge and the skills to fulfil their role in the implementation. They should also have the resources to do their implementation tasks. For example, they should have sufficient budget, staff, data, and equipment. The organizational structure and systems should enable the stakeholders to do their implementation work. For example, stakeholders should be empowered and have the mandate for their assigned implementation tasks.

Moreover, the required stakeholders, such as the managers and professionals in the principal's company, should have time for their implementation tasks. If the implementation work is on top of their everyday tasks, these stakeholders temporarily face an extra workload. Moreover, other implementation projects may take place at the same time. The simultaneous implementation projects ensure an accumulation of work for those involved. If these stakeholders are unable to implement the solutions, they will be frustrated.

 How To Do It?

You may assess stakeholder readiness by asking the principal. Managers can give you their judgment of the readiness of their subordinates. As managers they have an idea how ready their subordinates are. Moreover, the human resources (HR) department can be a valuable resource here. The stakeholders themselves are also a source of information. Observations of stakeholder behaviour can be helpful. If you do interviews with stakeholders, you must be critical. The stakeholders may give politically correct answers.

Create stakeholder awareness

The principal may also need to work with *external* stakeholders to implement a solution. Some examples of external stakeholders are suppliers, customers, and business partners. The external stakeholders whose support we require, must be aware, aligned, and able to provide that support. We therefore need to ensure that all required stake-holders, both internal and external, are ready to support the implementation. The principal must ensure that these stakeholders are aware, aligned, and able. Figure 10.18 provides some actions to ensure stakeholders' awareness, alignment, and ability.

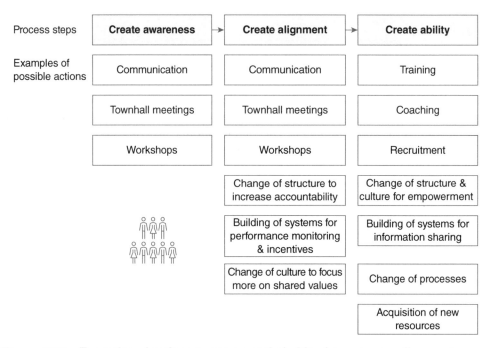

Figure 10.18   Examples of actions to ensure stakeholders' awareness, alignment, and ability

The stakeholders participating in the implementation should receive information about the solution, the implementation plan, and their role in the implementation. We inform the required stakeholders on a need-to-know basis.

A readiness assessment informs us about which stakeholders need (increased) awareness about what subject. We must inform these unaware stakeholders. But we also must answer any questions these stakeholders have. Therefore, we need to set up two-way communication.

The communication with the internal stakeholders should be multi-level. We need to address the different hierarchical levels of the principal's company: top managers, middle and lower managers, and frontline professionals. We may use multimedia, including online video meetings, and print communication. In the digital era, physical gatherings remain essential. We may organize workshops for small groups and town hall meetings – i.e., organization-wide business meetings – for large groups of employees. The principal should play a critical role in communication. We can prepare the tools and forms of communication, but the principal should be the one to communicate with her subordinates.

How To Do It? ————————————————————

Do not assume that telling a message *once* is enough. Many people will only pick up on the message after hearing it more than once. There can be all sorts of reasons for this. For example, people need to concentrate and listen better, they have other things on their mind, or the message is too complex for them. Therefore, you must say it at least three times to ensure the message gets through.

Create stakeholder alignment

The readiness assessment also informs us about which stakeholders need to be (more) aligned on what subject. The principal needs to align these stakeholders on the performance objectives, the solution, and the intended implementation. We advise the principal on how to engage and persuade these stakeholders. For solving *problems*, the principal must instil a sense of urgency in the stakeholders. So-called 'burning platforms' or crises will motivate stakeholders to accept solutions and support implementation.

Envision the future

For seizing *opportunities*, the principal may envision the company's future after successfully seizing that opportunity. In any case, we need to develop compelling stories about solutions. Such stories should contain clear and appealing ambitions or aspirations. Because maximizing profit may not inspire all stakeholders, we need to identify meaningful purposes for everybody. To motivate stakeholders, we should define the purpose of the implementation in terms of shared values and not-for-profit objectives, such as supporting society and saving the planet.

Take an inclusive approach

All required stakeholders should feel part of the implementation journey. Therefore, the implementation work must follow an *inclusive* approach. We engage these stakeholders with two-way communication and meetings. We may also need to adapt the organizational structure, systems, and culture.

- The principal may have to adapt the *organizational structure* to align the internal stakeholders. She must make individuals responsible and accountable for the results of their assigned implementation tasks. Shared responsibility often means no responsibility because the individuals involved may hide behind each other.

- We advise on how to adapt the *organizational systems* for performance management. The principal must measure implementation progress and reward satisfactory results.
- The principal may have to improve the *organizational culture* to create alignment. The principal will play an essential role in cultural change by modelling the new behaviour.

Align the required stakeholders with conflicting interests

The required stakeholders may need (more) confidence in the chosen solution. They may also disagree about the ethics of the solution. The solution may clash with stakeholders' norms and values. If these stakeholders do not align with the principal's solution, they will resist the implementation. We may ask: "How should the principal align stakeholders with conflicting interests?" We distinguish between three approaches.

- The principal may convince these stakeholders that the solution is also in their (long-term) interests. For example, the principal may convince unions that while the reorganization will cost jobs in the short term, it will create many more new jobs in the long term.
- The principal can provide incentives to these stakeholders if they collaborate. For example, the principal can promise bonuses and promotions to managers and frontline professionals.
- The principal can exert her power over these stakeholders to make them accountable for some critical results. If they consciously fail to deliver these results, the principal holds them responsible and imposes sanctions. For example, the principal will fire a manager or not extend a contract if that manager fails to meet her target.

There are limits to how much alignment we can achieve (recall the discussion about resolving stakeholder conflict in Chapter 6). For some stakeholders, alignment is impossible. Therefore, we must devise a plan to keep these powerful conflicting stakeholders at bay.

 ── **How To Do It?** ──────────────

Try to avoid getting everyone on board at all costs. You may fail, and the price will be too high.

Create stakeholder ability

The required stakeholders who are informed and motivated but lack capabilities and resources for their implementation role will become frustrated. Therefore, it is essential to enable these parties to do their implementation work. Enablement of stakeholders may concern new knowledge, information, skills, and personnel, but also a mandate to decide.

Engage change agents

The principal needs 'change agents' or people who can prepare and facilitate the implementation. These people should inspire and encourage the required stakeholders. They build consensus among these stakeholders and overcome any resistance. We can identify the potential change agents. Criteria include their skills (such as communication and collaboration), formal or informal leadership, and track record (past performance). These agents should get critical roles to drive the implementation. The principal must enable these people to fulfil a positive role in the implementation. These change agents form the implementation team.

Personal skills

The managers and frontline professionals need skills to conduct their assigned implementation actions. We distinguish between different skills, such as leadership skills, managerial skills, and technical skills. If the concerned managers and employees lack these skills, we may train and coach these people. Such training can take different forms. Besides traditional classroom training, we may offer more modern formats, such as computer simulations for experiential learning. Simulations may provide managers and employees with an immersive experience of their new working conditions after the implementation.

Organizational capabilities

We may upskill the principal's current employees, but the principal can also replace current employees who do not have and cannot or do not want to develop the required skills with new employees who have these skills. An ethical principal ensures a good social plan for the redundant staff.

The ability to implement solutions not only rests on the skills of individual managers or frontline professionals. The implementation also depends on *organizational* capabilities, which rely on the collaboration of skilled individuals. We may advise on organizational restructuring to create linkages between the people who need to collaborate for organizational capabilities. Moreover, we may recommend adjusting organizational systems, processes, resources, and culture to enable individuals to implement their actions together.

How To Do It?

Do not assume that all stakeholders will have time for your implementation plan. The best people never have time to spare because they are always in demand. Assigning an implementation role means you should also decide what work the concerned people should give up during implementation. Implementation is also choosing what actions people will *not* do (during the implementation).

Pause and Reflect

Use your own experience of a recent project from your study or work. Did you ask yourself: Are the assigned people really going to implement this solution?

SCHEDULE THE IMPLEMENTATION WORK

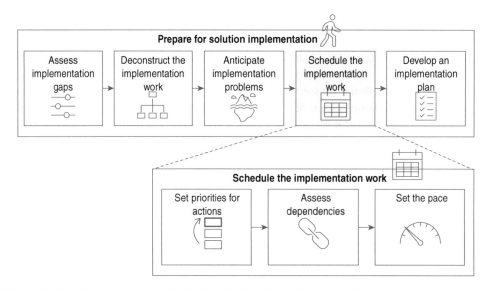

Figure 10.19   A process for scheduling the implementation work

Set the priorities for the actions

Rapid success of the implementation work is vital to create support for the required changes. The success convinces the required stakeholders that the principal is right. It helps if we show early in the implementation process that the solution works. Therefore, we evaluate the implementation actions on two criteria:

- the action's contribution to the principal's performance
- the ease of implementing the action

Figure 10.20 shows a simplified mapping of implementation actions on these criteria. The top-right quadrant houses the impactful and easy actions that are the 'low-hanging fruit' or 'quick wins'.

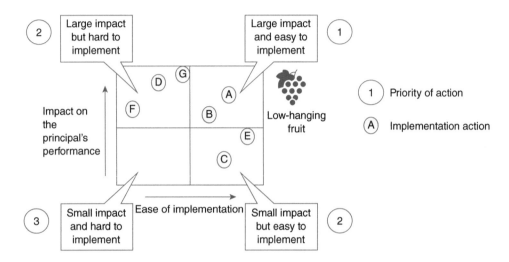

Figure 10.20   A simplified mapping of implementation actions

Assess the dependencies between the actions

In consultation with the principal, we need to schedule the implementation work. When should the implementation begin? When should it end? Besides the timing of the actions, we also need to consider the order or sequence of work. All actions are necessary to implement the solution but performing all actions simultaneously is beyond our resources and capabilities.

Moreover, we must complete some actions before new actions can start. We must account for any dependencies between the actions. For example, there may be an action of the third priority that is a condition for a higher priority action. For instance, before a bank can introduce a new customer service (a first-priority action), it must build a new IT system (a third-priority action). Therefore, we must determine an intelligent schedule of actions (see Figure 10.21), and in doing so, we distinguish between two vital parts of implementation planning:

- the actions to close the implementation gap(s)
- the actions to make the required stakeholders aware, aligned, and able to conduct these actions. The principal must inform, align, and enable the required stakeholders.

Figure 10.21 shows a simplified example of an implementation schedule.

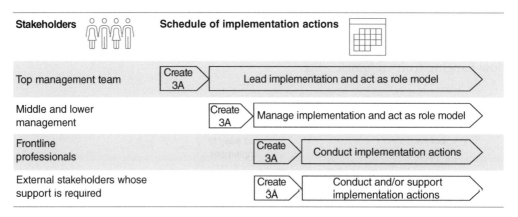

Figure 10.21   A simplified example of an implementation schedule

Note: 3A means the Awareness, Alignment, and Ability of stakeholders

Set the pace

The principal needs to decide about the pacing or speed of the implementation. How fast should she roll out the implementation plan? The desired speed depends on the nature of the problem or opportunity. In some cases, principals must quickly implement solutions. Sometimes haste is required. For example, quick action is vital if principals find themselves in a crisis that threatens their company's survival. Competitive pressure can also force principals to accelerate. But the quicker the implementation, the more resources we need. Moreover, a rapid implementation may entail risks, and the chance of errors increases under time pressure.

DEVELOP AN IMPLEMENTATION PLAN

We develop an implementation plan, which comprises the project scope (including desired results), budget, organization, and risk management plan (see Figure 10.22). It is a memorandum of shared understanding between the principal and us. The plan also acts as a contract between the principal, the project team, and key stakeholders.

Determine the project scope

In consultation with the principal, we define the scope of the project. It should be clear to all required stakeholders what the project's boundaries are. We must create a written IS/NOT list. This list shows what is in the project (the so-called 'in-scope' actions) and what is not (the 'out-scope' actions).

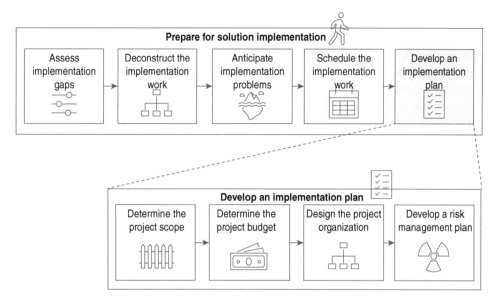

Figure 10.22   A process for developing an implementation plan

The purpose of the implementation is to close the principal's performance gap (see Figure 10.23). Since many other factors may influence the principal's performance, we must define clear project outcomes and deliverables. We need to determine objective and verifiable indicators of project success.

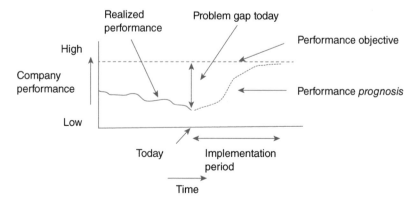

Figure 10.23   Solution implementation aims to close the performance gap

Determine the project budget

We must also determine what are the necessary resources to conduct the implementation project. Critical resources are people. People are about more than just the number of individuals and how many hours they may spend on the project. Equally important are the qualities of these individuals: knowledge, experience, skills, and attitude. In addition to human resources, projects require financial resources. Projects need budgets for investments (for example, in assets) and expenditures (for example, on external service providers).

Design the project organization

We define the *project team member profiles*: the required knowledge, and the experience, skills, and attitude of team members. These team members can be the principal's managers and frontline professionals. The principal must decide on the division of roles and responsibilities between them. The implementation project should have *sponsors*: decision-makers who have sufficient authority. In addition, large projects need *steering committees* consisting of the principal, the project sponsor, and other relevant internal stakeholders (typically senior managers).

We create *meeting schedules*: when and where to meet with whom to discuss what subjects. We also design *procedures for problem-solving*. When we say 'problems' in this context, we do not mean the key questions of Chapter 2, but problems that may arise during implementation. For example, we may come into conflict with stakeholders about access to data. In such scenarios, there must be an escalation procedure.

We also need to maintain a *project file*, which is the administration of all records relating to the project. Finally, we need to decide on *communication processes*. This process not only involves communication within the project team and with the steering committee, but also communication with the other stakeholders required for the implementation work.

Develop a risk management plan

Implementations are not without risks. Risks are specific events or developments which negatively impact projects. Examples of adverse events and developments are cost overruns, delays, out-of-scope actions, and deterioration of the quality of the project deliverables. We need to identify the implementation risks. Our solutions rest on assumptions that we cannot always test upfront with fact-based analyses. Some assumptions are about the future, and there are no data about the future. That is why uncertainty remains about whether solutions will work.

We must estimate the impact and likelihood of the risks. Next, we must develop preventive actions or contingency plans to deal with the negative consequences of materialized risks. We can mitigate risks by starting implementations with pilot tests. If a pilot is successful, we roll out the implementation plan. In case of failure, we learn from it and adapt our implementation approach. We may use a staged approach to implementation: we start small and, if successful, we scale up.

Pause and Reflect

Consider how you may use these techniques for preparing solution implementation in your studies, work, and personal life.

SUMMARY

We briefly outline the main takeaways of this chapter.

- Assess implementation gaps
  - deconstruct a solution into parts
  - assess the required values for each part
  - measure the existing values of each part
  - compare the required and existing values of each part
- Develop implementation actions
  - deconstruct the implementation work into concrete actions
  - identify analogical cases for structures
  - ask knowledgeable stakeholders and other experts for structures
  - identify frameworks from the literature for structures
- Schedule implementation actions
  - set priorities for actions
  - assess dependencies
  - set the pace
- Conduct a pre-mortem analysis of an implementation
  - the solution did not address the real problem
  - the solution was by design not implementable
  - the implementation failed for other reasons
    - the stakeholders did not collaborate
    - lack of resources and capabilities
    - unforeseen adverse developments
    - bad luck
- Assess the implementation readiness of stakeholders required for implementation
  - assess stakeholder awareness of the objective, problem, solution, and the implementation
  - assess stakeholder alignment with the objective, solution, and the implementation
  - assess stakeholder ability to implement the solution
- Develop an implementation plan
  - determine the project scope
  - determine the project budget
  - design the project organization
  - develop a risk management plan

Mini Exercise

Identify the key concepts and terms in this chapter, define them briefly and compile your own glossary.

REFERENCES AND FURTHER READING

Freeman, R. E. (1984). *Strategic Management: A Stakeholder Approach*. Boston, MA: Pitman.

Kaplan, R. S., Kaplan, R. E., & Norton, D. P. (2004). *Strategy Maps: Converting Intangible Assets into Tangible Outcomes*. Boston, MA: Harvard Business Press.

Kotter, J. P. (1996). *Leading Change*. Boston, MA: Harvard Business School Press.

Lewin, K. (1947). Frontiers in group dynamics: Concept, method and reality in social science; social equilibria and social change. *Human Relations*, *1*, 5–41.

Peters, T. J., & Waterman Jr, R. H. (1982). *In Search of Excellence*. London: Harper & Row.

Facilitate and Evaluate an Implementation

INTRODUCTION

After putting much effort into the implementation plan, people may believe that implementing is just ticking off the plan. A plan is necessary for a successful implementation, but we need more. No plan survives the confrontation with reality. We must be ready to adapt our plan if circumstances change. This chapter deals with a systematic approach to implementation, including adjusting the course when necessary.

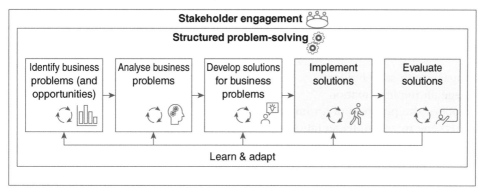

Figure 11.1   Implementing and evaluating solutions are the final steps of structured problem-solving

We facilitate the implementation while the required stakeholders do the actual implementation work (see Figure 11.2).

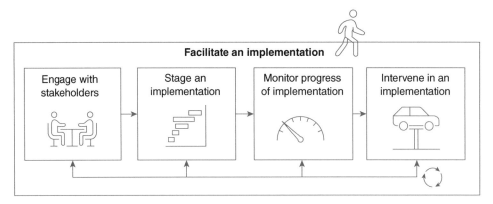

Figure 11.2   A process for facilitating an implementation

We also outline how to evaluate an implementation (see Figure 11.3).

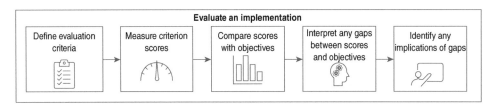

Figure 11.3   A process for evaluating an implementation

MAIN LEARNING OBJECTIVES

After studying this chapter, you should be able to:

- engage with stakeholders
- stage an implementation
- monitor the progress of an implementation
- intervene in an implementation
- evaluate an implementation

ENGAGE WITH STAKEHOLDERS

Chapter 6 outlined stakeholder engagement in problem-solving. Here we engage stakeholders in the solution implementation.

Chapter 6 introduced a process for stakeholder engagement (see Figure 11.4).

1. Identify critical stakeholder dependencies
    a. Identify what we need from stakeholders for implementation
    b. Identify vulnerabilities: how stakeholders can negatively affect the implementation

2. Decide on the stakeholder approach:

    a. Engage powerful aligned stakeholders
    b. Align powerful conflicting stakeholders
    c. Reduce vulnerability to powerful conflicting stakeholders
    d. Align weak, conflicting stakeholders
    e. Strengthen weak, aligned stakeholders

3. Ensure stakeholder collaboration

    a. Specify expectations
    b. Check for understanding and commitment
    c. Follow-up

4. Resolve stakeholder conflict

    a. Assertive-cooperative: collaborate
    b. Unassertive-cooperative: accommodate
    c. Assertive-uncooperative: compete
    d. Unassertive-uncooperative: avoid
    e. In-between assertiveness and cooperativeness: compromise

Here we discuss some implementation-specific topics.

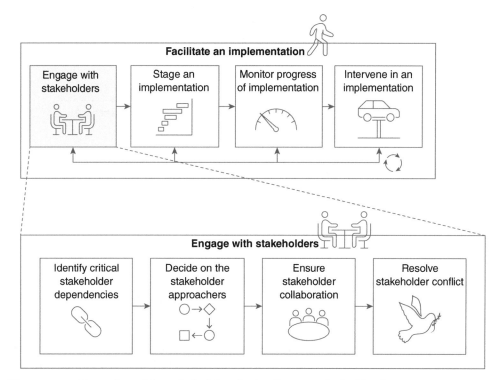

Figure 11.4 Engaging with stakeholders is the first step in facilitating an implementation

Set up an implementation office

If the implementation of a solution is complex, we set up an implementation office to facilitate the implementation. The implementation office is more than a project management office. The latter tracks a project's key performance indicators and monitors progress. In contrast, the implementation office has a more significant role than 'checking the boxes'. They are responsible for the implementation and must manage the trajectory.

The principal empowers the implementation office to steer the implementation if the office sees the need to do so. Therefore, the implementation office can intervene in implementations, challenge stakeholders, and impose sanctions on them if necessary. Such an office consists of the people who need to run the implementation. The head of this office reports to the steering committee of the implementation project. This committee includes the principal and any other top managers.

The implementation office deconstructs the implementation plan into workstreams. These streams are MECE groupings of implementation actions. A project team led by a manager or a senior professional implements a workstream. Figure 11.5 shows a simplified example of the organization of an implementation. The number of workstreams per project and the number of actions per workstream may vary.

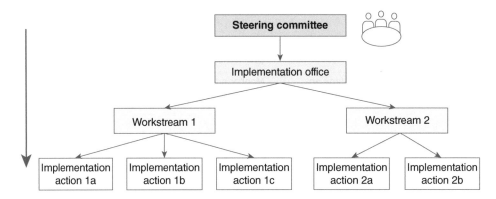

Figure 11.5   An example of the organization of an implementation

Prepare the leadership before the project kick-off

We need help to implement the project. Relevant stakeholders must accept, support, and sometimes approve the implementation. These stakeholders must be ready for implementation. Recall the 'triple As':

• Awareness of the objective, the problem, the solution, and the implementation plan
• Alignment of interests and values with the principal's objective, solution, and the implementation plan
• Ability to implement the solution

The leadership of the principal's company is critical to implementation success, and they must be ready. We will conduct workshops to inform and align the top managers around the objectives of the implementation process. Next, we will enable the principal and the other top managers to lead their organization into the implementation process. These leaders should act as role models for their organization and lead by example.

Engage the principal's organization during the project kick-off

Preferably, the principal should introduce the implementation in her organization. She should tell a compelling change story to the lower-level managers and the frontline professionals. Suppose the implementation concerns a solution to a problem. In that case, the principal should create a sense of urgency in her organization. But she should also energize these stakeholders. The principal should envision the bright future of the organization *after* the implementation. By creating an inspiring aspiration (not only about profit, but also about people and the planet), the principal can motivate the stakeholders to commit to the implementation. The principal and other top managers should develop the conviction among their subordinates that the solution is vital to the organization's future.

It is crucial that the lower-level managers and the frontline professionals feel included in the solution implementation. The implementation must be a joint effort of all relevant stakeholders: we need an inclusive approach.

Empower the lower-level managers and frontline employees

The implementation office should *enable* lower-level managers and frontline professionals to conduct the assigned actions. Therefore, the office should invest in these people. For example, individuals may need upskilling, and the implementation office may provide training and coaching to develop these people. The office may also have to adapt the principal's organizational processes, structure, systems, and culture to support the implementation.

Moreover, the office should empower internal stakeholders without a mandate to act. The implementation office may have to change the principal's organizational structure to empower these stakeholders. If the principal's organizational culture is inappropriate for the new solution, then the office must improve the culture. For example, the culture may be risk-averse, whereas the new solution requires a considerable tolerance for failure. Role modelling by the principal and top managers can be essential in changing the culture. Managers should not just tell people to change, but lead by example, and leaders should 'walk the talk'.

Communicate

The implementation office regularly communicates with the principal's organization during the implementation. These communications are frequent, for example, weekly updates to keep relevant stakeholders informed and engaged. Ideally, the principal or other top managers will communicate these messages. They should show the progress of the implementation. These leaders should also recognize and reward any stakeholders who perform well in the implementation. At the beginning of the implementation, the office needs some quick results. These are the so-called 'quick wins'. These successes are required to motivate the stakeholders. Early successes give confidence in the implementation plan. The organization should celebrate the implementation successes.

Pause and Reflect

Use your own experience of a recent project from your study or work. Did you ask yourself: Have people got the message, or should we repeat it?

STAGE AN IMPLEMENTATION

We distinguish between three forms of project staging: linear, parallel, and iterative.

Linear projects

A linear project is a sequence of steps: it is the simplest way to organize the project work. We presuppose a logical series of actions (see Figure 11.6). The linear form only works if the future is certain. Often there is a (long) preparation or planning phase before the implementation starts.

Figure 11.6   An example of a linear process model

Parallel projects

The parallel project is a more complex form of a linear project. This staging form consists of parallel sequences of actions that resemble a combination of linear projects (see Figure 11.7). We use it when we have independent implementation actions. We can run the actions in parallel if we are under time pressure and have enough resources.

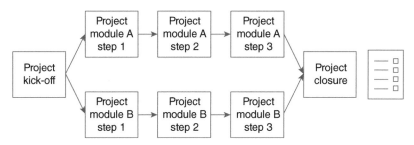

Figure 11.7 An example of a parallel process model

Iterative projects

If we face great uncertainty (level 3 or 4), then we cannot use linear staging. Because of the uncertainty, we cannot be sure that we will do everything right the first time. Therefore, we need to create space to make mistakes and learn from our errors. The planning phase is relatively short, and the implementation serves as a test. We alternate planning and implementation actions whereby the implementation lessons inform a new planning phase. Learning from errors means cycles or iterations. A famous example is the 'agile process model', which consists of predefined cycles of planning and implementation (the so-called 'time boxes'). Figure 11.8 shows an agile process model.

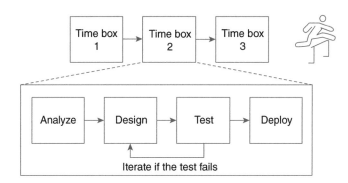

Figure 11.8 An example of an agile process model

How to decide on the staging approach?

Assess the level of uncertainty around the implementation

Chapter 8 introduced a process for assessing the level of uncertainty.

1. Identify the relevant variables for implementation
2. Assess the future values of these variables
3. Assess the probabilities of these values

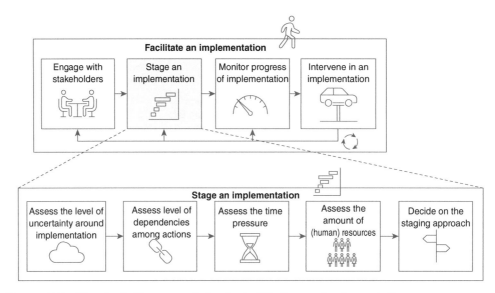

Figure 11.9   Staging is the second step in facilitating an implementation

Assess the level of dependencies among actions

To what extent are the actions dependent on each other? An action can be a condition for another action. For instance, we must build a new IT system before introducing a new customer service. We must perform these actions one after the other.

Assess the time pressure

How much time pressure do we face? In the event of a problem, the lack of financial reserves can create time pressure. Opportunities can be a race with the competition to be the first to introduce a new product.

Assess the number of resources

How many resources, such as people, equipment, and financial resources, do the different actions require? If we have sufficient resources, we can do the actions in parallel.

Decide on the staging approach

Figure 11.10 provides a decision tree for deciding on an appropriate approach.

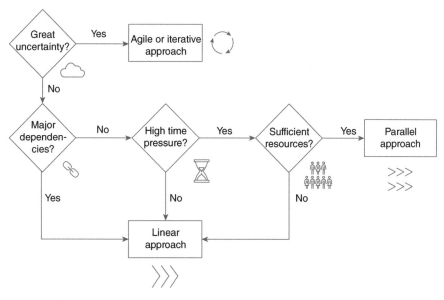

Figure 11.10   A process for deciding on the implementation approach

Mitigate the risks

An iterative model allows us to start small and then scale up. We will implement on a small scale to 'pilot test' our solution. It is a small-scale experiment to find out whether the solution works. We learn from the test results. Based on these outcomes we may adapt our implementation plan and even the solution. Adaptation is not a problem at this implementation stage, at least not compared to the later stages. This early adaptation prevents larger problems at later stages.

The implementation office will only roll out the plan if there is enough certainty that the plan will work. Otherwise, the risks will be too great. A successful pilot reduces the risks. After a successful pilot, we can have enough confidence in our solution and implementation plan. Now the implementation office is ready to 'scale up' the implementation. We will roll out our implementation plan on a large scale.

━━━━━━━━ **Running Case RobotCo** ━━━━━━━━

Identify the critical path of actions

Tara has set up an implementation office that is responsible for the staging of the implementation. A crucial concept in staging is the critical path. This path is the most extended sequence of *dependent* actions. Therefore, the critical path determines the

(Continued)

shortest possible duration of an implementation process. Tara can identify the critical path in the following steps:

1. List all implementation actions (actions A, B, and C in the example of Figure 11.11).
2. Assess the duration of each action. Tara estimates how much time it will take to complete an action (see the numbers between brackets in Figure 11.11).
3. Identify any dependencies between the actions. Can specific actions only start after we have completed other actions? For example, before the principal can introduce a new customer service, a new IT system must be ready. In Figure 11.11, B depends on A. C is not dependent on any other action.
4. Determine which actions are critical and which actions have a 'float'. Float is the amount of time we can delay a given action without delaying the entire project. We can delay actions with a float without making the project longer. But we cannot delay critical actions without making the project longer. Actions A and B are critical as they determine the project's eight-week duration. Action C has eight weeks to complete. As C's duration is only four weeks, C has four weeks spare. The four weeks is the float.
5. Define the sequence of critical actions as the critical path. The series of A and B is the critical path.

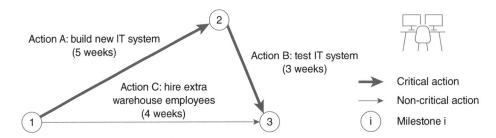

Figure 11.11   A simplified example of a critical path

Plan the actions

Tara must plan all actions for solution implementation. She distinguishes three essential guidelines for such planning:

*   The critical actions are the priority. Tara must plan and monitor the critical path with the utmost care.
*   Some actions require pilots before scaling up. Tara must reserve enough time for these pilots before the plan is rolled out.
*   A project needs 'quick wins' to boost morale. Tara must plan quick wins as early as possible in the implementation trajectory.

Tara can use a Gantt chart for planning the implementation actions. Figure 11.12 provides an example of the actions of Figure 11.11.

Action	Week							
	1	2	3	4	5	6	7	8
A: build IT system	■■■■■■■■■■■■■							
B: test system						■■■■■■■		
C: hire employees	■■■■■■■■							

Figure 11.12   A simplified example of a Gantt chart

MONITOR THE PROGRESS OF AN IMPLEMENTATION

The implementation office must track and manage the implementation project. The process may look as follows (see Figure 11.13).

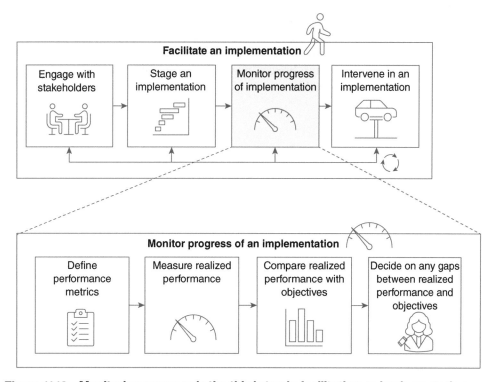

Figure 11.13   Monitoring progress is the third step in facilitating an implementation

Define the performance metrics

The office needs information about the status of the project schedule:

- progress of project actions
- costs of these actions
- timing of the actions

Moreover, we need updates on any open problems that arise during implementation. In addition, the office requires information about any risks. We use metrics that indicate the status of risks.

Create a performance management structure

We may create a performance management structure for the implementation process. The office will identify a set of key performance indicators that provide a good picture of the progress of the actions.

Measure the realized performance

The implementation office decides on the frequency of status information and assigns responsibilities to stakeholders for information collection. The office tracks these indicators to keep the score of the implementation actions. The scores can be presented on a performance management dashboard (see Figure 11.14). The implementation office checks the boxes, identifies any problems with progress, and develops solutions for these problems.

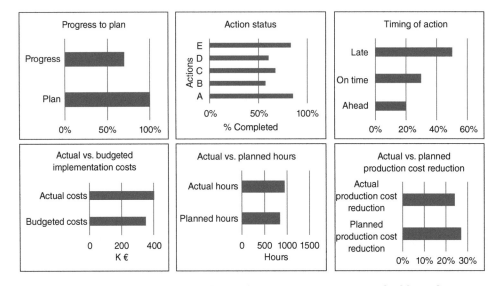

Figure 11.14   A simplified example of a performance management dashboard

───────────── **Running Case RobotCo** ─────────────

Tara monitors progress with a Gantt tracking chart which compares:

- the timing according to the plan
- the realized or actual timing for completed actions
- the expected timing for ongoing actions (see Figure 11.15)

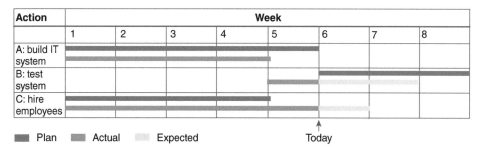

Action	Week							
	1	2	3	4	5	6	7	8
A: build IT system								
B: test system								
C: hire employees								

■ Plan   ■ Actual   ▨ Expected   Today

Figure 11.15   An example of a Gantt tracking chart

Compare the realized performance to the objectives

How does the realized performance compare to the performance objectives? Is implementation on track? Do we reach the objectives or not? We identify any gaps. Data visualisation (such as Figure 11.15) makes it easier to understand gaps and communicate with stakeholders.

Decide on gaps between the realized performance and the objectives

A gap points to a problem. We frame a problem as a gap between the realized performance and the objective. Should every gap lead to an intervention? We only intervene if a gap is substantial, and we expect it to be structural, meaning that it will not get smaller or disappear.

 ───── **Mini Exercise** ─────

Think of a recent strategic product introduction by a well-known company and use Internet research to identify the key performance indicators for monitoring progress of the implementation (no more than five).

Pause and Reflect

Use your own experience of a recent project from your study or work. Did you ask yourself: Is everybody putting in their best effort, or are some people only paying lip service to the implementation plan?

INTERVENE IN AN IMPLEMENTATION

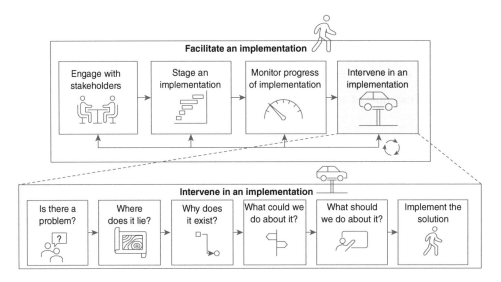

Figure 11.16   The Sequential Analysis Method for intervening in an implementation

Is there a problem?

The implementation office must follow through and keep people accountable for delays in actions and other problems during implementation. The office should not tolerate missed deadlines. Therefore, they frequently organize standardized meetings with the workstream leaders and their teams. The office head leads these discussions, and a representative from the principal's business control department will also be present for the reviews.

- The participants discuss the implementation *progress* and review the commitments that workstream leaders and their teams made in the previous meeting. Have these commitments been realized?

- If not (gaps between realization and commitments), they will discuss any *problems*, explaining why workstream leaders did not meet the promises.
- The workstream leaders also update the implementation office about *any relevant developments* that impact the implementation.
- Finally, the workstream leaders make *commitments* in front of their peers for the next period. Such public commitments increase the pressure on workstream leaders to keep their promises.

These meetings act as a moment of truth for the workstream leaders and thus provide the necessary discipline. Frequent and regular meetings, weekly or more often, create a rhythm for the involved stakeholders.

Where does the problem lie?

Workstream leaders may encounter various problems during implementation. There may have been delays in actions and deliverables. Additionally, the realized performances may not meet expectations. For example, the quality of the deliverables, outputs, or products and services may need improvement. Moreover, workstream leaders may exceed their budgets.

Why does the problem exist?

If workstream leaders have not achieved their commitments, they must discuss the underlying problems with the implementation office. Together with the office, the workstream leaders identify the problem causes (see Figure 11.17).

Figure 11.17   A logical structure of the possible causes of implementation problems

Problems with the implementation plan

Poor implementation can also stem from a flawed or inadequate implementation plan. The plan is not good enough. Plans can fall short in many ways, such as:

- the implementation office has overlooked certain aspects of the implementation
- the implementation office has not taken adequate action

- communication with the stakeholders is poor
- stakeholders do not carry out implementation actions well enough because of insufficient collaboration between the involved parties

Problems with the solution

Implementation can go according to plan, but the results for the principal can still be disappointing. A reason for this can be that the solution is not good. Remember that the solution rests on assumptions about the future. At the time of decision-making, the future is uncertain. Therefore, the principal must decide under uncertainty. When the principal implements the solution, it may become apparent that one or more of the solution's assumptions are incorrect. Things have turned out differently than we expected. Examples are customers reacting less positively than assumed or competitors responding more aggressively to the principal's solution than expected.

Even if we systematically assess the assumptions of our solution hypothesis, we cannot determine with certainty that these assumptions are correct. After all, assumptions are about beliefs about the future. Misjudging such assumptions is not a culpable and avoidable mistake but the inevitable consequence of uncertainty. Flawed solutions present severe problems for us. We need to analyse why our solution does not work. The cause can lie in the solution development, but it can also lie deeper. It may be that the problem analysis was flawed. In the latter case, we must redo the analysis. Based on the improved problem analysis, we must develop a new solution. These are serious setbacks that cause significant delays and budget overruns.

Problems with the stakeholders

Double tasks for the stakeholders

We need to account for the regular functions of the principal's managers and front-line professionals. The implementation of solutions comes on top of running the business. For example, 'during the store's renovation, sales must continue as usual'. These double tasks put extra pressure on the principal's workforce. Under this pressure, they can easily make mistakes. Overloading staff can also mean that these people:

- do not entirely perform implementation actions
- perform actions too late
- do not perform the actions at all

Exemplary implementation plans consider the double burden on the principal's workforce. *Either* the employees get help from external parties, such as external services providers, *or* the implementation office adjusts the deadlines to the available time that people have. Such plans fit the employees' agendas and workload.

Resistance by stakeholders

Despite our efforts to align stakeholders, some may resist the implementation plan. Stakeholders can openly or secretly resist the implementation. In the latter case, they publicly say yes to the implementation, but their actions show the opposite. We distinguish between the following reasons:

- *Disagreement*: This resistance arises because people disagree about the solution or the implementation plan. An example is the double tasks.
- *Opportunism*: People may also be opportunistic and follow their conflicting private agenda.
- *Cockiness and stubbornness*: Some stakeholders do not follow implementation plans because they are cocky or stubborn. These individuals go their way and only care a little about the implementation plan but do what they want.
- *Distraction*: Stakeholders start the implementation well but gradually get *distracted* by things other than the implementation plan.

Unforeseen changes

Other reasons why implementation does not solve the problem are unforeseen changes. After developing the implementation plan, some event or development has undermined the solution or the plan. It can be something within the principal's company, the principal's industry, or the macro-environment. An example of a harmful internal event is the unforeseen departure of two of the principal's most talented employees, who leave to establish a new company. We could not foresee these events or developments. These unforeseen changes undermine the implementation plan. Then we must go back to the drawing-board to develop a new plan. The principal will be disappointed, and we will have to explain that this was an *unavoidable* mistake and that we are *not* culpably guilty.

 How To Do It?

Provide flexibility for learning and adapting because your implementation plan will probably go differently than you hope.

Bad luck

Implementations can also go wrong due to bad luck. We can have everything well prepared, but things can go wrong. *Murphy's law* says that anything that can go wrong will go wrong. We can anticipate inevitable setbacks and bad luck by including buffers. These buffers make the plan less efficient, but increase the robustness of the plan.

Pause and Reflect

Use your own experience of a recent project from your study or work. Did you ask yourself: Is the implementation plan feasible, given the unforeseen changes?

What could we do about implementation problems?

The implementation office, together with the concerned workstream leaders, will develop solutions for these implementation problems. The office is empowered to make decisions about such solutions. In general, the office has three options in case of implementation problems:

- Repair or repeat the failed implementation actions and continue with the original implementation plan (if the plan did not cause the problem).
- Adapt the initial implementation plan (if the plan caused the problem): adapt resources, actions, or objectives.
- Abandon the implementation if adapting the plan will not help solve the problem. Abandonment is the last resort in the case of grave issues we cannot resolve.

We can outline the process for developing solutions (see Chapter 8):

1. Develop possible solutions for implementation problems
2. Prioritise the solutions
3. Develop a solution hypothesis
4. Test the hypothesis

What we could do about stakeholder resistance

As an example, we outline what we could do about implementation problems arising from stakeholder resistance.

1. We *identify* the resisting stakeholders. Identification can be challenging if the resistance is covert.
2. We *confront* the resisting stakeholders with their underperformance.
3. We *investigate* what causes the resistance (disagreement, opportunism, cockiness and stubbornness, or distraction).
4. Depending on the causes of the resistance, we can take different actions to *remedy* the resistance.
   a. In case of disagreement, we may *align* the resisting stakeholders to get these stakeholders on board.
   b. In other cases, we must confront stakeholders with the negative consequences of their resistance. Therefore, the implementation office must be mandated to impose negative *sanctions* on resisting stakeholders.

What should we do about implementation problems?

Chapter 8 also outlined evaluating the accepted hypotheses and deciding on the solution. Under uncertainty about the future, no implementation plan survives the confrontation with reality. Then, implementation cannot be a linear process. Instead, we use the iterative model: we implement solutions using a cyclical or loop-based process of learning and adapting. We distinguish between two cycles or loops (see Figure 11.18):

- There is a loop during the pilot phase. A pilot's failure means that the implementation office needs to adapt the pilot until it is successful. After a successful pilot, the implementation office will roll out the plan.
- The monitoring of the progress of the implementation leads to another loop. Suppose the realized performance of the implementation actions goes according to plan. In that case, the workstream leaders and their teams can continue to conduct the planned actions. Suppose the realized performance falls short of the objectives. In that case, the implementation office and the workstream leaders need to solve the implementation problem.

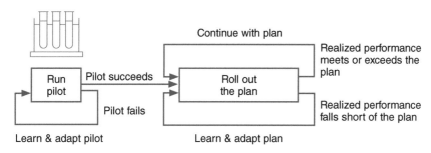

Figure 11.18   An iterative process of implementation under uncertainty

Implement the solution

Implementation means change. Lower-level managers and frontline professionals reverting to old behaviour is a well-known risk of organizational change processes. During the implementation project, participants are motivated, and the implementation office monitors the actions and performance of these people. But after the completion of the implementation, people have space to revert to their comfort zone of old, familiar behaviour. The space increases if the principal's attention has shifted to other matters.

To reinforce and sustain the required new behaviour of the lower-level managers and frontline professionals, the implementation office anchors the solution in the principal's organizational structure, systems, processes, and culture. For example, the office sets performance objectives, makes people accountable for realizing these objectives, and introduces regular performance reviews. Stakeholders can only perform well if they behave in the new, desired way.

Pause and reflect

Consider how you may use these techniques for facilitating a solution implementation in your studies, work, and personal life.

EVALUATE AN IMPLEMENTATION

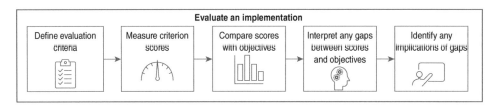

Figure 11.19   A process for evaluating an implementation

Define the criteria, measure the scores, and compare them with the objectives

Defining evaluation criteria, measuring scores, and comparing them with objectives for evaluating an implementation are the same steps as for monitoring implementation progress.

Interpret any gaps between the scores and the objectives

We frame a problem as a gap between the realized score and the higher objective. If the gap is substantial, it justifies a problem analysis. Figure 11.20 presents the Sequential Analysis Method. However, we may also opt for another approach, such as the Issue Tree or Hypothesis Tree Method.

So far, we have discussed realized scores falling short of the objectives. But the realized scores may also *exceed* objectives. This is success. It is essential to analyse success as we may learn from it. We may segment the success: where does the success lie? For example, which people were most successful? Then, we explain the success of these segments.

Identify any implications of gaps

In the case of implementation problems, how should we prevent them from happening again? If we have successes, how should we repeat them? The implications are solutions. We can use the Sequential Analysis Method to develop these solutions (see Figure 11.21).

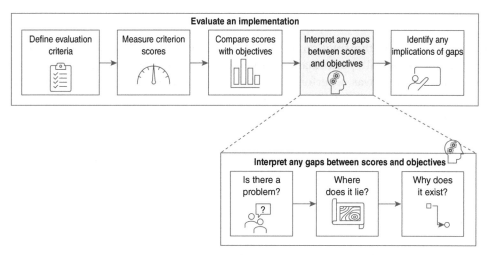

Figure 11.20   The Sequential Analysis Method for interpreting implementation problems

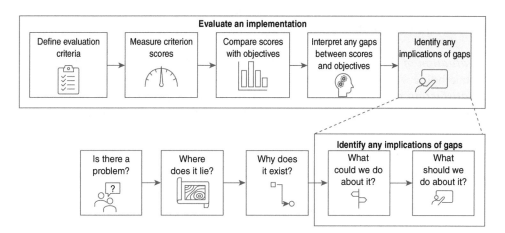

Figure 11.21   The Sequential Analysis Method for identifying the gap implications

 **Pause and Reflect**

Use your own experience of a recent project from your study or work. Did you ask yourself:

- To what extent could I have prevented specific implementation problems?
- What could or should I have done better?
- How can I improve next time?

Evaluate the solution's impact

After implementing the solution, the implementation office measures any improvements in the principal's performance. Did we close the performance gap? After all, the principal's problem was a performance gap. Implementation of the solution should close the gap. But closing the gap can take a long time after the implementation has ended. For example, compare cost reductions with revenue growth solutions. If we cut the principal's costs, they directly affect the principal's profit. But suppose we have a solution for growing the principal's revenue. Revenue growth may take more time for results to become visible. A price reduction can immediately increase sales, but research and development for product innovation usually take much more time.

Evaluate our Impact

Besides *our* solution, there may be other factors influencing the performance improvement of the principal. We must ask ourselves: 'What would the principal have realized *without* our solution?' Ideally, we would like to compare their principal's performance with and without our solution. Laboratory experiments where researchers can work with control groups are not feasible. We may ask the principal and other relevant stakeholders for their judgment.

- *Valuation of the solution impact*: How much do the principal and other relevant stakeholders value the performance impact of our solution?
- *Satisfaction with the solution*: How satisfied are the principal and other relevant stakeholders with our solution? Satisfaction results from exceeding expectations. Expectations are about the solution's performance impact but also about other factors.

Project evaluation is not only about the project's performance impact and other *outcomes*, but also about *inputs and processes*. Have we developed and implemented solutions on time and within budget? Are the principal and other relevant stakeholders satisfied with the process and their collaboration with us?

Close a project

During projects, we have documented our work well. After the completion of the project, we transfer the documentation to the principal. The principal now has all the project materials, and we instruct the principal on how to use these materials.

Problem-solving is a project with a beginning and an end. Once the project has reached closure, the principal must be able to continue with the solution independently. The principal should not remain dependent on us.

Often the principal will celebrate the successful completion of a project. The project team will have a festive closing of the project. After the hard work, it is time to relax. The finish can vary from a drink or dinner to a social event. We also use these events to acknowledge exceptional achievements publicly and reward those involved.

Identify lessons learned

After the closure of the project, the team may have a debriefing meeting. The team will discuss what went well and what should improve. The members learn from the experience and write down the lessons to share with colleagues within the company. Every project may add insights to the company's knowledge. We can create a knowledge management system to store that know-how. Of course, we will remove any sensitive and secretive information about the organization, the principal, or any other stakeholder. The company's knowledge management system makes the anonymized project information available. Colleagues working on similar projects can search the system and benefit from the relevant information. They can search the database of projects and topics. Of course, they can also contact the experts in the company. They should not reinvent the wheel.

 —— **Pause and Reflect** ——————————————

Consider how you may use these techniques for evaluating a solution implementation in your studies, work, and personal life.

SUMMARY

We briefly outline the main takeaways of this chapter.

- Engage with stakeholders
    - identify critical stakeholder dependencies
    - decide on the stakeholder approaches
    - ensure stakeholder collaboration
    - resolve stakeholder conflict
- Stage an implementation
    - assess the level of uncertainty around the implementation
    - assess the level of dependencies among actions
    - assess the time pressure
    - assess the amount of (human) resources
    - decide on the staging approach
- Monitor the progress of an implementation
    - define the performance metrics
    - measure the realized performance
    - compare the realized performance with the objectives
    - decide on any gaps between the realized performance and the objectives
- Intervene in an implementation
    - Is there an implementation problem?
    - Where does it lie?
    - Why does it exist?

    ○   What could we do about it?
    ○   What should we do about it?
- Evaluate an implementation
    ○   define evaluation criteria
    ○   measure the criterion scores
    ○   compare the scores with the objectives
    ○   interpret any gaps between the scores and the objectives
    ○   identify any implications of gaps

Mini Exercise

Identify the key concepts and terms in this chapter, define them briefly and compile your own glossary.

WRAP UP

We close the book with two overviews. First, we present an overview of the structured problem-solving method.

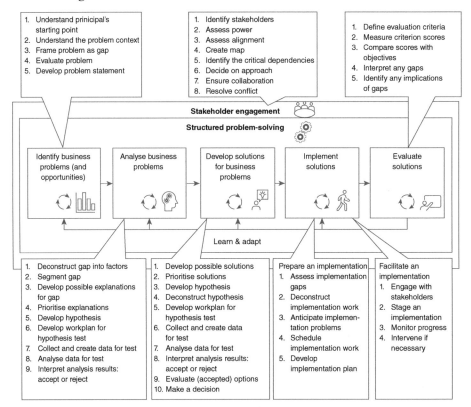

Figure 11.22   The structured problem-solving method at a glance

Finally, we present an overview of the four business skills for the twenty-first century that are the focus of this book.

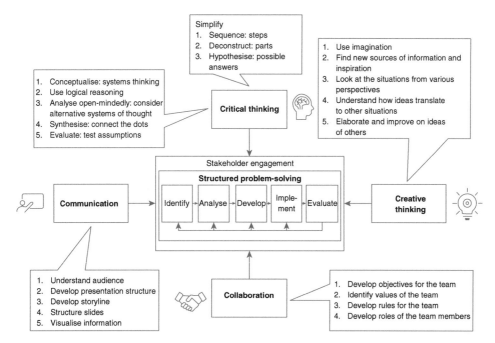

Figure 11.23   An overview of the four business skills for the twenty-first century at a glance

Good luck with the application of these skills!

REFERENCES AND FURTHER READING

Freeman, R. E. (1984). *Strategic Management: A Stakeholder Approach*. Boston, MA: Pitman.

Kaplan, R. S., Kaplan, R. E., & Norton, D. P. (2004). *Strategy Maps: Converting Intangible Assets into Tangible Outcomes*. Boston, MA: Harvard Business Press.

Kotter, J. P. (1996). *Leading Change*. Boston, MA: Harvard Business School Press.

Lewin, K. (1947). Frontiers in group dynamics: Concept, method and reality in social science; social equilibria and social change. *Human Relations, 1,* 5–41.

INDEX

Note: Page numbers followed by "f" represents figures.